P9-CBI-850

TECHNICAL COLLEGE OF THE LOWCOUNTRY
LEARNING RESOURCES CENTER
POST OFFICE BOX 1288
BEAUFORT, SOUTH CAROLINA 29901-1288

Bloom's Modern Critical Views

African American
 Poets: Wheatley–
 Tolson
African American
 Poets: Hayden–Dove
Dante Alighieri
Isabel Allende
American Women
 Poets, 1650–1950
Hans Christian
 Andersen
Maya Angelou
Asian-American Writers
Margaret Atwood
Jane Austen
Paul Auster
James Baldwin
Honoré de Balzac
The Bible
William Blake
Ray Bradbury
The Brontës
Gwendolyn Brooks
Elizabeth Barrett
 Browning
Robert Browning
Albert Camus
Truman Capote
Miguel de Cervantes
Geoffrey Chaucer
G.K. Chesterton
Kate Chopin
Joseph Conrad
Contemporary Poets
Julio Cortázar
Stephen Crane
Don DeLillo
Charles Dickens
Emily Dickinson
John Donne and the
 17th-Century Poets

Fyodor Dostoevsky
W.E.B. DuBois
George Eliot
T.S. Eliot
Ralph Ellison
Ralph Waldo Emerson
William Faulkner
F. Scott Fitzgerald
Robert Frost
William Gaddis
Thomas Hardy
Nathaniel Hawthorne
Robert Hayden
Ernest Hemingway
Hermann Hesse
Hispanic-American
 Writers
Homer
Langston Hughes
Zora Neale Hurston
Aldous Huxley
John Irving
James Joyce
Franz Kafka
John Keats
Jamaica Kincaid
Stephen King
Milan Kundera
Tony Kushner
Doris Lessing
C.S. Lewis
Sinclair Lewis
Norman Mailer
David Mamet
Christopher Marlowe
Gabriel García
 Márquez
Carson McCullers
Herman Melville
Arthur Miller
John Milton

Toni Morrison
Joyce Carol Oates
Flannery O'Connor
George Orwell
Octavio Paz
Sylvia Plath
Edgar Allan Poe
Katherine Anne Porter
Marcel Proust
Thomas Pynchon
Philip Roth
Salman Rushdie
J. D. Salinger
José Saramago
Jean-Paul Sartre
William Shakespeare
Mary Wollstonecraft
 Shelley
John Steinbeck
Amy Tan
Alfred, Lord Tennyson
Henry David Thoreau
J.R.R. Tolkien
Leo Tolstoy
Ivan Turgenev
Mark Twain
Kurt Vonnegut
Derek Walcott
Alice Walker
H.G. Wells
Eudora Welty
Walt Whitman
Tennessee Williams
Tom Wolfe
William Wordsworth
Jay Wright
Richard Wright
William Butler Yeats
Émile Zola

Bloom's Modern Critical Views

KATE CHOPIN
Updated Edition

Edited and with an introduction by
Harold Bloom
Sterling Professor of the Humanities
Yale University

BLOOM'S
LITERARY CRITICISM
An imprint of Infobase Publishing

Bloom's Modern Critical Views: Kate Chopin—Updated Edition

Copyright ©2007 Infobase Publishing

Introduction © 2007 by Harold Bloom

All rights reserved. No part of this publication may be reproduced or utilized in any form
or by any means, electronic or mechanical, including photocopying, recording, or by any
information storage or retrieval systems, without permission in writing from the publisher.
For more information contact:

Bloom's Literary Criticism
An imprint of Infobase Publishing
132 West 31st Street
New York NY 10001

ISBN-10: 0-7910-9369-7
ISBN-13: 978-0-7910-9369-6

Library of Congress Cataloging-in-Publication Data
Kate Chopin / Harold Bloom, editor. — Updated ed.
    p. cm. — (Bloom's modern critical views)
  Includes bibliographical references (p.   ) and index.
  ISBN 0-7910-9369-7
  1. Chopin, Kate, 1851-1904—Criticism and interpretation. 2. Women and literature—
Louisiana—History—19th century. 3. Louisiana—in literature. I. Bloom, Harold.
II. Title. III. Series.
  PS1294.C63Z73 2007
  813'.4—dc22   2006031968

Bloom's Literary Criticism books are available at special discounts when purchased in bulk
quantities for businesses, associations, institutions, or sales promotions. Please call our
Special Sales Department in New York at (212) 967-8800 or (800) 322-8755.

You can find Bloom's Literary Criticism on the World Wide Web at
http://www.chelseahouse.com

Contributing Editor: Camille-Yvette Welsch

Cover designed by Takeshi Takahashi

Cover photo © The Granger Collection, New York

Printed in the United States of America

Bang EJB 10 9 8 7 6 5 4 3 2 1

This book is printed on acid-free paper.

All links and web addresses were checked and verified to be correct at the time of publication. Because of the dynamic nature of the web, some addresses and links may have
changed since publication and may no longer be valid.

Contents

Editor's Note   vii

Introduction   1
  Harold Bloom

Tradition and the Female Talent:
The Awakening as a Solitary Book   7
  Elaine Showalter

Kate Chopin's Social Fiction   27
  Mary E. Papke

Semiotic Subversion in "Désirée's Baby"   75
  Ellen Peel

The Teeth of Desire:
The Awakening and *The Descent of Man*   89
  Bert Bender

The Quintessence of Chopinism   103
  Martha Fodaski Black

Kate Chopin: Ironist of Realism   119
  Kathleen Wheeler

A Writer, Her Reviewers, and Her Markets   145
  Emily Toth

'Local Color' Literature and *A Night in Acadie*   167
      Nancy A. Walker

Unraveling the Southern Pastoral Tradition:
A New Look at Kate Chopin's *At Fault*   191
      Maureen Anderson

Chronology   205
Contributors   207
Bibliography   209
Acknowledgments   213
Index   215

Editor's Note

My Introduction amiably suggests that *The Awakening* is a rather more flawed and less feminist a narrative than most current feminist critics care to recognize. Walt Whitman's auto-erotic stances and rhetoric profoundly inform Chopin's novel, whose essential story is Edna's awakening to a passion for her own body.

A good antidote to my interpretation can be found in the formidably feminist Elaine Showalter, who finds in Chopin a great figure no longer neglected by literary tradition, a view in which she is joined by almost all the other essayists in this volume.

Chopin's shorter fictions are commended by Mary E. Papke and Ellen Peel, while Bert Bender sees *The Awakening* as "correcting" Walt Whitman by Charles Darwin.

Martha Fodaski Black finds "uncompromising realism" in *The Awakening*.

Chopin's talent for irony is deftly traced by Kathleen Wheeler, while Emily Toth deals with considerations of the literary market confronted by *The Awakening*.

This volume concludes with two accounts of Chopin's achievements in the short story. Nancy A. Walker joins Kathleen Wheeler in appreciating ironies, after which Maureen Anderson credits Chopin with undoing the false idealizations of the Southern pastoral tradition.

HAROLD BLOOM

Introduction

I

The Complete Works of Kate Chopin (1969) comprise only two volumes. In her own lifetime (1850–1904), she published two novels, *At Fault* (1890), which I have not read, and the now celebrated *The Awakening* (1899), as well as two volumes of short stories, *Bayou Folk* (1894) and *A Night in Acadie* (1897). The short stories—out of Maupassant—are very mixed in quality, but even the best are fairly slight. *The Awakening*, a flawed but strong novel, now enjoys an eminent status among feminist critics, but I believe that many of them weakly misread the book, which is anything but feminist in its stance. It is a Whitmanian book, profoundly so, not only in its echoes of his poetry, which are manifold, but more crucially in its erotic perspective, which is narcissistic and even autoerotic, very much in Whitman's true mode. The sexual awakening that centers the novel involves a narcissistic self-investment that constitutes a new ego for the heroine. Unfortunately, she fails to see that her passion is for herself, and this error perhaps destroys her.

Lest I seem ironic, here at the start, I protest that irony is hardly my trope; that Walt Whitman, in my judgment, remains the greatest American writer; and that I continue to admire *The Awakening*, though a bit less at the second reading than at the first. Its faults are mostly in its diction; Chopin

1

had no mastery of style. As narrative, it is simplistic rather than simple, and its characters have nothing memorable about them. Chopin's exuberance as a writer was expended where we would expect a daughter of Whitman to locate her concern: the ecstatic rebirth of the self. Since Chopin was not writing either American epic or American elegy, but rather an everyday domestic novel, more naturalistic than Romantic, fissures were bound to appear in her work. The form of Flaubert does not accommodate what Emerson—who may be called Chopin's literary grandfather—named as the great and crescive self. Nevertheless, as a belated American Transcendentalist, Chopin risked the experiment, and what Emerson called the Newness breaks the vessels of Chopin's chosen form. I would call this the novel's largest strength, though it is also its formal weakness.

II

Walt Whitman the man doubtless lusted after what he termed the love of comrades, but Walt Whitman the poet persuades us rhetorically only when he lusts after himself. To state this more precisely, Walt Whitman, one of the roughs, an American, the self of *Song of Myself*, lusts after "the real me" or "me myself" of Walt Whitman. Chopin's heroine, Edna, becomes, as it were, one of the roughs, an American, when she allows herself to lust after her real me, her me myself. That is why Chopin's *The Awakening* gave offense to reviewers in 1899, precisely as *Leaves of Grass* gave offense from its first appearance in 1855, onwards to Whitman's death, and would still give offense, if we read it as the Pindaric celebration of masturbation that it truly constitutes. Edna, like Walt, falls in love with her own body, and her infatuation with the inadequate Robert is merely a screen for her overwhelming obsession, which is to nurse and mother herself. Chopin, on some level, must have known how sublimely outrageous she was being, but the level was not overt, and part of her novel's power is in its negation of its own deepest knowledge. Her reviewers were not stupid, and it is shallow to condemn them, as some feminist critics now tend to do. Here is the crucial paragraph in a review by one Frances Porcher (in *The Mirror* 9, May 4, 1899), who senses obscurely but accurately that Edna's desire is for herself:

> It is not a pleasant picture of soul-dissection, take it anyway you like; and so, though she finally kills herself, or rather lets herself drown to death, one feels that it is not in the desperation born of an over-burdened heart, torn by complicating duties but rather because she realizes that something is due to her children, that she cannot get away from, and she is too weak to face the issue.

Besides which, and this is the stronger feeling, she has offered herself wholly to the man, who loves her too well to take her at her word; "she realizes that the day would come when he, too, and the thought of him, would melt out of her existence," she has awakened to know the shifting, treacherous, fickle deeps of her own soul in which lies, alert and strong and cruel, the fiend called Passion that is all animal and all of the earth, earthy. It is better to lie down in green waves and sink down in close embraces of old ocean, and so she does.

The metaphor of "shifting, treacherous, fickle deeps" here, however unoriginal, clearly pertains more to Edna's body than to her soul, and what is most "alert and strong and cruel" in Edna is manifestly a passion for herself. The love-death that Edna dies has its Wagnerian element, but again is more Whitmanian, suggesting the song of death sung by the hermit thrush or solitary singer in "When Lilacs Last in the Dooryard Bloom'd." Edna moves in the heavy, sensual and sensuous atmosphere of Whitman's "The Sleepers," and she dies only perhaps as Whitman's real me or me myself dies, awash in a body indistinguishable from her own, the body of the mother, death, the ocean, and the night of a narcissistic dream of love that perfectly restitutes the self for all its losses, that heals fully the original, narcissistic scar.

Sandra M. Gilbert, who seems to me our most accomplished feminist critic, reads the novel as a female revision of the male aesthetic reveries of Aphrodite's rebirth. I would revise Gilbert only by suggesting that the major instances of such reverie—in Dante Gabriel Rossetti, Swinburne, Pater, and Wilde—are not less female than Chopin's vision is, and paradoxically are more feminist than her version of the myth. The autoerotic seems to be a realm where, metaphorically anyway, there are no major differences between male and female seers, so that Chopin's representation of Edna's psychic self-gratification is not essentially altered from Whitman's solitary bliss:

Edna, left alone in the little side room, loosened her clothes, removing the greater part of them. She bathed her face, her neck and arms in the basin that stood between the windows. She took off her shoes and stockings and stretched herself in the very center of the high, white bed. How luxurious it felt to rest thus in a strange, quaint bed, with its sweet country odor of laurel lingering about the sheets and mattress! She stretched her strong limbs that ached a little. She ran her fingers through her loosened hair for a while. She looked at her round arms as she held them straight up and rubbed them one after the other, observing closely, as if it were something she saw for the first time, the fine, firm quality and texture of her flesh. She clasped her hands easily above her head, and it was thus she fell asleep.

Edna observing, as a discovery, "the fine, firm quality and texture of her flesh," is the heir of Whitman proclaiming: "If I worship one thing more than another it shall be the spread of my own body, or any part of it." Chopin seems to have understood, better than most readers in 1899, what Whitman meant by his crucial image of the tally: "My knowledge my live parts, it keeping tally with the meaning of all things." As the erotic image of the poet's voice, the tally obeys Emerson's dark law of Compensation: "Nothing is got for nothing." If Edna awakens to her own passion for her own body and its erotic potential, then she must come also to the tally's measurement of her own death.

III

Some aspects of Whitman's influence upon *The Awakening* have been traced by Lewis Leary and others, but since the influence is not always overt but frequently repressed, there is more to be noticed about it. Edna first responds to "the everlasting voice of the sea" in chapter 4, where its maternal contrast to her husband's not unkind inadequacy causes her to weep copiously. At the close of chapter 6, the voice of the Whitmanian ocean is directly associated with Edna's awakening to self:

The voice of the sea is seductive; never ceasing, whispering, clamoring, murmuring, inviting the soul to wander for a spell in abysses of solitude; to lose itself in mazes of inward contemplation.
The voice of the sea speaks to the soul. The touch of the sea is sensuous, enfolding the body in its soft, close embrace.

This is a palpable and overt influence; far subtler, because repressed, is the Whitmanian aura with which Kate Chopin associates the ambivalence of motherhood. Whitman himself both fathered and mothered all of his mostly tormented siblings, as soon as he was able, but his own ambivalences toward both fatherhood and motherhood inform much of his best poetry. Something of the ambiguous strength of *The Awakening*'s conclusion hovers in its repressed relation to Whitman. Edna leaves Robert, after their mutual declaration of love, in order to attend her close friend Adèle in her labor pains:

Edna began to feel uneasy. She was seized with a vague dread. Her own like experiences seemed far away, unreal, and only half remembered. She recalled faintly an ecstasy of pain, the heavy odor of chloroform, a stupor which had deadened sensation, and an awakening to find a little new life to which she had given being, added to the great unnumbered multitude of souls that come and go.

She began to wish she had not come; her presence was not necessary. She might have invented a pretext for staying away; she might even invent a pretext now for going. But Edna did not go. With an inward agony, with a flaming, outspoken revolt against the ways of Nature, she witnessed the scene [of] torture.

She was still stunned and speechless with emotion when later she leaned over her friend to kiss her and softly say good-by. Adèle, pressing her cheek, whispered in an exhausted voice: "Think of the children, Edna. Oh think of the children! Remember them!"

The protest against nature here is hardly equivocal, yet it has the peculiar numbness of "the great unnumbered multitude of souls that come and go." Schopenhauer's influence joins Whitman's as Chopin shows us Edna awakening to the realization of lost individuality, of not wanting "anything but my own way," while knowing that the will to live insists always upon its own way, at the individual's expense:

Despondency had come upon her there in the wakeful night, and had never lifted. There was no one thing in the world that she desired. There was no human being whom she wanted near her except Robert; and she even realized that the day would come when he, too, and the thought of him, would melt out of her existence, leaving her alone. The children appeared before her like antagonists who had overcome her; who had overpowered and sought to drag her into the soul's slavery for the rest of her days. But she knew a way to elude them. She was not thinking of these things when she walked down to the beach.

The water of the Gulf stretched out before her, gleaming with the million lights of the sun. The voice of the sea is seductive, never ceasing, whispering, clamoring, murmuring, inviting the soul to wander in abysses of solitude. All along the white beach, up and down, there was no living thing in sight. A bird with a broken wing was beating the air above, reeling, fluttering, circling disabled down, down to the water.

The soul's slavery, in Schopenhauer, is to be eluded through philosophical contemplation of a very particular kind, but in Whitman only through a dangerous liaison with night, death, the mother, and the sea. Chopin is closer again to Whitman, and the image of the disabled bird circling downward to darkness stations itself between Whitman and Wallace Stevens, as it were, and constitutes another American approach to the Emersonian abyss of the self. Edna, stripped naked, enters the mothering sea with another recall of Whitman: "The foamy wavelets curled up to her white feet, and coiled like serpents about her ankles." In the hermit thrush's great song of death that is the apotheosis of "When Lilacs Last in the Dooryard Bloom'd," death arrives coiled and curled like a serpent, undulating round the world. Whitman's "dark mother always gliding near with soft feet" has come to deliver Edna from the burden of being a mother, and indeed from all burden of otherness, forever.

ELAINE SHOWALTER

Tradition and the Female Talent:
The Awakening *as a Solitary Book*

"Whatever we may do or attempt, despite the embrace and transports of love, the hunger of the lips, we are always alone. I have dragged you out into the night in the vain hope of a moment's escape from the horrible solitude which overpowers me. But what is the use! I speak and you answer me, and still each of us is alone, side by side but alone."[1] In 1895, these words, from a story by Guy de Maupassant called "Solitude," which she had translated for a St. Louis magazine, expressed an urbane and melancholy wisdom that Kate Chopin found compelling. To a woman who had survived the illusions that friendship, romance, marriage, or even motherhood would provide lifelong companionship and identity, and who had come to recognize the existential solitude of all human beings, Maupassant's declaration became a kind of credo. Indeed, *The Awakening*, which Chopin subtitled "A Solitary Soul," may be read as an account of Edna Pontellier's evolution from romantic fantasies of fusion with another person to self-definition and self-reliance. At the beginning of the novel, in the midst of the bustling social world of Grand Isle, caught in her domestic roles of wife and mother, Edna pictures solitude as alien, masculine, and frightening, a naked man standing beside a "desolate rock" by the sea in an attitude of "hopeless resignation" (Chap. 9). By the end, she has claimed a solitude that is defiantly feminine, returning to the nearly empty island off-season, to stand naked and "absolutely alone" by

From *New Essays on* The Awakening, Wendy Martin, ed., pp. 33–57. © 1988 by Cambridge University Press.

the shore and to elude "the soul's slavery" by plunging into the sea's embrace (Chap. 39).

Yet Edna's triumphant embrace of solitude could not be the choice of Kate Chopin as an artist. A writer may work in solitude, but literature depends on a tradition, on shared forms and representations of experience; and literary genres, like biological species, evolve because of significant innovations by individuals that survive through imitation and revision. Thus it can be a very serious blow to a developing genre when a revolutionary work is taken out of circulation. Experimentation is retarded and repressed, and it may be several generations before the evolution of the literary genre catches up. The interruption of this evolutionary process is most destructive for the literature of a minority group, in which writers have to contend with cultural prejudices against their creative gifts. Yet radical departures from literary convention within a minority tradition are especially likely to be censured and suppressed by the dominant culture, because they violate social as well as aesthetic stereotypes and expectations.

The Awakening was just such a revolutionary book. Generally recognized today as the first aesthetically successful novel to have been written by an American woman, it marked a significant epoch in the evolution of an American female literary tradition. As an American woman novelist of the 1890s, Kate Chopin had inherited a rich and complex tradition, composed not only of her American female precursors but also of American transcendentalism, European realism, and *fin-de-siècle* feminism and aestheticism. In this context, *The Awakening* broke new thematic and stylistic ground. Chopin went boldly beyond the work of her precursors in writing about women's longing for sexual and personal emancipation.

Yet the novel represents a literary beginning as abruptly cut off as its heroine's awakening consciousness. Edna Pontellier's explicit violations of the modes and codes of nineteenth-century American women's behavior shocked contemporary critics, who described *The Awakening* as "morbid," "essentially vulgar," and "gilded dirt."[2] Banned in Kate Chopin's own city of St. Louis and censured in the national press, *The Awakening* thus became a solitary book, one that dropped out of sight, and that remained unsung by literary historians and unread by several generations of American women writers.

In many respects, *The Awakening* seems to comment on its own history as a novel, to predict its own critical fate. The parallels between the experiences of Edna Pontellier, as she breaks away from the conventional feminine roles of wife and mother, and Kate Chopin, as she breaks away from conventions of literary domesticity, suggest that Edna's story may also be read as a parable of Chopin's literary awakening. Both the author and the heroine seem to be oscillating between two worlds, caught between contradictory definitions of femininity and creativity, and seeking either to synthesize them or to go beyond them to an emancipated womanhood and an emancipated fiction. Edna Pontellier's "unfocused yearning" for an autonomous life is akin to Kate Chopin's yearning to write works that go beyond female plots and feminine endings.

In the early stages of her career, Chopin had tried to follow the literary advice and literary examples of others and had learned that such dutiful efforts led only to imaginative stagnation. By the late 1890s, when she wrote *The Awakening*, Chopin had come to believe that the true artist was one who defied tradition, who rejected both the "convenances" of respectable morality and the conventions and formulas of literary success. What impressed her most about Maupassant was that he had "escaped from tradition and authority ... had entered into himself and looked out upon life through his own being and with his own eyes."[3] This is very close to what happens to Edna Pontellier as she frees herself from social obligations and received opinions and begins "to look with her own eyes, to see and to apprehend the deeper undercurrents of life" (Chap. 32). Much as she admired Maupassant, and much as she learned from translating his work, Chopin felt no desire to imitate him. Her sense of the need for independence and individuality in writing is dramatically expressed in *The Awakening* by Mademoiselle Reisz, who tells Edna that the artist must possess "the courageous soul that dares and defies" (Chap. 21) and must have strong wings to soar "above the level plain of tradition and prejudice" (Chap. 27).

Nonetheless, in order to understand *The Awakening* fully, we need to read it in the context of literary tradition. Even in its defiant solitude, *The Awakening* speaks for a transitional phase in American women's writing, and Chopin herself would never have written the books she did without a tradition to admire and oppose. When she wrote *The Awakening* in 1899, Chopin could look back to at least two generations of female literary precursors. The antebellum novelists, led by Harriet Beecher Stowe, Susan Warner, and E. D. E. N. Southworth, were the first members of these generations. Born in the early decades of the nineteenth century, they began to publish stories and novels in the 1850s and 1860s that reflected the dominant expressive and symbolic models of an American woman's culture. The historian Carroll Smith-Rosenberg has called this culture the "female world of love and ritual," and it was primarily defined by the veneration of motherhood, by intense mother–daughter bonds, and by intimate female friendships. As Smith-Rosenberg explains: "Uniquely female rituals drew women together during every stage of their lives, from adolescence through courtship, marriage, childbirth and child rearing, "death and mourning. Women revealed their deepest feelings to one another, helped one another with the burdens of housewifery and motherhood, nursed one another's sick, and mourned for one another's dead."[4] Although premarital relationships between the sexes were subject to severe restrictions, romantic friendships between women were admired and encouraged. The nineteenth-century ideal of female "passionlessness"—the belief that women did not have the same sexual desires as men—had advantages as well as disadvantages for women. It reinforced the notion that women were the purer and more spiritual sex, and thus were morally superior to men. Furthermore, as the historian Nancy F. Cott has argued, "acceptance of the idea of passionlessness created sexual solidarity among women; it allowed women to consider their love relationships with one another of higher character than heterosexual relationships because they excluded (male) carnal passion."[5] "I do not believe that men can ever feel so pure an enthusiasm for women as we can feel for one another," wrote the novelist Catherine Sedgwick, "Ours is nearest to the love of angels."[6] The homosocial world of women's culture in fact allowed much leeway for physical intimacy and touch; "girls routinely slept together, kissed and hugged one another."[7] But these caresses were not interpreted as erotic expressions.

The mid-nineteenth-century code of values growing out of women's culture, which Mary Ryan calls "the empire of the mother," was also sustained by sermons, child-rearing manuals, and sentimental fiction.[8] Women writers advocated motherly influence—"gentle nurture," "sweet control," and "educating power"—as an effective solution to such social problems as alcoholism, crime, slavery, and war. As Harriet Beecher Stowe proclaimed, "The 'Woman Question' of the day is: Shall MOTHERHOOD ever be felt in the public administration of the affairs of state?"[9]

As writers, however, the sentimentalists looked to motherhood for their metaphors and justifications of literary creativity. "Creating a story is like bearing a child," wrote Stowe, "and it leaves me in as weak and helpless a state as when my baby was born."[10] Thematically and stylistically, pre–Civil War women's fiction, variously described as "literary domesticity" or the "sentimental novel," celebrates matriarchal institutions and idealizes the period of blissful bonding between mother and child. It is permeated by the artifacts, spaces, and images of nineteenth-century American domestic culture: the kitchen, with its worn rocking chair; the Edenic mother's garden, with its fragrant female flowers and energetic male bees; the caged songbird, which represents the creative woman in her domestic sphere. Women's narratives were formally composed of brief sketches joined together like the pieces of a patchwork quilt; they frequently alluded to specific quilt patterns and followed quilt design conventions of repetition, variation, and contrast. Finally, their most intense representation of female sexual pleasure was not in terms of heterosexual romance, but rather the holding or suckling of a baby;

for, as Mary Ryan points out, "nursing an infant was one of the most hallowed and inviolate episodes in a woman's life.... Breast-feeding was sanctioned as 'one of the most important duties of female life,' 'one of peculiar, inexpressible felicity,' and 'the sole occupation and pleasure' of a new mother."[11]

The cumulative effect of all these covert appeals to female solidarity in books written by, for, and about women could be a subversive critique of patriarchal power. Yet aesthetically the fiction of this generation was severely restricted. The sentimentalists did not identify with the figure of the "artist," the "genius," or the "poet" promulgated by patriarchal culture. As Nina Baym explains, "they conceptualized authorship as a profession rather than a calling.... Women authors tended not to think of themselves as artists or justify themselves in the language of art until the 1870s and after."[12] In the writing of the sentimentalists, "the dimensions of formal self-consciousness, attachment to or quarrel with a grand tradition, aesthetic seriousness, are all missing. Often the women deliberately and even proudly disavowed membership in an artistic fraternity."[13] Insofar as art implied a male club or circle of brothers, women felt excluded from it. Instead they claimed affiliation with a literary sorority, a society of sisters whose motives were moral rather than aesthetic, whose ambitions were to teach and to influence rather than to create. Although their books sold by the millions, they were not taken seriously by male critics.

The next generation of American women writers, however, found themselves in a different cultural situation. After the Civil War, the homosocial world of women's culture began to dissolve as women demanded entrance to higher education, the professions, and the political world. The female local colorists who began to publish stories about American regional life in the 1870s and 1880s were also attracted to the male worlds of art and prestige opening up to women, and they began to assert themselves as the daughters of literary fathers as well as literary mothers. Claiming both male and female aesthetic models, they felt free to present themselves as artists and to write confidently about the art of fiction in such essays as Elizabeth Stuart Phelps's "Art for Truth's Sake".[14] Among the differences the local colorists saw between themselves and their predecessors was the question of "selfishness," the ability to put literary ambitions before domestic duties. Although she had been strongly influenced in her work by Harriet Beecher Stowe's *Pearl of Orr's Island*, Sarah Orne Jewett came to believe that Stowe's work was "incomplete" because she was unable to "bring herself to that cold selfishness of the moment for one's work's sake."[15]

Writers of this generation chose to put their work first. The 1870s and 1880s were what Susan B. Anthony called "an epoch of single women,"[16] and many unmarried women writers of this generation lived alone; others were involved in "Boston marriages," or long-term relationships with another woman. But despite their individual lifestyles, many speculated in their writing on the conflicts between maternity and artistic creativity. Motherhood no longer seemed to be the motivating force of writing, but rather its opposite. Thus artistic fulfillment required the sacrifice of maternal drives, and maternal fulfillment meant giving up artistic ambitions.

The conflicts between love and work that Edna Pontellier faces in *The Awakening* were anticipated in such earlier novels as Louisa May Alcott's unfinished *Diana and Persis* (1879) an Elizabeth Stuart Phelps's *The Story of Avis* (1879). A gifted painter who has studied in Florence and Paris, Avis does not intend to marry. As she tells her suitor, "My ideals of art are those with which marriage is perfectly incompatible. Success—for a woman—means absolute surrender, in whatever direction. Whether she paints a picture, or loves a man, there is no division of labor possible in her economy. To the attainment of any end worth living for, a symmetrical sacrifice of her nature is compulsory upon her." But love persuades her to change her mind, and the novel records the inexorable destruction of her artistic genius as domestic responsibilities, maternal cares, and her husband's failures use up her energy. By the end of the novel, Avis has become resigned to the idea that her life is a sacrifice for the next generation of women. Thinking back to her mother, a talented actress who gave up her profession to marry and died young, and looking at her daughter, Wait, Avis takes heart in the hope that it may take three generations to create the woman who can unite "her supreme capacity of love" with the "sacred individuality of her life."[17] As women's culture declined after the Civil War, moreover, the local colorists mourned its demise by investing its traditional images with mythic significance. In their stories, the mother's garden has become a paradisal sanctuary; the caged bird a wild white heron, or heroine of nature; the house an emblem of the female body, with the kitchen as its womb; and the artifacts of domesticity virtually totemic objects. In Jewett's *Country of the Pointed Firs*, for example, the braided rag rug has become a kind of prayer mat of concentric circles from which the matriarchal priestess, Mrs. Todd, delivers her sybilline pronouncements. The woman artist in this fiction expresses her conflicting needs most fully in her quasi-religious dedication to these artifacts of a bygone age.

The New Women writers of the 1890s no longer grieved for the female bonds and sanctuaries of the past. Products of both Darwinian skepticism and aesthetic sophistication, they had an ambivalent or even hostile relationship to women's culture, which they often saw as boring and restrictive. Their attitudes toward female sexuality were also revolutionary. A few radical feminists had always maintained that women's sexual apathy was not an innately feminine attribute but rather the result of prudery and repression; some women's rights activists too had privately confessed that, as Elizabeth Cady Stanton wrote in her diary in 1883, "a healthy woman has as much passion as a man."[18] Not all New Women advocated female sexual emancipation; the most zealous advocates of free love were male novelists such as Grant Allen, whose best-seller, *The Woman Who Did* (1895), became a byword of the decade. But the heroine of New Woman fiction, as Linda Dowling has explained, "expressed her quarrel with Victorian culture chiefly through sexual means—by heightening sexual consciousness, candor, and expression."[19] No wonder, then, that reviewers saw *The Awakening* as part of the "overworked field of sex fiction" or noted that since "San Francisco and Paris, and London, and New York had furnished Women Who Did, why not New Orleans?"[20]

In the form as well as the content of their work, New Women writers demanded freedom and innovation. They modified the realistic three-decker novels about courtship and marriage that had formed the bulk of mid-century "woman's fiction" to make room for interludes of fantasy and parable, especially episodes "in which a woman will dream of an entirely different world or will cross-dress, experimenting with the freedom available to boys and men."[21] Instead of the crisply plotted short stories that had been the primary genre of the local colorists, writers such as Olive Schreiner, Ella D'Arcy, Sarah Grand, and "George Egerton" (Mary Chavelita Dunne) experimented with new fictional forms that they called "keynotes," "allegories," "fantasies," "monochromes," or "dreams." As Egerton explained, these impressionistic narratives were efforts to explore a hitherto unrecorded female consciousness: "I realized that in literature everything had been done better by man than woman could hope to emulate. There was only one small plot left for herself to tell: the *terra incognita* of herself, as she knew herself to be, not as man liked to imagine her—in a word to give herself away, as man had given himself away in his writings."[22]

Kate Chopin's literary evolution took her progressively through the three phases of nineteenth-century American women's culture and women's writing. Born in 1850, she grew up with the great best-sellers of the American and English sentimentalists. As a girl, she had wept over the works of Warner and Stowe and had copied pious passages from the English novelist Dinah Mulock Craik's *The Woman's Kingdom* into her diary. Throughout her adolescence, Chopin had also shared an intimate friendship with Kitty Garasché, a classmate at the Academy of the Sacred Heart. Together, Chopin recalled, the girls had read fiction and poetry, gone on excursions, and "exchanged our heart secrets."[23] Their friendship ended in 1870 when Kate Chopin married and Kitty Garasché entered a convent. Yet when Oscar Chopin died in 1883, his young widow went to visit her old friend and was shocked by her blind isolation from the world. When Chopin began to write, she took as her models such local colorists as Sarah Orne Jewett and Mary Wilkins Freeman, who had not only mastered technique and construction but had also devoted themselves to telling the stories of female loneliness, isolation, and frustration.

Sandra Gilbert has suggested that local color was a narrative strategy that Chopin employed to solve a specific problem: how to deal with extreme psychological states without the excesses of sentimental narrative and without critical recrimination. At first, Gilbert suggests, "local color" writing "offered both a mode and a manner that could mediate between the literary structures she had inherited and those she had begun." Like the anthropologist, the local colorist could observe vagaries of culture and character with "almost scientific detachment." Furthermore, "by reporting odd events and customs that were part of a region's 'local color' she could tell what would ordinarily be rather shocking or even melodramatic tales in an unmelodramatic way, and without fear of ... moral outrage."[24]

But before long, Chopin looked beyond the oddities of the local colorists to more ambitious models. Her literary tastes were anything but parochial. She read widely in a variety of genres—Darwin, Spencer, and Huxley, as well as Aristophanes, Flaubert, Whitman, Swinburne, and Ibsen. In particular, she associated her own literary and psychological awakening with Maupassant. "Here was life, not fiction," she wrote of his influence on her; "for where were the plots, the old fashioned mechanism and stage trapping that in a vague, unthinking way I had fancied were essential to the art of story making."[25] In a review of a book by the local colorist Hamlin Garland, Chopin expressed her dissatisfaction with the restricted subjects of regional writing: "Social problems, social environments, local color, and the rest of it" could not "insure the survival of a writer who employs them."[26] She resented being compared to George Washington Cable or Grace King.[27] Furthermore, she did not share the female local colorists' obsession with the past, their desperate nostalgia for a bygone idealized age. "How curiously the past effaces itself for me!" she wrote in her diary in 1894. "I cannot live through yesterday or tomorrow."[28] Unlike Jewett, Freeman, King, or Woolson, she did not favor the old woman as narrator.

Despite her identification with the New Women, however, Chopin was not an activist. She never joined the women's suffrage movement or belonged to a female literary community. Indeed, her celebrated St. Louis literary salon attracted mostly male journalists, editors, and writers. Chopin resigned after only two years from a St. Louis women's literary and charitable society. When her children identified her close friends to be interviewed by her first biographer, Daniel Rankin, there were no women on the list.[29]

Thus Chopin certainly did not wish to write a didactic feminist novel. In reviews published in the 1890s, she indicated her impatience with novelists such as Zola and Hardy, who tried to instruct their readers. She distrusted the rhetoric of such feminist best-sellers as Sarah Grand's *The Heavenly Twins* (1893). The eleventh commandment, she noted, is "Thou shalt not preach."[30] Instead she would try to record, in her own way and in her own voice, the *terra incognita* of a woman's "inward life" in all its "vague, tangled, chaotic" tumult.

Much of the shock effect of *The Awakening* to the readers of 1899 came from Chopin's rejection of the conventions of women's writing. Despite her name, which echoes two famous heroines of the domestic novel (Edna Earl in Augusta Evans's *St. Elmo* and Edna Kenderdine in Dinah Craik's *The Woman's Kingdom*), Edna Pontellier appears to reject the domestic empire of the mother and the sororal world of women's culture. Seemingly beyond the bonds of womanhood, she has neither mother nor daughter, and even refuses to go to her sister's wedding.

Moreover, whereas the sentimental heroine nurtures others, and the abstemious local color heroine subsists upon meager vegetarian diets, Kate Chopin's heroine is a robust woman who does not deny her appetites. Freeman's New England nun picks at her dainty lunch of lettuce leaves and currants, but Edna Pontellier eats hearty meals of paté, pompano, steak, and broiled chicken; bites off chunks of crusty bread; snacks on beer and Gruyere cheese; and sips brandy, wine, and champagne.

Formally, too, the novel has moved away from conventional techniques of realism to an impressionistic rhythm of epiphany and mood. Chopin abandoned the chapter titles she had used in her first novel, *At Fault* (1890), for thirty-nine numbered chapters of uneven length, ranging from the single paragraph of Chapter 28 to the sustained narrative of the dinner party in Chapter 30. The chapters are unified less by their style than by their focus on Edna's consciousness, and by the repetition of key motifs and images: music, the sea, shadows, swimming, eating, sleeping, gambling, the lovers, birth. Chapters of lyricism and fantasy, such as Edna's voyage to the Chênière Caminada, alternate with realistic, even satirical, scenes of Edna's marriage.

Most important, where previous works ignored sexuality or spiritualized it through maternity, *The Awakening* is insistently sexual, explicitly involved with the body and with self-awareness through physical awareness. Although Edna's actual seduction by Arobin takes place in the narrative neverland between Chapters 31 and 32, Chopin brilliantly evokes sexuality through images and details. In keeping with the novel's emphasis on the self, several scenes suggest Edna's initial autoeroticism. Edna's midnight swim, which awakens the "first-felt throbbings of desire," takes place in an atmosphere of erotic fragrance, "strange, rare odors ... a tangle of the sea-smell and of weeds and damp new-ploughed earth, mingled with the heavy perfume of a field of white blossoms" (Chap. 10). A similarly voluptuous scene is her nap at Chênière Caminada, when she examines her flesh as she lies in a "strange, quaint bed with its sweet country odor of laurel" (Chap. 13).

Edna reminds Dr. Mandalet of "some beautiful, sleek animal waking up in the sun" (Chap. 23), and we recall that among her fantasies in listening to music is the image of a lady stroking a cat. The image both conveys Edna's sensuality and hints at the self-contained, almost masturbatory, quality of her sexuality. Her rendezvous with Robert takes place in a sunny garden where both stroke a drowsy cat's silky fur, and Arobin first seduces her by smoothing her hair with his "soft, magnetic hand" (Chap. 31).

Yet despite these departures from tradition, there are other respects in which the novel seems very much of its time. As its title suggests, *The Awakening* is a novel about a process rather than a program, about a passage rather than a destination. Like Edith Wharton's *The House of Mirth* (1905), it is a transitional female fiction of the *fin-de-siècle*, a narrative of and about the passage from the homosocial women's culture and literature of the nineteenth century to the heterosexual fiction of modernism. Chopin might have taken the plot from a notebook entry Henry James made in 1892 about "the growing divorce between the American woman (with her comparative leisure, culture, grace, social instincts, artistic ambition) and the male American immersed in the ferocity of business, with no time for any but the most sordid interests, purely commercial, professional, democratic and political. This divorce is rapidly becoming a gulf."[31] The Gulf where the opening chapters of *The Awakening* are set certainly suggests the "growing divorce" between Edna's interests and desires and Léonce's obsessions with the stock market, property, and his brokerage business.

Yet in turning away from her marriage, Edna initially looks back to women's culture rather than forward to another man. As Sandra Gilbert has pointed out, Grand Isle is an oasis of women's culture, or a "female colony": "Madame Lebrun's pension on Grand Isle is very much a woman's land not only because it is owned and run by a single woman and dominated by 'mother-women' but also because (as in so many summer colonies today) its principal inhabitants are actually women and children whose husbands and fathers visit only on weekends ... [and it is situated,] like so many places that are significant for women, outside patriarchal culture, beyond the limits and limitations of the city where men make history, on a shore that marks the margin where nature intersects with culture."[32]

Edna's awakening, moreover, begins not with a man, but with Adèle Ratignolle, the empress of the "mother-women" of Grand Isle. A "self-contained" (Chap. 7) woman, Edna has never had any close relationships with members of her own sex. Thus it is Adèle who belatedly initiates Edna into the world of female love and ritual on the first step of her sensual voyage of self-discovery. Edna's first attraction to Adèle is physical: "the excessive physical charm of the Creole had first attracted her, for Edna had a sensuous susceptibility to beauty" (Chap. 7). At the beach, in the hot sun, she responds to Adèle's caresses, the first she has ever known from another woman, as Adèle clasps her hand "firmly and warmly" and strokes it fondly. The touch provokes Edna to an unaccustomed candor; leaning her head on Adèle's shoulder and confiding some of her secrets, she begins to feel "intoxicated" (Chap. 7). The bond between them goes beyond sympathy, as Chopin notes, to "what we might well call love" (Chap. 7).

In some respects, the motherless Edna also seeks a mother surrogate in Adèle and looks to her for nurturance. Adèle provides maternal encouragement for Edna's painting and tells her that her "talent is immense" (Chap. 18). Characteristically, Adèle has rationalized her own "art" as a maternal project: "she was keeping up her music on account of the children ... a means of brightening the home and making it attractive" (Chap. 9). Edna's responses to Adèle's music have been similarly tame and sentimental. Her revealing fantasies as she listens to Adèle play her easy pieces suggest the restriction and decorum of the female world: "a dainty young woman ... taking mincing dancing steps, as she came down a long avenue between tall hedges"; "children at play" (Chap. 9). Women's art, as Adèle presents it, is social, pleasant, and undemanding. It does not conflict with her duties as a wife and mother, and can even be seen to enhance them. Edna understands this well; as she retorts when her husband recommends Adèle as a model of an artist, "She isn't a musician and I'm not a painter!" (Chap. 19).

Yet the relationship with the conventional Adèle educates the immature Edna to respond for the first time both to a different kind of sexuality and to the unconventional and difficult art of Mademoiselle Reisz. In responding to Adèle's interest, Edna begins to think about her own past and to analyze her own personality. In textual terms, it is through this relationship that she becomes "Edna" in the narrative rather than "Mrs. Pontellier."

We see the next stage of Edna's awakening in her relationship with Mademoiselle Reisz, who initiates her into the world of art. Significantly, this passage also takes place through a female rather than a male mentor, and, as with Adèle, there is something more intense than friendship between the two women. Whereas Adèle's fondness for Edna, however, is depicted as maternal and womanly, Mademoiselle Reisz's attraction to Edna suggests something more perverse. The pianist is obsessed with Edna's beauty, raves over her figure in a bathing suit, greets her as "ma belle" and "ma reine," holds her hand, and describes herself as "a foolish old woman whom you have captivated" (Chap. 21). If Adèle is a surrogate for Edna's dead mother and the intimate friend she never had as a girl, Mademoiselle Reisz, whose music reduces Edna to passionate sobs, seems to be a surrogate lover. And whereas Adèle is a "faultless madonna" who speaks for the values and laws of the Creole community, Mademoiselle Reisz is a renegade, self-assertive and outspoken. She has no patience with petty social rules and violates the most basic expectations of femininity. To a rake like Arobin, she is so unattractive, unpleasant, and unwomanly as to seem "partially demented" (Chap. 27). Even Edna occasionally perceives Mademoiselle Reisz's awkwardness as a kind of deformity, and is sometimes offended by the old woman's candor and is not sure whether she likes her.

Yet despite her eccentricities, Mademoiselle Reisz seems "to reach Edna's spirit and set it free" (Chap. 26). Her voice in the novel seems to speak for the author's view of art and for the artist. It is surely no accident, for example, that it is Chopin's music that Mademoiselle Reisz performs. At the *pension* on Grand Isle, the pianist first plays a Chopin prelude, to which Edna responds with surprising turbulence: "the very passions themselves were aroused within her soul, swaying it, lashing it, as the waves daily beat upon her splendid body. She trembled, she was choking, and the tears blinded her" (Chap. 9). "Chopin" becomes the code word for a world of repressed passion between Edna and Robert that Mademoiselle Reisz controls. Later the pianist plays a Chopin impromptu for Edna that Robert has admired; this time the music is "strange and fantastic—turbulent, plaintive and soft with entreaty" (Chap. 21). These references to "Chopin" in the text are on one level allusions to an intimate, romantic, and poignant musical *oeuvre* that reinforces the novel's sensual atmosphere. But on another level, they function as what Nancy K. Miller has called the "internal female signature" in women's writing, here a literary punning signature that alludes to Kate Chopin's ambitions as an artist and to the emotions she wished her book to arouse in its readers.[33]

Chopin's career represented one important aesthetic model for his literary namesake. As a girl, Kate Chopin had been a talented musician, and her first published story, "Wiser Than a God," was about a woman concert pianist who refused to marry. Moreover, Chopin's music both stylistically and thematically influences the language and form of *The Awakening*. The structure of the impromptu, in which there is an opening presentation of a theme, a contrasting middle section, and a modified return to the melodic and rhythmic materials of the opening section, parallels the narrative form of *The Awakening*. The composer's techniques of unifying his work through the repetition of musical phrases, his experiments with harmony and dissonance, his use of folk motifs, his effects of frustration and delayed resolution can also be compared to Kate Chopin's repetition of sentences, her juxtaposition of realism and impressionism, her incorporation of local color elements, and her rejection of conventional closure. Like that of the composer's impromptu, Chopin's style seems spontaneous and improvised, but it is in fact carefully designed and executed.[34]

Madame Ratignolle and Mademoiselle Reisz not only represent important alternative roles and influences for Edna in the world of the novel, but as the proto-heroines of sentimental and local color fiction, they also suggest different plots and conclusions. Adèle's story suggests that Edna will give up her rebellion, return to her marriage, have another baby, and by degrees learn to appreciate, love, and even desire her husband. Such was the plot of many late-nineteenth-century sentimental novels about erring young women marred to older men, such as Susan Warner's *Diana* (1880) and Louisa May Alcott's *Moods* (1882). Mademoiselle Reisz's story suggests that Edna will lose her beauty, her youth, her husband, and children—everything, in short, but her art and her pride—and become a kind of New Orleans nun.

Chopin wished to reject both of these endings and to escape from the literary traditions they represented; but her own literary solitude, her resistance to allying herself with a specific ideological or aesthetic position, made it impossible for her to work out something different and new. Edna remains very much entangled in her own emotions and moods, rather than moving beyond them to real self-understanding and to an awareness of her relationship to her society. She alternates between two moods of "intoxication" and "languor," expansive states of activity, optimism, and power and passive states of contemplation, despondency, and sexual thralldom. Edna feels intoxicated when she is assertive and in control. She first experiences such exultant feelings when she confides her history to Adèle Ratignolle and again when she learns how to swim: "intoxicated with her newly conquered power," she swims out too far. She is excited when she gambles successfully for high stakes at the race track, and finally she feels "an intoxication of expectancy" about awakening Robert with a seductive kiss and playing the dominant role with him. But these emotional peaks are countered by equally intense moods of depression, reverie, or stupor. At the worst, these are states of "indescribable oppression," "vague anguish," or "hopeless ennui." At best, they are moments of passive sensuality in which Edna feels drugged; Arobin's lips and hands, for example, act "like a narcotic upon her" (Chap. 25).

Edna welcomes both kinds of feelings because they are intense, and thus preserve her from the tedium of ordinary existence. They are in fact adolescent emotions, suitable to a heroine who is belatedly awakening; but Edna does not go beyond them to an adulthood that offers new experiences or responsibilities. In her relationships with men, she both longs for complete and romantic fusion with a fantasy lover and is unprepared to share her life with another person.

Chopin's account of the Pontellier marriage, for example, shows Edna's tacit collusion in a sexual bargain that allows her to keep to herself. Although she thinks of her marriage to a paternalistic man twelve years her senior as "purely an accident," the text makes it clear that Edna has married Léonce primarily to secure a fatherly protector who will not make too many domestic, emotional, or sexual demands on her. She is "fond of her husband," with "no trace of passion or excessive or fictitious warmth" (Chap. 7). They do not have an interest in each other's activities or thoughts, and have agreed to a complete separation of their social spheres; Léonce is fully absorbed by the business, social, and sexual activities of the male sphere, the city, Carondelet Street, Klein's Hotel at Grand Isle, where he gambles, and especially the New Orleans world of the clubs and the red-light district. Even Adèle Ratignolle warns Edna of the risks of Mr. Pontellier's club life and of the "diversion" he finds there. "It's a pity Mr. Pontellier doesn't stay home more in the evenings," she tells Edna. "I think you would be more—well, if you don't mind my saying it—more united, if he did." "Oh! dear no!" Edna responds, "with a blank look in her eyes. 'What should I do if he stayed home? We wouldn't have anything to say to each other'" (Chap. 23). Edna gets this blank look in her eyes—eyes that are originally described as "quick and bright"—whenever she is confronted with something she does not want to see. When she joins the Ratignolles at home together, Edna does not envy them, although, as the author remarks, "if ever the fusion of two human beings into one has been accomplished on this sphere it was surely in their union" (Chap. 18). Instead, she is moved by pity for Adèle's "colorless existence which never uplifted its possessor beyond the region of blind contentment" (Chap. 18).

Nonetheless, Edna does not easily relinquish her fantasy of rhapsodic oneness with a perfect lover. She imagines that such a union will bring permanent ecstasy; it will lead, not simply to "domestic harmony" like that of the Ratignolles, but to "life's delirium" (Chap. 18). In her story of the woman who paddles away with her lover in a pirogue and is never heard of again, Edna elaborates on her vision as she describes the lovers, "close together, rapt in oblivious forgetfulness, drifting into the unknown" (Chap. 23). Although her affair with Arobin shocks her into an awareness of her own sexual passions, it leaves her illusions about love intact. Desire, she understands, can exist independently of love. But love retains its magical aura; indeed, her sexual awakening with Arobin generates an even "fiercer, more overpowering love" for Robert (Chap. 28). And when Robert comes back, Edna has persuaded herself that the force of their love will overwhelm all obstacles: "We shall be everything to each other. Nothing else in the world is of any consequence" (Chap. 36). Her intention seems to be that they will go off together into the unknown, like the lovers in her story. But Robert cannot accept such a role, and when he leaves her, Edna finally realizes "that the day would come when he, too, and the thought of him, would melt out of her existence, leaving her alone" (Chap. 39).

The other side of Edna's terror of solitude, however, is the bondage of class as well as gender that keeps her in a prison of the self. She goes blank too whenever she might be expected to notice the double standard of ladylike privilege and oppression of women in southern society. Floating along in her "mazes of inward contemplation," Edna barely notices the silent quadroon nurse who takes care of her children, the little black girl who works the treadles of Madame Lebrun's sewing machine, the laundress who keeps her in frilly white, or the maid who picks up her broken glass. She never makes connections between her lot and theirs.

The scene in which Edna witnesses Adèle in childbirth (Chap. 37) is the first time in the novel that she identifies with another woman's pain, and draws some halting conclusions about the female and the human condition, rather than simply about her own ennui. Edna's births have taken place in unconsciousness; when she goes to Adèle's childbed, "her own like experiences seemed far away, unreal, and only half remembered. She recalled faintly an ecstasy of pain, the heavy odor of chloroform, a stupor which had deadened sensation" (Chap. 37). The stupor that deadens sensation is an apt metaphor for the real and imaginary narcotics supplied by fantasy, money, and patriarchy, which have protected Edna from pain for most of her life, but which have also kept her from becoming an adult.

But in thinking of nature's trap for women, Edna never moves from her own questioning to the larger social statement that is feminism. Her ineffectuality is partly a product of her time; as a heroine in transition between the homosocial and the heterosexual worlds, Edna has lost some of the sense of connectedness to other women that might help her plan her future. Though she has sojourned in the "female colony" of Grand Isle, it is far from being a feminist utopia, a real community of women, in terms of sisterhood. The novel suggests, in fact, something of the historical loss for women of transferring the sense of self to relationships with men.

Edna's solitude is one of the reasons that her emancipation does not take her very far. Despite her efforts to escape the rituals of femininity, Edna seems fated to reenact them, even though, as Chopin recounts these scenes, she satirizes and revises their conventions. Ironically, considering her determination to discard the trappings of her role as a society matron—her wedding ring, her "reception day," her "charming home"—the high point of

Edna's awakening is the dinner party she gives for her twenty-ninth birthday. Edna's birthday party begins like a kind of drawing-room comedy. We are told the guest list, the seating plan, the menu, and the table setting; some of the guests are boring, and some do not like each other; Madame Ratignolle does not show up at the last minute, and Mademoiselle Reisz makes disagreeable remarks in French.

Yet as it proceeds to its bacchanalian climax, the dinner party also has a symbolic intensity and resonance that makes it, as Sandra Gilbert argues, Edna's "most authentic act of self-definition."[35] Not only is the twenty-ninth birthday a feminine threshold, the passage from youth to middle age, but Edna is literally on the threshold of a new life in her little house. The dinner, as Arobin remarks, is a *coup d'état*, an overthrow of her marriage, all the more an act of aggression because Léonce will pay the bills. Moreover, she has created an atmosphere of splendor and luxury that seems to exceed the requirements of the occasion. The table is set with gold satin, Sevres china, crystal, silver, and gold; there is "champagne to swim in" (Chap. 29), and Edna is magnificently dressed in a satin and lace gown, with a cluster of diamonds (a gift from Léonce) in her hair. Presiding at the head of the table, she seems powerful and autonomous: "There was something in her attitude which suggested the regal woman, the one who rules, who looks on, who stands alone" (Chap. 30). Edna's moment of mastery thus takes place in the context of a familiar ceremony of women's culture. Indeed, dinner parties are virtual set pieces of feminist aesthetics, suggesting that the hostess is a kind of artist in her own sphere, someone whose creativity is channeled into the production of social and domestic harmony. Like Virginia Woolf's Mrs. Ramsay in *To the Lighthouse*, Edna exhausts herself in creating a sense of fellowship at her table, although in the midst of her guests she still experiences an "acute longing" for "the unattainable" (Chap. 30).

But there is a gap between the intensity of Edna's desire, a desire that by now has gone beyond sexual fulfillment to take in a much vaster range of metaphysical longings, and the means that she has to express herself. Edna may look like a queen, but she is still a housewife. The political and aesthetic weapons she has in her *coup d'état* are only forks and knives, glasses and dresses.

Can Edna, and Kate Chopin, then, escape from confining traditions only in death? Some critics have seen Edna's much-debated suicide as a heroic embrace of independence and a symbolic resurrection into myth, a feminist counterpart of Melville's Bulkington: "Take heart, take heart, O Edna, up from the spray of thy ocean-perishing, up, straight up, leaps thy apotheosis!" But the ending too seems to return Edna to the nineteenth-century female literary tradition, even though Chopin redefines it for her own purpose. Readers of the 1890s were well accustomed to drowning as the fictional punishment for female transgression against morality, and most contemporary critics of *The Awakening* thus automatically interpreted Edna's suicide as the wages of sin.

Drowning itself brings to mind metaphorical analogies between femininity and liquidity. As the female body is prone to wetness, blood, milk, tears, and amniotic fluid, so in drowning the woman is immersed in the feminine organic element. Drowning thus becomes the traditionally feminine literary death.[36] And Edna's last thoughts further recycle significant images of the feminine from her past. As exhaustion overpowers her, "Edna heard her father's voice and her sister Margaret's. She heard the barking of an old dog that was chained to the sycamore tree. The spurs of the cavalry officer clanged as he walked across the porch. There was the hum of bees, and the musky odor of pinks filled the air" (Chap. 39). Edna's memories are those of awakening from the freedom of childhood to the limitations conferred by female sexuality.

The image of the bees and the flowers not only recalls early descriptions of Edna's sexuality as a "sensitive blossom," but also places *The Awakening* firmly within the traditions of American women's writing, where it is a standard trope for the unequal sexual relations between women and men. Margaret Fuller, for example, writes in her journal: "Woman is the flower, man the bee. She sighs out of melodious fragrance, and invites the winged laborer. He drains her cup, and carries off the honey. She dies on the stalk; he returns to the hive, well fed, and praised as an active member of the community."[37] In post–Civil War fiction, the image is a reminder of an elemental power that women's culture must confront. *The Awakening* seems particularly to echo the last lines of Mary Wilkins Freeman's "A New England Nun," in which the heroine, having broken her long-standing engagement, is free to continue her solitary life, and closes her door on "the sounds of the busy harvest of men and birds and bees; there were halloos, metallic clatterings, sweet calls, long hummings."[38] These are the images of a nature that, Edna has learned, decoys women into slavery; yet even in drowning, she cannot escape from their seductiveness, for to ignore their claim is also to cut oneself off from culture, from the "humming" life of creation and achievement.

We can re-create the literary tradition in which Kate Chopin wrote *The Awakening*, but of course, we can never know how the tradition might have changed if her novel had not had to wait half a century to find its audience. Few of Chopin's literary contemporaries came into contact with the book. Chopin's biographer, Per Seyersted, notes that her work "was apparently unknown to Dreiser, even though he began writing *Sister Carrie* just when *The Awakening* was being loudly condemned. Also Ellen Glasgow, who was at this time beginning to describe unsatisfactory marriages, seems to have been unaware of the author's existence. Indeed, we can safely say that though she was so much of an innovator in American literature, she was virtually unknown by those who were now to shape it and that she had no influence on them."[39] Ironically, even Willa Cather, the one woman writer of the *fin-de-siècle* who reviewed *The Awakening*, not only failed to recognize its importance but also dismissed its theme as "trite."[40] It would be decades before another American woman novelist combined Kate Chopin's artistic maturity with her sophisticated outlook on sexuality, and overcame both the sentimental codes of feminine "artlessness" and the sexual codes of feminine "passionlessness."

In terms of Chopin's own literary development, there were signs that *The Awakening* would have been a pivotal work. While it was in press, she wrote one of her finest and most daring short stories, "The Storm," which surpasses even *The Awakening* in terms of its expressive freedom. Chopin was also being drawn back to a rethinking of women's culture. Her last poem, written in 1900, was addressed to Kitty Garasché and spoke of the permanence of emotional bonds between women:

To the Friend of My Youth

It is not all of life
To cling together while the years glide past.
It is not all of love
To walk with clasped hands from the first to last.
That mystic garland which the spring did twine
Of scented lilac and the new-blown rose,
Faster than chains will hold my soul to thine
Thro' joy, and grief, thro' life—unto its close.[41]

We have only these tantalizing fragments to hint at the directions Chopin's work might have taken if *The Awakening* had been a critical success or even a *succès de scandale*, and if her career had not been cut off by her early death. The fate of *The Awakening* shows only too well how a literary tradition may be enabling, even essential, as well as confining. Struggling to escape from tradition, Kate Chopin courageously risked social and literary ostracism. It is up to contemporary readers to restore her solitary book to its place in our literary heritage.

NOTES

1. Guy de Maupassant, "Solitude," trans. Kate Chopin, *St. Louis Life* 12 (December 28, 1895), 30; quoted in Margaret Culley, "Edna Pontellier: 'A Solitary Soul,'" in *The Awakening*, Norton Critical Edition (New York: Norton, 1976), p. 224.

2. See the contemporary reviews in the Norton Critical Edition, pp. 145–55.

3. "Confidences," in *The Complete Works of Kate Chopin*, ed. Per Seyersted (Baton Rouge: Louisiana State University Press, 1969), Vol. II, p. 701.

4. Carroll Smith-Rosenberg, *Disorderly Conduct: Visions of Gender in Victorian America* (New York: Knopf, 1985), p. 28.

5. Nancy R. Cott, "Passionlessness: An Interpretation of Victorian Sexual Ideology, 1790–1850," *Signs* 4 (1978): 233.

6. Catherine Maria Sedgwick, manuscript diary, quoted in Cott, "Passionlessness," 233.

7. Smith-Rosenberg, *Disorderly Conduct*, p. 69.

8. See Mary P. Ryan, *The Empire of the Mother: American Writing about Domesticity* (New York: Haworth Press, 1982).

9. Harriet Beecher Stowe, *My Wife and I*, quoted in Mary Kelley, *Private Woman, Public Stage: Literary Domesticity in Nineteenth-Century America* (New York: Oxford University Press, 1984), p. 327.

10. Ibid., p. 249.

11. Mary P. Ryan, *Womanhood in America from Colonial Times to the Present* (New York: Franklin Watts, 1983), p. 144.

12. Nina Baym, *Women's Fiction: A Guide to Novels by and about Women in America 1820–1870* (Ithaca, N.Y.: Cornell University Press, 1978), p. 32.

13. Ibid., p. 32.

14. Elizabeth Stuart Phelps, "Art for Truth's Sake," in her autobiography, *Chapters from a Life* (Boston: Houghton Mifflin, 1897).

15. Sarah Orne Jewett, *Letters*, ed. Annie Adams Field (Boston: Houghton Mifflin, 1911), p. 47; quoted in Josephine Donovan, *Sarah Orne Jewett* (New York: Frederick Ungar, 1980), p. 124.

16. Susan B. Anthony, "Homes of Single Women," 1877, quoted in Carol Farley Kessler, "Introduction" to Elizabeth Stuart Phelps, *The Story of Avis* (repr. New Brunswick, N.J.: Rutgers University Press, 1985), xxii.

17. Phelps, *The Story of Avis*, pp. 126, 246.

18. Elizabeth Cady Stanton, diary for 1883, quoted in Cott, "Passionlessness," 236 n. 60.

19. Linda Dowling, "The Decadent and the New Woman in the 1890s," *Nineteenth-Century Fiction* 33 (1979): 441.

20. Frances Porcher, "Kate Chopin's Novel," *The Mirror* (May 4, 1899) and "Books of the Day," *Chicago Times-Herald* (June 1, 1899), in Norton Critical Edition, pp. 145, 149.

21. Martha Vicinus, "Introduction" to George Egerton, *Keynotes and Discords* (repr. London: Virago Books, 1983), xvi.

22. George Egerton, "A Keynote to *Keynotes*," in *Ten Contemporaries*, ed. John Gawsworth (London: Ernest Benn, 1932), p. 60.

23. Per Seyersted, *Kate Chopin: A Critical Biography* (New York: Octagon Books, 1980), p. 18.

24. Sandra Gilbert, "Introduction" to *The Awakening and Selected Stories* (Harmondsworth: Penguin, 1984), p. 16.

25. "Confidences," in Chopin, *Complete Works*, Vol. II, pp. 700–1.

26. "Crumbling Idols," in Chopin, *Complete Works*, Vol. II, p. 693.

27. Seyersted, *Kate Chopin*, p. 83.

28. Ibid., p. 58.

29. Ibid., p. 209, n. 55.

30. "Confidences," in Chopin, *Complete Works*, Vol. II, p. 702.

31. Henry James, November 26, 1892, quoted in Larzer Ziff, *The American* 1890s (New York: Viking, 1966), p. 275.

32. Gilbert, "Introduction," p. 25.

33. Thanks to Nancy K. Miller of Barnard College for this phrase from her current work on the development of women's writing in France. I am also indebted to the insights of Cheryl Torsney of the University of West Virginia, and to the comments of the other participants of my NEH Seminar on "Women's Writing and Women's Culture," Summer 1984.

34. Thanks to Lynne Rogers, Music Department, Princeton University, for information about Frédéric Chopin.

35. Gilbert, "Introduction," p. 30.

36. See Gaston Bachelard, *L'eau et les rêves* (Paris, 1942), pp. 109–25.

37. Margaret Fuller, "Life Without and Life Within," quoted in Bell G. Chevigny, *The Woman and the Myth* (Old Westbury, N.Y.: Feminist Press, 1976), p. 349. See also Wendy Martin, *An American Triptych: Anne Bradstreet, Emily Dickinson, Adrienne Rich* (Chapel Hill: University of North Carolina Press, 1984), pp. 154–9.

38. "A New England Nun," in Mary Wilkins Freeman, *The Revolt of Mother*, ed. Michele Clark (New York: Feminist Press, 1974), p. 97.

39. Seyersted, *Kate Chopin*, p. 196.

40. "Sibert" [Willa Cather], "Books and Magazines," *Pittsburgh Leader* (July 8, 1899), in Norton Critical Edition, p. 153.

41. Chopin, *Complete Works*, Vol. II, p. 735.

MARY E. PAPKE

Kate Chopin's Social Fiction

Kate Chopin's fictional world encompasses all of the nineteenth-century South and is one contemporaneous with her life. She is writing, then, within a period of enormous transmogrification: the pre-capitalist, patriarchal plantation economy built on slavery giving way to industrialization of the land and economic assimilation of the South into a post–Civil War "united" state built on a new class system and based, in part, on the retention of a large working class and the subordination of women of all classes. Concomitantly, she addresses myths of nostalgia and progress, examining the seductive stasis of the old order and the uncertain authority of the new, as evinced both in the private and public spheres. In addition, she depicts social stratification—for example, the social, economic, and sexual segregation of Creoles, Arcadians, poor whites, frontierspeople, new money southerners, and blacks—as both the cause and effect of individual and collective alienation.

Her South is not the romantic vision put forth by many of her contemporary regionalist writers; instead, the real metamorphoses occurring in her time stand as constant background and touchstone to her major subject: the emergent selves of women defying the social securities and strictures of the old South, judging and being judged by the ideological parameters of the true womanhood code. Chopin writes across class and color lines, portraying virtually every southern "type," but she, like Wharton, focuses in her major

From *Verging on the Abyss: The Social Fiction of Kate Chopin and Edith Wharton*, pp. 31–88. Copyright © 1990 by Mary E. Papke.

works on her own class and sex: Creole or upper middle-class society and the
position of women within it. The ideology of true womanhood is as basic to
her work as women are central within society.

It is common knowledge that the cult of domesticity and true
womanhood outlined earlier was particularly exaggerated in the antebellum
South. As historian Anne Firor Scott points out, "Women, like slaves, were
an intrinsic part of the patriarchal dream" (53). Plantation life in order to
be profitable necessitated strict hierarchic systemization of all social/sexual
relationships—master/mistress to slave, man to woman—as well as ideological
justification for ruling class practices. The ideal southern woman was not
just an imaginary distortion of male demands but a realizable construct of
immense value to the patriarchy. To cite Scott again, "Motherhood, happy
families, omnipotent men, satisfied slaves—all were essential parts of the
image of the organic patriarchy." She goes on to say that "in none of these
areas did the image accurately depict the whole reality" (63). One can argue,
however, that women's lived reality was extremely limited, subject as it
was in multiple ways to hegemonic rule. More crucial in the experience of
many white southern women was their apprehension of the irreconcilable
contradictions between ideological theory and social practice. The moral
double standard inherent within true womanhood tenets made glaringly
apparent the disparities between ideological abstraction and lived experience;
in particular, "miscegenation was the fatal flaw in the patriarchal doctrine"
(Scott 59). Male sexual practices refuted the hegemonic hierarchy, breaking
down the distinction between woman and slave; both nonracist and racist
women felt the threat of that breach. Furthermore, if women were to fulfill
their ideological function as moral guardians, they could perhaps support
slavery as a system of labor, since slavery then is seen as an issue of economics
within the male sphere, but could not do so if that system were also one based
on physical and spiritual oppression, since the maintenance of slavery then
raised issues falling within woman's sphere. For example, as noted earlier,
Harriet Beecher Stowe's *Uncle Tom's Cabin, or Life Among the Lowly* stands as
a model for the true womanhood literary response to unchristian acts but not
to slavery as a productive if exploitative system of labor. Chopin evoked the
slavery issue and woman's response to it in several stories—notably "Désirée's
Baby" and "La Belle Zoraïde," but in general, such catastrophic socioeconomic
problems serve as background in her fiction to larger philosophical issues
made comprehensible by their individualization. Chopin saw that for women
of any color life in the antebellum and postbellum South was potentially
abysmal. The struggle against cultural imperatives is a fierce one, made even
more notable in Chopin's representation of it through her focus on states of
liminality.

Cynthia Griffin Wolff, in her "Kate Chopin and the Fiction of Limits," points this out in her overview:

> A majority of Chopin's fictions are set in worlds where stability or permanence is a precarious state: change is always threatened— by the vagaries of impassive fate, by the assaults of potentially ungovernable individual passions, or merely by the inexorable passage of time. More generally, we might say that Chopin construes existence as necessarily uncertain. (125)

More specifically and reinterpreting Wolff, one can see that because Chopin chose to portray women schooled in piety, purity, and passivity, she could not have produced anything other than a fiction of limits and, in many cases, of defeat. Social and sexual ideology which had never fully acknowledged the self-will and personal aspiration of women could prove only more alienating to the individual confronting the shifting reality of the old patriarchal order giving way to a modern, amoral world that yet maintained contradictory prescriptions concerning women. Within this shifting reality, there is seemingly no place for the inscription of woman's desire; or, as Wolff writes of Chopin, "what she sees is the ominous and insistent presence of the margin: the inescapable fact that even our most vital moments must be experienced on the boundary—always threatening to slip away from us into something else, into some dark, undefined contingency" (126). Indeed, in Chopin's world view and fiction, the marginalization of women's lives and desires, the consequent alienation of these individuals within and from their social collectives, becomes the central issue, the boundaries suddenly brought into sharp, clear focus.

As most critics point out, Chopin's earliest stories effectively delimit a range of responses to womanhood ideology and offer characterizations of women that will inform her entire opus. There is, in other words, a direct link between her earliest complete story "Emancipation: A Life Fable" (ca. 1869–1870) and *The Awakening* (1899); Chopin begins and ends with works that dare and defy, simultaneously deconstructing romantic rebellion and elucidating the pragmatics and penalties of particular individual revolts against society. Stories written by early 1891 set out in microcosm the grander pattern of Chopin's later literary explorations and effectively introduce all the central concerns therein: the awakening of woman to her true self (or selves) and the abysses of solitude or alienation into which that self wanders in her quest for fulfillment.

Chopin's women are not as easily compartmentalized as Wharton's: not for her the straightforward portrayal of ideologically stereotypical women—

martyr, mistress, masterpiece. However, Chopin does make up her own continuum of females responding to ideology: woman as "true woman," a seemingly helpless being who is defined only through relationships to and with men; woman as outsider, an artist of a new world view; woman as dual self, a female precariously balanced between submission and self-will.

Chopin first created a patently romantic response to entrapment, a rebellion that is neither willful revolt nor, indeed, female or human in body or soul. Nonetheless, and even though it can be read as naive wish-fulfillment, the animal and animalistic fable of "Emancipation" cannot be denied its importance to Chopin's development. This early work acts as contrast to and kernel for *The Awakening*; further, it offers the sentimentalist, romantic response to life that Chopin will reconstruct, analyze, and then destroy in her later fiction.

In "Emancipation: A Life Fable," an animal born and bred in a cage moves from satisfied, solipsistic existence to isolation in and partial consciousness of a larger world. The male animal while entrapped is nurtured by "an invisible protecting hand" (37) and believes himself to be the center of the universe: the hand that feeds him and the light that warms him exist, he believes, only for those purposes. By chance his cage door is left open. Since he is a "pet" animal and also a creature without knowledge or consciousness, he cannot either close the door or ignore the intrusive effect on his world; more and more "Light" (37) shines in on him until he leaps out into it. Still without consciousness of his true self, "heedless that he is wounding and tearing his sleek sides" (37), he rushes into the world and experiences a sudden and dangerous sensuous awakening. He is no longer kept and cossetted but must now seek his own sustenance and discover his own substance. Despite his isolation and suffering, the animal remains in the world: "the cage remains forever empty!" (38)

Chopin's moral is clear: one must live in the world and be of it; one must discover a self in body (the senses) and in mind (Light) even though that quest be painful and, at first, disillusioning. However, Chopin's romantic means toward this radically open-ended statement are clearly unsophisticated choices. The first false note that points to her lack of authorial self-consciousness and philosophical maturity is the chosen form for her self-expression: the allegorization of her concerns—entrapment within a society and alienation from a true self—and the distanciation of sex and species, both of which formalize, sentimentalize, and undermine her social critique. The emphasis placed on purely animalistic or sensuous self-knowledge also clouds her vision of rebellion: the animal moves away from selfishness and towards consciousness, but that movement is one which remains limited despite Chopin's attempt to suggest the emergence of total selfhood (consciousness of mind and body rather than body split from mind). Furthermore, that the "revolt" of her brute antagonist is effected by accident romanticizes the actual process of coming to consciousness, making of it an aleatory, spontaneous leap of faith from an accepted and good enclosure to an accepted and better "Unknown" (37). Finally, and to be expected from so young a writer, such an emancipation is rewarded, and even suffering is ameliorated by the "seeking, finding, joying" (38) of the animal's continued journey through life. Chopin was clearly aware of the seductive power of nonconsciousness implicitly revealed in the protected life of a nurtured pet just as she was sympathetic to defiance. However, she was not yet able to elucidate the dialectical tension between submission and rebellion, the process of coming to consciousness that informs and is *The Awakening*. The seeds of revolt, in any case, are sown, her focus on ideological conflict begun. Having once romanticized the struggle for selfhood, Chopin would thereafter deromanticize ideological entrapment, meticulously disclosing in her later works the individual's painful journey toward true self through abysses of solitude.

Three of her earliest stories flesh out in female characters her first brutal reading of individual within and without society. All are built upon the ideology of true womanhood; yet each is strikingly dissimilar in its portrayal of woman reaching toward self-consciousness. "A No-Account Creole," first written as "Euphrasie" in 1888 and rewritten in 1890 and in January–February 1891, reveals a woman within the traditional patriarchy. "Wiser Than a God," written in June 1889, draws the world of the woman as artist. "A Point at Issue!", written in August 1889, examines the woman as divided self desirous of both self-fulfillment and union with another.

Chopin's renaming of "Euphrasie" as "A No-Account Creole" perhaps best reveals her theme and self-consciousness, in the negative sense, as a writer. Although Euphrasie is the center of the story, she is, like the animal in "Emancipation," a paragon of passivity. Despite Chopin's female allegiance, it must have seemed obvious finally both to editor and to writer that a title indicating the agent of the plot would be more acceptable to conventional, ideologically bound readers.

Euphrasie inadvertently instigates the action and conflict detailed in the story when she writes her father's New Orleans creditors about the sorry state of their plantation. She does not do so out of sheer willfulness but for the sake of duty, justice, and, perhaps, for a bit of excitement. In any case, this action takes place before the story proper begins, thus marginalizing Euphrasie's will in a curious way even though this is her story. The conflict and drama depicted relies upon, instead, the actions of Euphrasie's two men: Placide Santien, the darkly handsome, violent Creole of the second title; and Wallace Offdean, the "well-clipped and groomed," cool creditor (88). Who will win

Euphrasie is the central question, and the oppositeness of the two men is the dramatic mechanism of the tale. Euphrasie is at the center of their conflict, yet she does not move nor is she particularly moved or moving as a character. A dutiful daughter, student, plantation mistress, she wishes only to become a dutiful wife. She is first affianced to Placide: it is an almost predetermined union, and he loves her. Although she is attracted to Wallace, and he to her, she is content to fulfill her obligation to Placide. In short, Euphrasie believes in the ideological precept that a woman's fate is effected by men and that first come are first served with the opportunity to determine a woman's destiny.

Indeed, Euphrasie would be taken care of well by either of these two men. Placide prepares assiduously for the moment he is to bring her to his plantation home. Wallace, in turn, promises her a better plantation when he offers his hand. She can choose, of course, only one and that one has already been named, a fact which Wallace is oblivious to until she blurts it out at his proposal. While Chopin incorporates passages on love and romance within the text, it becomes clear at this point of disclosure that Chopin's story is, finally, not about love but about honor in the abstract: not Euphrasie's sense of honor which is touched upon as being somehow tainted because she has kissed a man she does not love, not Placide's honor which would have been insulted by Wallace's behavior had Wallace acted knowingly against him, not Wallace's honor since he also has been done no willful wrong. Chopin's ostensible subject is, instead, male honor in the abstract as it is expressed through love for woman or, as Wallace tells Placide, "The way to love a woman is to think first of her happiness" (101). So, when Placide jilts Euphrasie, he proves doubly honorable: he leaves the door open for Wallace, the man who has awakened his sense of honor; and he saves Euphrasie, as she makes clear, from the sin of having to make love to the wrong man (102).

Finally, the last "action" of the story is telling. Wallace asks Euphrasie if he can return to her, and this time she says nothing. He tells her that if she does *not* speak, he will know he can return. Again, she says nothing. It is clear, then, that she is a "true" woman, one who does nothing yet all good comes to her. She is one of Chopin's few perfect Southern belles, women who would keep to their place although it means the ruination of their souls.

It is interesting that this story takes "Emancipation" one step further without freeing itself completely of romantic melodramatics. Here the door to Euphrasie's senses is opened by Wallace; here the way for Wallace to win Euphrasie is made clear by Placide, who does so by following Wallace's advice. In both actions, the power comes from without Euphrasie—notably, from men. Most striking is that Euphrasie's nonconsciousness of her own power, that over men and thus over her own fate, never changes, never becomes even a partial consciousness but remains marginal throughout the plot. Yet the trace of Euphrasie's power and the fact that her passivity masks an inner torment reflect both Chopin's own authorial passivity and desire. The reader is made aware, even in this conventional tale, that surface does not necessarily reveal substance: the assumption that silence equates with acquiescence need not be true. That Chopin will later offer detailed portrayal of the ideologically true woman who speaks of and to her situation, notably in her characterization of Adèle Ratignolle in *The Awakening*, suggests that even in her earliest and seemingly most conventional fiction, Chopin was subtly subversive, if not speaking clearly her discontent or disbelief at least murmuring the same in her submerged text.

"Wiser Than a God" presents the highly dramatic and at times also melodramatic moment of crisis in the life of pianist Paula Von Stoltz: she must choose between the call of art and the call of love. Again, Chopin draws the mind/body split, this time, however, without recourse to fabular conceit or fairy-tale ending. Chopin will allow no conventional compromise here. It is mildly astonishing to read Paula's refusal of George Brainard's proposal. At the same time, it is not unexpected, at the end, to see Paula rewarded for her show of will with the admiration of Professor Max Kuntzler, "her teacher of harmony" (44).

Chopin's revelation coupled with unconventional resolution and conventional conclusion is that of Paula's character, the pragmatic but determined artist. Paula is neither the dilettante nor the starving bohemian (characterizations seen in Wharton's similar art versus marriage stories). It is true that she stands outside of high society because of her art: she produces on demand what George Brainard's class desires. More important, however, is the fact that she is socially alienated because of her class, nationality, and—by the story's middle point—her solitude.

Despite her negative background of neither wealth nor community, Paula perceives herself as a self-fulfilled and self-fulfilling individual. Since marriage to George would necessitate her response to the call of true womanhood rather than that of artist, Paula's rejection reveals her determination to support herself, albeit through temporary compromise of her full aspirations, and to produce art but not to be consumed by its buyers (a decision strikingly similar to Chopin's case). She is a woman artist who addresses her mental powers to the realization of deep desire: to speak her body through her art. In the story, she comes to understand fully the opposition between and interrelationship of illusion and reality, sentiment and emotion, desire and need. Paula then chooses to follow the purpose of her life even though she be deemed "a mad woman" (46) by George and his ilk, to position herself in a state of liminality. By the conclusion, it is clear that the narrator/author, not one of George's world, believes Paula to be wiser than a god.

Foreshadowing another important subtext in *The Awakening*, Chopin here also develops a continuum of relationships obtained between men and women by deconstructing abstract male attitudes toward women into particular types of social practices. In brief, Chopin separates men into friends or lovers, companions or husbands, stereotypes again but ones less reliant on fairy-tale romantics. Chopin also sets out different female responses to the call of womanhood: women either become wives and mothers, as George's unnamed "pretty little black-eyed fairy" (43) does, eschewing even the mundane art she appreciates; or exiles, as Paula becomes when she purposely moves to Europe. Of course, Chopin suggests that a woman might have the best of both worlds, harmony in every sense of the word, if she meets a man who could be both friend and lover, but this union of opposites is not effected within the story itself. Paula's abyss of solitude is brightened by her eventual renown and Max's presence in her life. We are not, however, led to believe that her self-exile is any less real and painful. Chopin makes clear, then, that women love, but for the salvation of their selves, they might not allow themselves to live out that love. Such will be the dilemma facing Edna Pontellier, and such will be the life choice of Mademoiselle Reisz in *The Awakening*.

In "A Point at Issue!" Chopin further complicates the theme of pure intellect in conflict with pure emotion as well as her neat bifurcation of male roles. Charles Faraday, a mathematics professor, meets student Eleanor Gail, is first physically attracted to her, and then comes to perceive her as "his ideal woman," "a logical woman" (49). In short, she shatters his ideological expectations, "an adorned picture of woman as he had known her" (49), and becomes the new woman of whom he has heretofore only dreamed. Perceiving her as his ideal equal, he would be both friend and lover, beyond ideological constraints:

> Marriage was to be a form, that while fixing legally their relation to each other, was in no wise to touch the individuality of either; that was to be preserved intact. Each was to remain a free integral of humanity, responsible to no dominating exactions of so-called marriage laws. And the element that was to make possible such a union was trust in each other's love, honor, courtesy, tempered by the reserving clause of readiness to meet the consequences of reciprocal liberty. (50)

Eleanor wholly acquiesces to this, finding Charles equally ideal, although in different ways. Charles is notably conservative, is a man of reason despite his desire to make a different kind of union. He is also a secure member of his society, academia. Eleanor, on the other hand, is the true revolutionary despite her decision to be, at first, led by Charles into an "intellectual existence" (50). She is outside his established world but also determined to remain free of "public notice" (48). She is weary of compromising social proprieties and instead wishes her union to effect "the satisfying consciousness of roaming the heights of free thought, and tasting the sweets of a spiritual emancipation" (48). For her, solitude and contemplation are to be transformed into intercourse and revelation; transcendence is all. For him, the best of both worlds remains desirable. It is this incompatibility between the desires of conventional men and of radical women that ruptures their new marriage and destroys Eleanor.

Both ostensibly live up to their pact. Eleanor stays in France after their honeymoon to perfect her French; Charles returns to the university. The difference of view is immediately obvious. Eleanor progresses; Charles regresses. She surrounds herself with books and throws herself into a new world; Charles returned to his old one, "to his duties at the university, and resumed his bachelor existence as quietly as though it had been interrupted but by the interval of a day" (51). Furthermore, Eleanor continues to see them as two selves with one purpose; Charles makes them one—"She was himself" (52), thus denying their individuality. Most important, Charles returns not only to his secure, staid world, but he also begins to act and to communicate as one deeply entrenched within society. He becomes attracted to another woman and writes Eleanor of her, knowing himself that his is not a serious interest but merely social flirtation and ego-gratification. Eleanor, since she lives outside society and is unaware of Charles' reconstitution of his conservative, social self, assumes their pact has begun in earnest, that they are living an open marriage. And she follows suit. When they reunite several months later, it becomes clear that they can no longer communicate but that neither understands nor wishes to comprehend why.

Charles' true possessive nature has, by the end, come to the fore: he has not thought this out, but "he began to wonder if there might not be modifications to this marital liberty of which he was so staunch an advocate" (56). Eleanor has also surrendered her intellect to her emotions: she reveals, "'I have been over the whole ground myself, over and over, but it is useless. I have found that there are certain things which a woman can't philosophize about, any more than she can about death when it touches that which is near to her!'" (58). Charles communes only with himself and remains deluded in the end; however, he loses neither self nor Other: "'I love her none the less for it, but my Nellie is only a woman, after all!'" (58). Eleanor explores her self and reveals it to Charles, yet in doing so, she effaces herself and then can no longer philosophize about her own self-death: "'I think nothing!'" (58).

Chopin here delimits the boundaries of ideology and elaborates upon the results both of traversing those boundaries and of compromising the self. She reveals a possible alternative to patriarchal convention and then how impossible, at least in this case, it is to attain. Close examination of her character development further reveals that it is the boundaries of a woman's life that are the points at issue. Charles is from beginning to end at the secure center of the societal web. Eleanor who begins almost beyond it and who attempts to reform its boundaries by her very act of living is finally brought into the center as well: she becomes not Charles, as he romanticizes, but merely his reflection, the shadow of her true self. The mind/body split seen in the first story is reenacted, but this time the mind is surrendered, the inner self lost through capitulation. Chopin here rewrites the fable and romances of her earlier work as pessimistic realism, the lightness of those tales transformed into darkness. Except in those works wherein Chopin falls back upon myths and melodrama, there will be no more simple happy endings.

At Fault, written between 5 July 1889 and 20 April 1890, marks Chopin's first full-scale attempt at controversial content expressed through conventional form. Like her earliest stories, this first novel shows her artistic and philosophical development as well as her shortcomings. *At Fault* is both unexpected revelation and partial compromise. As with any woman's work that straddles in unladylike fashion the gap between sentimental and social fiction, it is necessary to pay attention both to what Chopin explicitly says and to what she cannot or will not yet say but which she embeds in her text. To do so, one must pull apart the multiple layers of her novel to get at her core concerns.

Simply, *At Fault* is a story of problematic love. Thérèse Lafirme, a widow in her thirties, inherits her husband's Cane River plantation, Place-Du-Bois. Through a business venture, she meets David Hosmer, a northerner, and they quickly fall in love. So too do Grégoire Santien, Thérèse's nephew, a hot-blooded, overly romantic Creole (and brother of the equally hot-blooded Placide in "A No-Account Creole") and Melicent Hosmer, David's sister, an "independent" woman who lives off her brother and who is a melodramatic sap, an almost caricatural new woman. David, however, is divorced from an alcoholic, and his ex-wife Fanny still lives. Thérèse, a Catholic southerner of the old morality, cannot accept new mores and, in essence, forces David to re-wed Fanny and to bring her to Cane River so that Thérèse can have David with her while they ostensibly live out her moral code by making Fanny happy. Fanny eventually succumbs to her weakness and, in a highly melodramatic climax, drowns. Similarly, Grégoire's and Melicent's affair is destroyed when he kills a racially-mixed firebrand who burns down David's sawmill. That cold-blooded murder, even if of a dangerous terrorist, morally disgusts Melicent, and she leaves Grégoire. Grégoire then dies violently, leaving Melicent to do a moral about-face as she grieves for him in melodramatic fashion. Finally, as in the best of all sentimental romances, Thérèse and David are married and, one assumes, live happily ever after.

It should be evident from the above that Chopin's experimentation lies in her premises and not in her close. Perhaps because she chose to focus on such a controversial issue as divorce while she also critiqued the rise of industrial capitalism, she felt compelled to end her various plots with convenient and seemingly conventional conclusions—in other words, to make a last curtsy to propriety and popular taste. But just how enervating are her textual compromises in the light of such radical content? It is hard to deny the revisionary intent of her text, and, indeed, the title of her work is, one might argue, consciously self-reflexive. Just as the reader is led to see that everyone in the novel is flawed in some crucial way, so too does Chopin suggest that conventional literature and the world it depicts and glorifies are dangerously at fault.

The few critics who have done serious study of this work tend to bypass questions of form and to focus instead on the most obvious yet crucially innovative level of the text: the economic critique. Unlike many local colorists, Chopin is not intent on painting a picture of an idyllic South. Instead, she places her novel in the post-Reconstruction South and focuses on the changes occurring on the land and in the industry because of the arrival of northern capitalist methods and ethics. *At Fault*, then, can be seen as a political and economic battleground. Furthermore, as Joyce Ruddel Ladenson writes:

> The dialectic is right out of Marx: feudal power conflicts with rising bourgeois power, with the inevitable triumph of the latter. The catch here is that contrary to the standard class conflict which at the highest levels takes place between men, this conflict combines class and sex, the feudal world represented by a woman tied to an older European culture. (32)

In this type of reading, Thérèse and David are not merely romantic or colorful individuals; more importantly, they are members of two different but now conjoined ensembles of human and economic relations. Chopin's presentation and development of characters thus complementarily offer socio-political analysis and criticism.

For example, Thérèse's world is seen, on the one hand, as built on firm and high morals, on individual sacrifice for the common good, the "sacredness of a trust" Thérèse shares with other living and dead southerners to uphold the old true way, feudal agrarianism (741). On the other hand, that Thérèse's morality is relative and, indeed, based on oppression of the common people and not always willful self-sacrifice is also shown: on her land lies the grave of McFarlane, a character based on the real-life Robert McAlpin who was, in turn, the inspiration for Stowe's Simon Legree; not all her ex-slaves or their descendants, notably the rebel Joçint, are as content as her old mammy, Marie Louise, is with their state of powerlessness in her world; more explicitly, Grégoire, her blood relative, stands as a negative exemplar of southern consciousness. Similarly, David's world is seen from opposing viewpoints. That his true world, industrial capitalism, allows new freedom for workers and women is obvious, particularly so in the case of his sister who is both a conspicuous consumer and a woman of leisure. That his system is also based on oppression and relative morality is again made clear through the actions of Joçint, the slave's son become wage slave; through description of Fanny's bourgeois, morally corrupt friends; and through his sister Melicent's own response to events, particularly her hypocritical "mourning" of her moral counterpart, Grégoire. As Lewis Leary makes clear, it is not for either world a case of absolute good or evil: "The fault may be interpreted as that of an agrarian, land-preserving South, lulled by traditions of ease and morality and religion, as it fails to respond to the industrial, land-destroying North, whose morality is modern and utilitarian. Or it may be the other way round" (178).

Chopin's acknowledgment of moral relativity and self-doubt in times of social and economic transformation is farsighted; it is her movement away from absolutes which informs her superficially romantic text and makes of it more than what it at first appears to be. Indeed, to understand fully Chopin's final political position and statement necessitates moving to another level of the text, that of the story of the individual's search for a moral, socially responsible, and self-fulfilling existence. It is also at this level of Thérèse's and David's love story that Chopin's critique of socio-sexual politics, particularly that of true womanhood ideology, implicit in the economic subtext, becomes evident.

Thérèse Lafirme is, first and foremost, a southern lady of the old tradition. She is fully complicit with womanhood ideology, so much so that she moves residence away from the newly built railroad to avoid the encroaching hordes of northern capitalist barbarians of whom David Hosmer is one. She rebuilds in the old style and, in fact, attempts to uphold single-handedly the old way of plantation life even while she capitalizes, personally and financially, on her relationship with David. Though she passes a singular year in his company, she still advocates true womanhood precepts: she reminds him continuously that she is no individualist and that she gladly effaces herself for the sake of others. Her self-martyrdom excuses her powerful position as plantation mistress: she acts as overlord merely to comply with duty and not as an expression of self-will. Similarly, once she learns of David's marital situation, she again sacrifices her own desire for the sake of another and in doing so simultaneously acts as martyr and moral guardian to David and Fanny. Thérèse thus appears to be morally and spiritually superior, sexually pure, the womanly ideal. By the novel's end, however, Chopin exposes such self-effacement as morally ambiguous (at best), socially negligent, individually destructive, and, in the case of Fanny, death-dealing.

As Thérèse's ideological counterpart, David is equally pure in his behavior. Once Thérèse tells him that he must be a man and face the consequences of his actions, he willingly accepts her as moral guide: "He felt her to be a woman with moral perceptions keener than his own and his love, which in the past twenty-four hours had grown to overwhelm him, moved him now to a blind submission" (769). Though he is in "anguish of spirit" (770), he returns to Fanny, remarries her, and attempts to live up to Thérèse's standards for him. He continues to do so even after he realizes he hates Fanny, even after he moves Fanny to Place-Du-Bois and must then see both women each day, even after Fanny descends into alcoholic schizophrenia again. By the novel's end, Chopin makes clear once more that such self-martyrdom is not only repressive but also hypocritical and, again for Fanny, lethal.

It is through the disturbed character of Fanny that Chopin disorders the neat sexual and moral hierarchies at the base of womanhood ideology and of her text. One can read Fanny as pure stereotype: Fanny as the fallen woman. Chopin makes her more than that by offering in a minimum of words Fanny's side of the story. She is a woman fallen into alienation, a true woman in that she is powerless and self-less. Through Fanny's eyes, the reader sees another David, as real a man as Thérèse's lover, and learns why after the first marriage Fanny "began to dread him and defy him" (779). David's relationship with Fanny had been superficial from the start. David had quickly labelled her as beneath him in class, and Fanny had just as quickly "felt herself as of little consequence, and in a manner, overlooked" (798). Her desire and self-will are deemed unimportant, especially after the death of their only child, a son; she is at most David's helpmeet and, during the second marriage, treated as *his* child. In essence, David, following Thérèse's will, drives Fanny to desperate means and to her eventual despairing end. For example, after their reunion and despite his knowledge of her "sensitivity," he uproots Fanny from her secure if morally tainted world and forces her move to an alien and alienating land. It is not surprising, then, that on her first night in Thérèse's world Fanny finds "a certain mistrust was creeping into her heart with the nearing darkness" (794). The coming of night suggests not only the mental darkness of Fanny's stupors; it also foreshadows Fanny's end as well as recognition of the truth of her existence and perceptions: the moral murkiness of her marriage, the rude erasure of her hope when she later hears

David who becomes at one point deliriously ill call Thérèse's name instead of her own and who later threatens to kill her if she take Thérèse's name in vain, the moral and spiritual blindness she faces as she realizes that neither David nor Thérèse acknowledges her desire, the irreparable loss of herself in her constant position of otherness, the final inky darkness that is her death.

The destruction of Fanny's precariously maintained sense of self because of the moral theories and practices of Thérèse and David judges darkly both womanhood ideology and the patriarchal, whether feudal or capitalist. If an individual, even if only a weak woman, can be driven into solitude and alienation by accepted morality for her own good, what then is the difference between morality and immorality? Similarly, if a man sacrifices his life only to destroy another's, what is the social value of such self-effacement? Finally, if a woman were to realize the cost of womanhood morality and that there is not one true, faultless way of being, how then does she or anyone live? Chopin's answer to the last is the "moral" of her tale: some women and men do not survive; some do, but only after questioning authority, admitting self-will, and accepting self-doubt and continual self-transformation as the basis of existence in an, at best, amoral world.

Chopin suggests such a survivor in the character counterpart to Fanny: Homeyer, the man closest to David. Homeyer's philosophy of life and reaction to David's actions are continually recalled by David at crucial moments. For instance, David reviews Homeyer's response to his remarriage and the moral issues involved:

> And what had Homeyer said of it? He had railed of course as usual, at the submission of a human destiny to the exacting and ignorant rule of what he termed moral conventionalities. He had startled and angered Hosmer with his denunciation of Thérèse's sophistical guidance. Rather—he proposed—let Hosmer and Thérèse marry, and if Fanny were to be redeemed—though he pooh-poohed the notion as untenable with certain views of what he called the rights to existence: the existence of wrongs— sorrows—diseases—death—let them all go to make up the conglomerate whole—and let the individual man hold on to his personality. But if she must be redeemed—granting this point to their littleness, let the redemption come by different ways than those of sacrifice: let it be an outcome from the capability of their united happiness. (777)

David, the slave to "Love's prophet," Thérèse, cannot at this point in the story accept Homeyer's advice, but neither can he totally cast it from his mind (777). Later, David recalls another conversation concerning religions, applicable to Thérèse's Catholicism, and social evolution, ideas unheard of in his and Thérèse's philosophy:

> "Homeyer would have me think that all religions are but mythological creations invented to satisfy a species of sentimentality—a morbid craving in man for the unknown and undemonstrable.... he believes in a natural adjustment... In an innate reserve force of accommodation. What we commonly call laws in nature, he styles accidents—in society, only arbitrary methods of expediency, which, when they outlive their usefulness to an advancing and exacting civilization, should be set aside. He is a little impatient to always wait for the inevitable natural adjustment." (792–793)

Homeyer, then, is a man beyond the manners and morals of David and Thérèse, a sophisticated realist coupling a long-range optimism with immediate pessimism. Homeyer is also a character beyond the text: he neither appears, nor is he given a verifiable existence. Homeyer is such an illusory and visionary being, in fact, that Thérèse early on surmises he is David's alter-ego. Chopin never corroborates this interpretation in her narration but instead leaves Homeyer a voice deeply embedded in David and strangely distanced within the text. However, just as Thérèse speculates that Homeyer is David's inner voice, it is textual counterpoint to conjecture that Homeyer is the text's other narrator, Chopin's secret critical voice. This theory is given substance by Thérèse's awakening to new consciousness and by the lovers' final discourse.

Thérèse begins to question her moral allegiance and purposes once Fanny arrives at Place-Du-Bois. She hears Fanny's story and thereafter sees before her the effects of her moral stance. Her self-sacrifice is shown to be futile and selfish; her morals become less self-glorifying: she thinks, "Were Fanny, and her own prejudices, worth the sacrifice which she and Hosmer had made?" (808). Later she ponders whether her morality is finally a nurturance or a denial of life: "the doubt assailed her whether it were after all worth while to strive against the sorrows of life that can be so readily put aside" (810). At the same time David comes to realize that their morality costs too much but that he cannot break faith with Thérèse. At this point, however, it clearly becomes solely Thérèse's duty to offer moral support to both of them since it was her will that their lives be so and it is now only within her power to make those lives bearable. Shortly thereafter, Thérèse dreams that her actions to save David had only served to kill him. She here subconsciously recognizes the relativity of her morality:

She had always thought this lesson of right and wrong a very
plain one. So easy of interpretation that the simplest minded
might solve it if they would. And here had come for the first time
in her life a staggering doubt as to its nature.... She continued
to ask herself only "was I right?" and it was by the answer to
that question that she would abide, whether in the stony content
of accomplished righteousness, or in an enduring remorse that
pointed to a goal in whose labyrinthine possibilities her soul lost
itself and fainted away. (840)

But there are no easy either–or answers available to Thérèse, and she
consciously enters a state of contemplation and self-doubt. Grégoire's death,
as well as Joçint's murder, makes righteousness impossible: Grégoire is of
her blood, and she therefore believes that she shares responsibility for all
the bloodshed. She accepts then that the ideology which she has advocated
has proven to be at least partially based on immorality and hypocrisy. Her
relationship with David and Fanny serves to foreground this realization. As
she tells David after Fanny's death, "'I have seen myself at fault in following
what seemed the only right. I feel as if there were no way to turn for the
truth. Old supports appear to be giving way beneath me. They were so
secure before'" (872). And so Thérèse precariously balances between self-
recrimination and self-loss.

David offers Thérèse and himself a way out but not, as one would
expect of a less complicated work, by offering his new supports—bourgeois
ethics—as alternative world view. David has also seen into the heart of his
morality which is, obviously, not that dissimilar from Thérèse's. For all their
seemingly crucial differences—sex, class, mores—David and Thérèse are still
identically caught in the deadly web of hegemonic ideology, and, as David
points out, it is not within those traditional boundaries that they will acquire
self-knowledge:

"Thérèse," said Hosmer firmly, "the truth in its entirety isn't given
to man to know—such knowledge, no doubt, would be beyond
human endurance. But we make a step towards it, when we learn
that there is rottenness and evil in the world, masquerading as
right and morality—when we learn to know the living spirit from
the dead letter. I have not cared to stop in this struggle of life to
question. You, perhaps, wouldn't dare to alone. Together, dear
one, we will work it out. Be sure there is a way—we may not find
it in the end, but we will at least have tried." (872)

It is a declaration such as Homeyer might have made.

The novel's conclusion reestablishes difference and offers a quick glimpse at transcendence of separation. David and Thérèse marry and begin a new life which incorporates the best of their old worlds but which is beyond the strictures and norms of the traditional. David while still the sensible capitalist has learned sensitivity through his experience with Thérèse. Similarly, Thérèse while yet the plantation mistress is no longer a firm frozen saint but has instead come to acknowledge and to express her individual desire. The joining of old and new worlds, the marriage of land and industry, of South and North, of woman and man result finally in a utopic union of promising and profitable love. Chopin, however, does not descend into sentimental romance here. She makes clear that transcendence coupled with self-fulfillment is possible but that the potentiality lies solely within the power and will of each individual: the reader is not privy to David's and Thérèse's last whispered words. Self-fulfillment is not presented as a finished product, a commodity that one can purchase cheaply, but as a process one must effect. Chopin only indicates that some words of desire and will can be said and heard by those who refuse self-effacement, those who continually strive to understand the "living spirit"; but these words cannot be inscribed in traditional texts, cannot be spelled out in "dead letter." The conclusion of *At Fault*—unlike the dead ending of "A Point at Issue!"—is open-ended "natural adjustment" and offers not so much a resolution as a glimpse of a new world, one of unspeakable delight.

The partial compromise of the text lies in the forms and techniques Chopin uses. Chopin was not yet such a sufficiently sophisticated writer and social critic to be able to produce a completely unified work of social fiction. Too often her central concerns play second role to stereotypical characterization, witty stabs at minor issues, and her expert but disruptive introduction of dialect. The melodramatic Grégoire–Melicent love story does not finally add as much as it distracts from the development of the realistic main plot and the ethical issues therein. The conflation of fate and self-will is also heavy-handed since it is abruptly and violently forced as climax. Most problematic is Chopin's use of Black characters. Thérèse's lived experience is predicated upon the use of Blacks as labor power, as constituents of the feudal slave culture with which she is first identified. One of the most disturbing elements of the novel is that Black characters must die, in essence be sacrificed, so that she may relinquish her sense of totality to the new ideology embodied in David; one may look to Helen Taylor's critique of *At Fault* for a fuller account of this problem. *At Fault* was, of course, Chopin's first novel, and in several sections it reads as such.

That Chopin herself felt the inadequacy of her novelistic skills can be intuited from her return to the short story form. She seemed to comprehend that her own critical impatience with large-scale plot manipulation made her resort to textual methods of expediency in order to foreground her philosophical end statements, that she had attempted too much too soon. She might, as well, also have been discouraged by the reception accorded her first novel. Whatever the case, she turned back to short fiction and used it once more as a testing ground for the themes, images, and techniques introduced here and later brought together so well in her final masterpiece, *The Awakening*. She continued to call attention to the process of coming to consciousness, a critical process only partially realized and elaborated in *At Fault*.

Though Kate Chopin would continue to experiment with various fictional forms, her post–1891 work focuses more and more on the oppressiveness of womanhood ideology and the arduousness of woman's quest for self. This development is particularly striking when one considers the popularity of Chopin's less adventurous work, her local color stories. That Chopin had more to say than what could be said through conventional fiction is patent; that she had the courage to do so, risking the loss of reputation and audience, is both strange and rare.

One cannot know what made Chopin follow the literary course she did. One can speculate that after the total rejection of her second novel, *Young Dr. Gosse*, begun almost immediately after *At Fault* and finished in November 1890, she realized what was acceptable and what was not. One can go further, however, and theorize that her post–1891 stories reveal that she chose nonetheless to make central in her fiction that which was not to be written or said in genteel literature. The increasingly revisionary subject matter on which her mid-career stories depend suggests that Chopin wished both to subvert and to challenge true womanhood ideology in her work and that she was herself progressively informed by the critical process she persistently pursued despite censure. Her major stories of this period can be categorized as addressing three themes under the heading of ideology: the solitary awakening of the alienated individual, the virtues and failings of motherhood as a means to self-fulfillment, and the realm of the senses as the battleground for the self.

Her 1891 stories for the most part break no new ground and read as fairly conventional historical and local color tales. Her main energy was then going toward the promotion of her two novels. There are, to be sure, unconventional heroines even here: Marianne in "The Maid of Saint Phillippe" (written 19 April 1891), Fifine in "A Very Fine Fiddle" (13 September 1891), Boulotte in "Boulôt and Boulotte" (20 September 1891), Lolotte Bordon in

"A Rude Awakening" (13 July 1891). All are social exiles because of class or circumstance; except for the mythic Marianne, all are pragmatic survivors who break convention for good reason and thus are finally not such rebellious figures as may appear so on first reading. Less easily rationalized are those stories in which Chopin purposely focuses on alienation; these works rise above the ordinary, though not all do so to the same degree. Two of her earliest stories in this vein, "Beyond the Bayou" (7 November 1891) and "After the Winter" (31 December 1891), fail to show the roots of social conflict that effect an alienated life. In both, the protagonists, the African-American La Folle and the ruined southerner Michel, have been driven insane by their experiences of war and its atrocities. Both reject society until, by accident, they are brought back into the fold through the acts of children. Chopin does not investigate the causes of self-exile in these particular cases, nor does she seem to desire anything less than full reconciliation of individual with society. There is a hint, however, that society has changed its ways at least partially because of the actions of its self-exiled; in both stories, society waits with open arms for the return of its critics, and it is a warm world of "infinite peace" and childlike innocence (188). At the same time, it is a radiant world only at its center; as Michel perceives, even in his transcendent moment, there is always "the hill far off that was in black shadow against the sky" (188). Chopin hereafter concerns herself almost obsessively with the black shadows on the social margins. In this line of her work, she is no longer content with emancipation from alienation if it only leads to return to the old world that is still bordered in darkness.

"Ma'ame Pélagie," written 27–28 August 1892, and "Désirée's Baby," written 24 November 1892, clearly mark her break with traditional reconciliation themes and superficially happy endings. In both, she takes up the true woman paradigm, sets it in the historical contexts of an antebellum and a postbellum South, and subtly exposes the destructive will-to-power which relies upon womanhood ideology for its realization.

"Désirée's Baby" takes place in the old South, and the reader is presented with two portraits of that time and place. One centers on the genteel and peaceful Valmondé, grand plantation of a couple of the same name. Here Désirée is abandoned as a baby and taken up as the Valmondés' own child. At the outset of the story, she is eighteen, has grown "to be beautiful and gentle, affectionate and sincere,—the idol of Valmondé" (240). She has just left her perfect world for L'Abri, the plantation of her impassioned husband, Armand Aubigny.

L'Abri is the black horizon glimpsed in Chopin's earlier story. Unlike Valmondé, it is a dark world of sadness and barely restrained brutality. The passions of its master result not in love and fruitfulness for this world, as they do at first for Désirée, but in ruthlessness and sterility. It is a world of power in which Armand's will and desire color everything, just as the oaks around his house "shadowed it like a pall" (241). Désirée's conflicting emotions of happiness and fear felt early on in their marriage (242) foreshadow their fall into individual darkness and despair. It comes as no surprise at the end that the one symbol of a bright new world, Désirée's newborn son, should prove death-dealing precisely because it has been darkened, both figuratively and literally, by Armand.

Once it becomes evident that their son is a mulatto, Désirée loses everything: Armand throws her from the pedestal on which he had placed her down to the lowest level of animal, though Chopin immediately clarifies for the reader that it is Armand who is the inhuman beast and not Désirée (243). The checked cruelty of Armand, reined in after his marriage, is unleashed: the slaves suffer as does their supposed sister, Désirée, and it is all her fault. That Désirée is blamed for the impurity of their son is both circumstantial and telling. Monsieur Valmondé had foreseen such a situation before the wedding, stressing the uncertainty of her parentage. Armand had responded to his warnings about her obscure past by saying that the Aubigny name would make Désirée into the compleat ideal. Here Chopin reveals the base of true womanhood, male power, and the agency of feminine self-fulfillment, male desire. Even though Armand himself has a somewhat shadowy past and an equally dark present, there is never a moment, until the final disclosure, that suspicion falls on anyone but Désirée. In this way Chopin utilizes the theme of racism to illuminate her critical reading of woman's extreme vulnerability if she chooses to live according to patriarchal prescriptives. Chopin drives home the truth that no matter how such a woman might live, no matter what she might make herself to be, she can be destroyed, and with full social sanction, if she does not fit the specified model in every particular way, even in those ways outside her control. In Armand's world, Désirée deserves social oblivion or death since she has passed herself off as other than what she should have been: her reality, rooted in her body, is a black stain on him and his world, "upon his home and his name" (244).

Désirée also comes to believe herself doomed, though not at fault. Ever a true woman, she remains oblivious to the very last of her rights and her nascent power as well as profoundly limited in her consciousness, both of her situation and of herself. She is the last to realize her child is black; she is the last to acquiesce to the "fact" that she must be the cause of this since her husband has said it is so. However, she also never accepts her fall from true womanhood, and this is what finally destroys her. Her identity is inextricably dependent upon her relationship to Armand as his wife and mother of his child. If he denies his child and no longer desires her, Désirée is not only abandoned, but she is no longer Désirée; as Peggy Skaggs argues in *Kate Chopin*, "her place and even her name depend upon man's regarding her as a prized possession" (26). "Schooled too well in the manners and constraints of true womanhood, Désirée herself denies the possibility of life outside Armand's world and instead chooses a suicidal descent into and not beyond the bayou. Even though Chopin makes clear at the end that Désirée was not "at fault"—Armand's mother was racially mixed—Chopin also indicates that her exoneration is not the point at issue but that her self-destruction is: Anna Shannon Elfenbein points out, "It does not really matter whether she is white or black, since her very life depends on the whims, social class, and race of her husband" (127). Her "total powerlessness" is "the result of the life-and-death power of the husband in her society" (131).

Chopin does suggest ways of escape for women. One is the path chosen by Armand's mother, again a woman whose life was dependent on male compassion and power. The father proves more humane than the son, but this does not compensate for the mother's life of exile and her burial in an alien land. Another way is offered by Madame Valmondé. Though she accepts the "fact" of Désirée's race, she does not deny Désirée's personhood. After Désirée writes her for self-confirmation and solace, Madame Valmondé answers: "'My own Désirée: Come home to Valmondé; back to your mother who loves you. Come with your child'" (243). She does not verify Désirée's whiteness because she cannot; she does not deny Désirée's relationship to her because she chooses not to do so. She is the character with the most liberated consciousness, then, a woman who would transcend racist and sexist ideology to protect her own, in this case the female. Désirée, of course, does not even perceive the possibility of a female world; unlike her mother, she proves to have less consciousness of her innate self. She had identified herself, as Armand did, as an idol, and like all idols is "silent, white, motionless" (243), nonconscious, easy to destroy. Once accused and abandoned, once marked as an undesirable, she cannot, as she tells her mother, survive: "'I shall die. I must die. I cannot be so unhappy, and live'" (243). And, as in *At Fault*, Chopin leaves the reader with an awareness of where the fault for this lies: not merely in the frail hands of powerless individuals but in the actions of all individuals who support this patriarchal, racist world the social faults of which finally widen into the black abyss that engorges Désirée.

"Ma'ame Pélagie" more openly points to the ruin effected by adherence to such reactionary ideology. The story is set in a postbellum South and portrays two sisters caught between the old and new worlds seen in *At Fault*. Pélagie and Pauline Valmêt, respectively fifty and thirty-five years old, live in a comfortless log cabin beside the ruins of their mansion which was torched during the Civil War. Pélagie's only desire is to rebuild the mansion and to

die there. Their niece La Petite comes to visit and despite her love of life tries
to fit into their backward looking existence, finally rebelling against living
solely in the past. Pauline, who has come to love La Petite, tells her sister
she will die if the niece leaves since there will then be no present or future
for Pauline on the Côte Joyeuse. The conflict is thus seen to be that between
two worlds, both embodied within and reflected through women: the old true
womanhood reality of Pélagie versus the new life, "the pungent atmosphere
of an outside and dimly known world," which La Petite introduces to her and
which is desired by Pauline (233). Unlike that in "Désirée's Baby," the battle
here is simple and the outcome almost a given; however, the final resolution
for Pélagie is a striking parallel to Désirée's last walk away from the old
world.

Pélagie is the embodiment of the true southern woman, though she is
not by any means the frail flower of womanhood. Despite the loss of home,
wealth, and power, she clings tenaciously to the past and the dream of what
once was. Even though she eventually perceives the falseness of her dream,
the basic corruptness of that world view, she never renounces her past or
her true womanhood conception of self as queen and martyr. She remains
imperious and self-alienated to the end.

From the outset of the story, it is also clear that Pélagie is an extremely
willful woman blind to her own selfishness. She has effectively ruled and
ruined her sister's life for thirty years in her attempt to train her to be "a true
Valmêt" (233). She forces her sister to efface herself for the sake of Pélagie's
passionate goal: to reconstitute daily her own past, one that Pauline does not
share since she cannot remember it. That past seductively offers a place of
privilege for Pélagie, if not for her sister, one through which she would be
socially secure, part of a whole that serves as a collective only in that it shelters
each individual from accusation and consciousness of fault. Like Thérèse in
At Fault, Pélagie thinks the old way is the only way and that remuneration for
her own loss sanctions the forcing of her will on others.

Pélagie's denial of present reality is strong even in the face of La Petite,
the girl from the world outside. In one of their first embraces, Pélagie looks
only for "a likeness of the past in the living present" (234), refusing to see
anything other than her dream. She is similarly untouched when her niece
later grieves that life at Côte Joyeuse is killing them and when she argues
against the necessity of such self-entrapment:

> "it is as though a weight were pressing me backward here. I must
> live another life; the life I lived before. I want to know things
> that are happening from day to day over the world, and hear
> them talked about. I want my music, my books, my companions.

If I had known no other life but this one of privation, I suppose it would be different. If I had to live this life, I should make the best of it. But I do not have to; and you know, tante Pélagie, you do not need to. It seems to me," she added in a whisper, "that it is a sin against myself." (234–235)

For Pélagie, La Petite is easily discounted as a new woman; she is not a true Valmêt. La Petite thinks of herself instead of Pélagie's imaginary collective, and it is of no consequence to Pélagie that that community is nearly dead. In stark contrast, Pauline sees her niece as her "'saviour; like one who had come and taken me by the hand and was leading me somewhere—somewhere I want to go'" (235). This response suggests that she has been a hostage to her sister's territorial imperative; she has been made to live in a world not her own. It is only when Pauline says that she will die if La Petite is forced to leave because of Pélagie's morbidity that Pélagie's dream and world fall apart. Pauline is the last but for Pélagie, and she is also Pélagie's charge, for whom she believes she has always sacrificed herself. Once Pauline rejects her sister's dream world, Pélagie has no one to reflect her self-constitution, no one with whom she can dramatize herself. Yet once Pélagie has been called upon to make the ultimate sacrifice, to give up her dream for someone who no longer loves her in the old way, as a true woman she does so and in that way is obviously similar to Désirée. However, unlike Désirée, Pélagie is finally revealed to be a perversely dark womanhood exemplar, for in her final act of self-effacement, she defies all comprehension.

As was suggested earlier, Chopin portrays Pélagie throughout as a harsh and narrow-minded woman. Despite her calculated appearance as a concerned and self-sacrificing sister, Pélagie is continually exposed as an unmoved and self-seeking tyrant. She is thus also similar to Armand, both bound to concepts of honor and loyalty that deny individual desire or being beyond their own. It is after her scene with Pauline that the reader sees the true Pélagie: a living ghost whose reality lies not in this world but in the ruined and ruinous past. She walks through the destroyed mansion, oblivious to actual "light or dark" (236), "to see the visions that hitherto had crowded her days and nights, and to bid them farewell" (236). She relives her past, her initial denial of war threats, her romanticized memories of the slaves' lot. Even as she recalls the slaves' revolt, she embraces nonconsciousness, complicit denial of the knowledge that her world could be built on violence and oppression. Abruptly, she feels again her desire to kill a Black woman, then to die in the fire "to show them how a daughter of Louisiana can perish before her conquerors" (237). Her visions are both grotesquely cruel and wildly sentimental, and her dream is revealed as a superficial whitewashing of the actual nightmare past. The reader also sees that Pélagie's reactionary and racist nonconsciousness constitutes her past and her relation to life, that it is actually Pauline, and not her dream, that has made her live on precisely because Pauline, like the Black woman, has never fit into Pélagie's vision of self and world. Pauline once kept her from the perfect heroine's death; Pauline, no matter what now occurs, will thus always keep her from recapturing the past potential of self-perfectability. Yet Pélagie is a survivor, and she ultimately finds a new use for Pauline. Pauline will be the recipient of Pélagie's greatest gift. Pélagie will give her Côte Joyeuse to refashion into her own new world; she will give up her dream and herself for her sister. Pélagie thus creates an almost equally romantic and repressive vision of total self-martyrdom with which to replace her primal dream. She chooses to live alienated and alienating to the very last.

At the end, the land lives up to its name: a new house stands on the site of the ruins, one filled with pleasant companions and music. Pauline is reborn as an independent woman, and La Petite no longer need deny her true self. However, like the shadows of L'Abri, Pélagie stands alone, draped in black, just on the edge of this new world. As Chopin concludes, "How could it be different! While the outward pressure of a young and joyous existence had forced her footsteps into the light, her soul had stayed in the shadow of the ruin" (239). Unlike Madame Valmondé, Pélagie cannot transcend her social prejudices, ideological upbringing; and her limited consciousness of self in relation to others. Chopin presents nothing positive in Pélagie's past, present, or future. Furthermore, at the end Pélagie is seen to have aged suddenly as if she has been denied sustenance, perhaps an allusion to her vampiric living off the past and those who made her past possible. It is Pauline and her reality that will live, just as Thérèse does in *At Fault* within her new world at the end; it is a time and place of unknowns, but it is at least of "the living spirit." More important, that the new world is born through the influence of a new woman, small but sure of self, is indicative of Chopin's belief in the positive effects of some women's own will-to-power if that reflects defiance against the old ways and leads to self-realization rather than self-effacement.

Chopin had earlier written another story, "Miss McEnders" (7 March 1892), on this theme of moral guardianship and blind social consciousness, and would continue to explore this topic in later pieces. Woman's complicity with corrupt social systems and totalizing ideologies would also remain a central subject throughout Chopin's career. So too would Chopin continually return to the dilemma of desire versus duty, self-realization versus socially sanctioned self-sacrifice. She does so in such stories as "La Belle Zoraïde" (21 September 1893) and "Lilacs" (14–16 May 1894). Her most complex stories, however, take up the secondary characters introduced in the works discussed above: the Paulines, the Madame Valmondés, the women who experience some sort of personal and social awakening. In these works, Chopin offers concentrated descriptions of moments that shatter social complacency, that quickening of consciousness which gives birth to self-desire, self-recognition, and, in Chopin's fictive world, consequent despair and self-alienation. Chopin's "The Story of an Hour," written 19 April 1894, is undoubtedly her most famous and intense reading in this line.

Before discussing that story and those that follow and clearly point to *The Awakening*, one should note that Chopin first penned another portrait of a highly unconventional woman. Her development as a writer can be marked by these singular pieces: "Wiser Than a God," coming at the beginning of her career; "Azélie" written on 22–23 July 1893, both closing off the second stage and introducing the pre-*Awakening* stories; "An Egyptian Cigarette" written in April 1897 just before she began *The Awakening*; and "The Storm" written 19 July 1898 soon after she had finished her masterpiece. One could argue that each story acts as Chopin's release from the pessimistic vision developing in her work; each piece centers on a strong woman who is virtually untouched by the despair found in Chopin's more realistic fiction.

"Azélie" is conspicuously unlike Chopin's other work, a rustic fable with an almost feminist but also extremely subtle moral. Azélie is a poor farmer's daughter who neither acts nor thinks at all like Chopin's conventional women: she is a seemingly amoral, nearly Amazonian female who barely acknowledges male reality or desire. She first offends the shop-tender 'Polyte when she refuses to act according to his ideological expectations: "There was no trace of any intention of coquetry in her manner. He resented this as a token of indifference toward his sex, and thought it inexcusable" (291). Later she further disorders his physical world and his ideological world view when she breaks into his store and takes what she and her father need: "She seemed to have no shame or regret for what she had done, and plainly did not realize that it was a disgraceful act. 'Polyte often shuddered with disgust to discern in her a being so wholly devoid of moral sense" (295). Despite this assault on his masculinity and morals, he falls in love with her, primarily because he misreads her actions and presentation of self as those of a helpless damsel in distress who needs a knight in shining armor to tame and protect her:

He would keep her with him when the others went away. He longed to rescue her from what he felt to be the demoralizing influences of her family and her surroundings. 'Polyte believed he would be able to awaken Azélie to finer, better impulses when he should have her apart to himself. (296)

These romantic and ideologically conventional notions are given short shrift by Azélie, who coolly dismisses his advances: "She was not indignant; she was not flustered or agitated, as might have been a susceptible, coquettish girl; she was only astonished, and annoyed" (295). Refusing his proposal and, thus, entrance into his world, she suddenly leaves with her family for warmer climes. She is throughout her relationship with him untouched and untouchable. Though the reader is offered little insight into Azélie's personal sense of self and world, it is obvious that she, like Paula in "Wiser Than a God," chooses to position herself outside society and is content to remain there. She is alien to 'Polyte's class, undesiring of his offers of love and redemptive salvation, and, unlike Paula, she is firmly attached to and responsible toward her small community. In fact, she is so strong in will and self-constitution that her power finally draws 'Polyte away from his world at the end as he quits his store to follow in her footsteps.

Chopin perhaps suggests in this open ending that despite appearances and expectations, the alienate may lead a desirable, even enviable, existence based on responsible and responsive affection and concern. But, of course, Azélie is forever a social anomaly, like the animal in "Emancipation." Her particular case implicitly critiques conventional morality, but it does not offer an explicit model for new consciousness. Hers is a complete, self-contained, self-sufficient world; yet her very act of living changes the world around her, and one senses that all good things will come to her in the end. This is not the typical condition explored in Chopin's fiction.

"The Story of an Hour," for instance, details a very ordinary reality and conscientiously analyzes that moment in a woman's life when the boundaries of the accepted everyday world are suddenly shattered and the process of self-consciousness begins. Louise Mallard, dutiful wife and true woman, is gently told that her husband has been killed in a train accident. Her response is atypical, however, and that is the subject of the story: what Louise thinks and feels as she finds herself thrust into solitude and self-contemplation for the first time.

Louise appears in the opening as the frail, genteel, devoted wife of a prosperous businessman; she is at first only named as such: Mrs. Mallard. However, her first response to the tragedy indicates a second Louise nestling within that social shell: "she did not hear the story as many women have heard the same, with a paralyzed inability to accept its significance. She wept at once, with sudden, wild abandonment, in her sister's arms" (352). Chopin thus implies that perhaps some part of Louise readily accepts the news. She also intimates that since Louise unconsciously chooses to enfold herself in a female embrace and not in the arms of the male friend who tells her of Mallard's death, Louise has already turned to a female world, one in which she is central. It is in the mid-section of the story, set in Louise's room, that Louise and Chopin's reader explore and come to understand reaction and potential action, social self—Mrs. Mallard—and private, female self—Louise.

Louise sits before an open window at first thinking nothing but merely letting impressions of the outer and inner worlds wash over her. She is physically and spiritually depleted but is still sensuously receptive. She sees the "new spring life" (352) in budding trees, smells rain, hears human and animal songs as well as a man "crying his wares" (352). She is like both a tired child dreaming a sad dream (353) and a young woman self-restrained but with hidden strengths. She is yet Mrs. Mallard.

As she sits in "a suspension of intelligent thought" (353), she feels something unnameable coming to her through her senses. It is frightening because it is not of her true womanhood world; it reaches to her from the larger world outside and would "possess her" (353). The unnameable is, of course, her self-consciousness that is embraced once she names her experience as emancipation and not destitution: "She said it over and over under her breath: 'free, free, free!' ... Her pulses beat fast, and the coursing blood warmed and relaxed every inch of her body" (353). It is at this point that she begins to think, the point at which she is reborn through and in her body, an experience analogous to that of Edna Pontellier in *The Awakening*.

Louise then immediately recognizes her two selves and comprehends how each will co-exist, the old finally giving way to the one new self. Mrs. Mallard will grieve for the husband who had loved her, but Louise will eventually revel in the "monstrous joy" (353) of self-fulfillment, beyond ideological strictures and the repressive effects of love:

> she would live for herself. There would be no powerful will bending hers in that blind persistence with which men and women believe they have a right to impose a private will upon a fellow-creature. A kind intention or a cruel intention made the act seem no less a crime as she looked upon it in that brief moment of illumination.
>
> And yet she had loved him—sometimes. Often she had not. What did it matter! What could love, the unsolved mystery, count for in face of this possession of self-assertion which she suddenly recognized as the strongest impulse of her being! (353)

It is only after Louise embraces this new consciousness, her sense of personal and spiritual freedom in a new world, that she is named as female self by her sister. This is no doubt ironic since her sister only unconsciously recognizes her; she can have little idea of the revolution that has taken place in Louise's own room. Yet Chopin does not allow simple utopian endings, and Louise's sister's intrusion into Louise's world also prefigures the abrupt end to her "drinking in a very elixir of life through that open window" (354).

Louise leaves her room and descends again into her past world. Though she carries herself "like a goddess of Victory" (354) and has transcended the boundaries of her past self, she is not armed for the lethal intrusion of the past world through her front door. Brently Mallard unlocks his door and enters unharmed. His return from the dead kills Louise, and Chopin's conclusion is the critical and caustic remark that all believed "she had died of heart disease—of joy that kills" (354).

It is easy for the reader to be overwhelmed by the pathos of the story, a natural response since the reader comes to consciousness of the text just as Louise awakens to self-consciousness. Chopin offers the reader only that one point of identification—Louise, whose powers of reflection have been repressed, suddenly shocked into being, and then brutally cut off. It is a disorienting reading experience to be cut off as well after being awakened to Louise's new self-possibilities. It is also beyond irony to be left at the conclusion with the knowledge that only Louise and the reader perceived the earlier "death" of the true woman Mrs. Mallard; and that what murdered her was, indeed, a monstrous joy, the birth of individual self, and the erasure of that joy when her husband and, necessarily, her old self returned. Far from being a melodramatic ending, the conclusion both informs and warns: should a woman see the real world and her individual self within it only to be denied the right to live out that vision, then in her way lies non-sense, self-division, and dissolution. Chopin's analysis of womanhood ideology and quest for self here takes on a darker hue. Her earlier stories examined the destruction of women who lived within traditional society; this piece offers no escape for those who live outside that world but who do so only in a private world in themselves. Either way, Chopin seems to be saying, there lies self-oblivion if only the individual changes and not the world.

At this time, Chopin also explored motherhood in several stories, no doubt as part of her own process of coming to consciousness. Louise was alone and had no other acceptable world—as ideology had pictured the world of mothers and children—in which to fulfill herself. In such works as "Regret," written 17 September 1894, and "Athénaïse," written 10–28 April 1895, Chopin depicts the female strength granted to mothers. Athénaïse, for example, is transformed by her pregnancy, which is described as both her self-contained experience and her sensuous awakening which leads to her reunion with her husband. However, as Peggy Skaggs points out in *Kate Chopin*, Athénaïse pays a price for attaining wifehood and motherhood: "She has sacrificed her name and more; she has sacrificed also her autonomy, her right to live as a discrete individual. Athénaïse Miché exists no longer" (38). Further, as Patricia Hopkins Lattin argues, Athénaïse's positive experience of pregnancy is qualified by several other motherhood stories, those in which women give birth or have given birth. One such representation of motherhood as yet another form of ideological entrapment that some women accept, along with the loss of self, and some do not is "A Pair of Silk Stockings," written in April 1896. The story shows the dark side of motherhood and builds on the major elements from "The Story of an Hour," with only a few shifts in class and setting.

In this piece, a genteel but poor woman, seemingly without support and alone except for her children, experiences an awakening of sensuous self. Mrs. Sommers is a woman born to a better class than the one she married into, but she is also a true woman who neither shirks sacrifice for her family nor thinks of anything beyond her immediate life as mother and martyr: "Se had no time—no second of time to devote to the past. The needs of the present absorbed her every faculty. A vision of the future like some dim, gaunt monster sometimes appalled her, but luckily to-morrow never comes" (500–501). As in "The Story of an Hour," the unexpected occurs: Mrs. Sommers comes into a veritable fortune, fifteen dollars, which she at first plans to spend on her children. Like Louise Mallard, she is physically and spiritually exhausted when she arrives at the moment of contemplation and action. One begins to see more clearly Chopin's definition of the usual effect of womanhood ideology: self-depletion. Again just like Louise, she experiences a sensuous moment—here the particularly female response to a specifically feminine luxury, silk stockings—which reawakens her female self, an experience which simultaneously embraces her and engulfs her in monstrous joy from which there is no desire for escape.

After she buys and puts on the stockings, she too comes to a suspension of intellectual thought prior to rebirth of her self:

> She was not going through any acute mental process or reasoning with herself, nor was she striving to explain to her satisfaction the motive of her action. She was not thinking at all. She seemed for the time to be taking a rest from that laborious and fatiguing function and to have abandoned herself to some mechanical impulse that directed her actions and freed her of responsibility. (502)

She feels, she is sensuously alive, she begins to be her old self made new by her greater enjoyment of self-fulfillment. Of course, tomorrow does come for her just as Brently Mallard did return to Louise. While the realization of her momentary freedom—the pleasure of spending money on herself— and her permanent obligation—her duty to her children—does not kill Mrs. Sommers, she is thrown into a despair from which there is no rescue. For Chopin, there is never an easy resolution to woman's quest for self and fulfillment of desire.

The major stories written immediately prior to Chopin's work on *The Awakening* share this focus on the negativity of unreflective passion as well as Chopin's increasingly complex manipulation of symbols for limitations and despair born out of denied desire. Even as she celebrates the senses as the breaking ground for consciousness, Chopin also portrays the purely sexual as another trap into which both men and women fall, a theme central to Maupassant's "mad" stories that Chopin translated and greatly admired. Desire becomes obsessive passion in these works, and passion proves as much an entrapment, a form of madness, as is ideologically conventional love.

"Her Letters," written 29 November 1894, is important both because it examines male and female responses to passion and because it contains what will become the central image and act of *The Awakening*. In this short story, a woman "pained and savage" with passion goes to destroy her lover's letters (399). It is a leaden day of "no gleam, no rift, no promise" (398), when she can no longer think but only feel and act as a wounded animal would: "With her sharp white teeth she tore the far corner from the letter, where the name was written; she bit the torn scrap and tasted it between her lips and upon her tongue like some god-given morsel" (399). Unable to give up the letters, she entrusts them to her husband's care, willing that he will destroy them without reading a line.

A year later she has died, and on another leaden day of "no gleam, no promise" (400), her husband finds the letters, suffers a conflict of will about reading them, and finally throws them unopened into a river. His initial discovery illuminates for us the relationship and rift between husband and wife, a point brought home by the bleak refrain, and his later journey to water emphasizes the emptiness of ordinary life and the despair that goes hand in hand with willful nonconsciousness. He realizes that he will never know her true self and that he is forever alienated from her: "The darkness where he stood was impenetrable ... leaving him alone in a black, boundless universe" (402). His passion for the now unattainable union and his "man-instinct of possession" (401) lead him to see her as his only salvation: to know "the secret of her existence" (404) will be to know his own self and the meaning of his existence. This desire is the romantic dream of *At Fault* become nightmare, madness, and self-destruction.

It is now that Chopin empowers her water symbol, as will occur in *The Awakening*, here making it the unnatural subject of a madman's obsessive passion to know and to be known by another. The husband returns to the river and the darkness, emasculated by his inability to know, savage in his need for consummation. He believes he hears the call of the water: "It babbled, and he listened to it, and it told him nothing, but it promised all. He could hear it promising him with caressing voice, peace and sweet repose. He could hear the sweep, the song of the water inviting him" (405). He answers by drowning himself, "to join her and her secret thought in the immeasurable rest" (405). Both now "rest" in the same final state but not, as the romantic madman would have it, together; instead, they are forever alienated in death, the ultimate dissolution, just as they were in life. Passion makes no new worlds. The dark side of desire illuminates only the funereal breach of self-faith and the impenetrable state of demented nonconsciousness that passion gives birth to and nurtures. For Chopin, passion alone is eventual self-death and not an avenue toward self-fulfillment.

The themes of mind split from body; dual and conflicting selves; the entrapment of wifehood, motherhood, and sex; the pull of desire and the pain of passion introduced in the stories discussed above will all become central issues in *The Awakening*. Through the creation of these works, Chopin informed herself of subjects crucial to woman and, at times, men. She taught herself to apprehend and to portray precisely the fissures in the social fabric of her world; she then proceeded to tear apart that neat cover cloth after one last, strange fictional release in a story that both incorporates the last major images of *The Awakening* and remains distanced from the comprehension obtained in that work.

"An Egyptian Cigarette," written in April 1897, is Chopin's concentrated primal version of *The Awakening*, a dream within a tale in which the dreamer escapes the nightmare. Again, Chopin creates a highly unconventional woman and situation that allow a nontragic if perplexing ending. That the female character who dreams is similar to the female writer who creates is obvious; indeed, that the fictional woman maintains a firm grasp of her self-possession despite her visions must have been a desire and dream of her creator as well.

In this short work, a cosmopolitan woman is given a box of Egyptian cigarettes that contain some sort of hallucinogenic drug. She smokes one and immediately experiences a distorted and perverse vision of passion and despair. In the dream, another woman driven wild with longing lies in a desert abandoned by her lover. She, in turn, dreams of following him to entrap him once more with her love. Ensnared by her obsession, she lies dying in the heat and thinks finally only of reaching the river. She also considers the irony of her life and its end: "I laughed at the oracles and scoffed at the stars when they told that after the rapture of life I would open my arms inviting death, and the waters would envelop me" (571). Like Edna at the end of *The Awakening*, she reviews her life, how she lived outside of religion and society for the sake of her love and how she is now abandoned by all. While she is physically tormented by sun and sand, she experiences a momentary shift in consciousness: "It seems to me that I have lain here for days in the sand, feeding upon despair. Despair is bitter and it nourishes resolve" (572). Above her, as will be above Edna, she hears "the wings of a bird flapping above [her] head, flying low, in circles" (572). She too reaches water and goes into it; like Edna she suffers a moment of fear at its embrace, but like Edna, she moves toward resolution and into "the sweet rapture of rest" (572), her senses alive and fulfilled at last.

The dreamer awakens at this point, disoriented and distressed after having thus "tasted the depths of human despair" (572). She contemplates the other dreams waiting for her in the remaining cigarettes: "what might I not find in their mystic fumes? Perhaps a vision of celestial peace; a dream of hopes fulfilled; a taste of rapture, such as had not entered into my mind to conceive" (573). But she is not, finally, a seer. She destroys the cigarettes and is only "'a little the worse for a dream ...'" (573). Chopin, however, did not deny her visions or forget those that had come before. She was moved to final exploration of woman's complicity in her own self-oppression and her ability to overcome self-repression. Two months after writing this story, Chopin began *The Awakening*.

The Awakening, originally entitled "A Solitary Soul" and written between June 1897 and 21 January 1898, begins with an assault on the senses and intellect. A brightly colored parrot caged just outside the door of a Grand Isle resort screams "'*Allez vous-en! Allez vous-en!* Sapristi! That's all right!'" as another pet beside it, a mocking bird, sings "with maddening persistence" (881). Thus, ambiguous warnings and wild elation open Edna Pontellier's experience of self-awakening and Chopin's accounting of the dangers inherent in such attempted self-fulfillment. That Edna's history is tied inextricably to that of men and patriarchal ideology is made clear by the characters introduced first—her husband, children, and future lover. That her story will not be a simply happy one is foreshadowed by the music chosen for the opening, a tune from *Zampa*, a highly sentimental opera of romance and death by water. Furthermore, that Edna is at the point of rebellion, at the moment before the quickening of consciousness, is made evident in the very first pages of this brief but intensely antiromantic work.

Again, Chopin presents us with a woman as outsider, Edna, whose case is made more complex by her apparent security in and attachment to her husband's world. Married to the consummate businessman, Léonce

Pontellier, she is accepted in his Creole society as an enchanting if somewhat naive lady. In actuality, she is foreign to that society but simultaneously complicit with the social and sexual business of that world. Hers is, then, an extremely unstable position, based on contingency and her proximity to authority. Raised in Kentucky and Mississippi, she is neither Creole nor part of the old way; instead, she is "an American woman, with a small infusion of French which seemed to have been lost in dilution" (884). Though she is authorized to become part of Creole society by virtue of her marriage, it is markedly clear she is alien: she, unlike the other women in the novel, is named the American way, as *Mrs.* Pontellier. Later, the reader learns that Edna herself is "not thoroughly at home in the society of Creoles" (889), that the supposed freedom of that people coupled with their steady repression of female self-will confuses her. Indeed, she is unlike the other women and, as is pointed out in the first incident of the novel, does not play her ideological roles well.

In the first chapter, Edna has been swimming in the heat of the day with Robert Lebrun, son of the Creole hotel proprietess; a man strikingly similar to Edna in appearance, age, and temperament. This harmless experience coupled with Léonce's annoyance at the womanhood world of leisure leads to a series of accusations and arguments between the Pontelliers. Léonce first admonishes her for her devaluation of the wife self he owns: "'You are burnt beyond recognition,' he added, looking at his wife as one looks at a valuable piece of personal property which has suffered some damage" (882). She responds by looking at her tanned hands, realizes she lacks her wedding rings, which Léonce is keeping safe for her, and submissively puts them back on, putting on her wifehood role as well. However, Edna cannot long keep up the show of compliance, instead turning her attention to Robert. Léonce then goes to a men's club, returning late in the night and willing to play husband again to Edna. She disappoints him by giving less than full attention to his anecdotes, failing a second time as wife: "He thought it very discouraging that his wife, who was the sole object of his existence, evinced so little interest in things which concerned him, and valued so little his conversation" (885). His second line of attack is to fault her mother self; he tells her a patent lie that one of their sons is deathly ill, and when this elicits no quick response, Léonce "reproached his wife with her inattention, her habitual neglect of the children" (885). In a parodic echo of the birds in the opening—those which, ironically, drove Léonce out of the hotel with their noise—he steadfastly and verbally assaults her in "a monotonous, insistent way" (885) until he drives her from bed and rest. He then sleeps, and, of course, Edna discovers that there is nothing amiss, not, at least, with her children.

This, as Chopin makes clear, is the stuff of normal marriages, incidents such as the above that occur and are as quickly forgiven and forgotten. Léonce, for all his boorishness, is not at all a poor husband. He is a conscientious provider, a distantly affectionate father, a true man who pulls his weight in the business world and expects his familial sphere to give proof of this while offering him respite. According to the standards of hegemonic ideology, he is, in fact, an ideal husband, the truth of which assertion, as Chopin ironically shows, even Edna cannot dispute (887). That he cannot personally understand his wife nor fully "define to his own satisfaction or any one else's wherein his wife failed in her duty toward their children" (887) is perplexing but not, finally, solely his problem. For, as Chopin makes obvious, Léonce's feelings are correct: Edna is not the ideal helpmeet or mother.

Edna is, instead, a solitary soul, "different from the crowd" (894). She is described as young, light, with eyes that are "quick and bright" (883), possessing a clear gaze unencumbered by the spectacles Léonce must wear to correct his vision. She sees things in a markedly different way than others do, albeit not necessarily at first with insight but, on the other hand, with inner sight: "She had a way of turning [her eyes] swiftly upon an object and holding them there as if lost in some inward maze of contemplation or thought" (883). Just so does Edna perceive the first altercation with Léonce; that night she sits alone outside, surrounded by "the everlasting voice of the sea" which comes to her like "a mournful lullaby" (886), and like Chopin's other water creatures, she begins to feel the entrapment of self: "An indescribable oppression, which seemed to generate in some unfamiliar part of her consciousness, filled her whole being with a vague anguish. It was like a shadow, like a mist passing across her soul's summer day. It was strange and unfamiliar; it was a mood" (886). Thus does Edna's apprehension of self begin, as with Chopin's other rebel women, out of a state of physical and spiritual depletion. This self-dramatization, however, is cut short by a too real invasion of mosquitoes. Chopin will not now descend into romanticization unless it be to detail and expose it as such. Her central concern is, instead, to portray the process of willful nonconsciousness giving way to self-consciousness, and despite the sometimes ironic stance of the narrator, she makes clear throughout the difference between reaction and action, stasis and self-discovery. Chopin would have the reader see, just as Edna comes to understand herself, that Edna is feeling but not thinking: "She was just having a good cry all to herself" (888).

Shortly thereafter, Chopin indicates that Edna does begin to think, in part because of her relationships with Adèle Ratignolle and Robert. Adèle is what Edna is not: "a mother-woman" (887), one of the reigning types at Grand Isle. For all Edna's glorification of Adèle—for example, she limns her as a Madonna—Edna also realizes that Adèle is a willing self-martyr: she is one of those "women who idolized their children, worshiped their husbands, and esteemed it a holy privilege to efface themselves as individuals and grow wings as ministering angels" (888). Edna is too much a sensual individualist to deny immediate experience for self-subordination. She is also incapable of devaluing her emotions and playing games of love; her knowledge that Adèle does so—for example, in past flirtations with Robert—merely serves to confuse her. Though drawn to Robert who appears to be almost her male soul, Edna herself cannot play romantically in order to pass the time but must take up with Robert wholeheartedly or not at all; as Adèle later warns Robert, "'She is not one of us; she is not like us. She might make the unfortunate blunder of taking you seriously'" (900). Since Edna's friends act upon her as living reminders of her self-alienation and limited consciousness, she seeks some individual or entity beyond these to help her understand that which she feels is suffocating her.

The sea which surrounds her, sings to her in her sadness, and engulfs her in "seductive odor" (892) is that which awakens her senses and self. It mirrors her own philosophical predispositions, like the rivers in earlier stories do for their listeners, and offers beyond self-confirmation the sensual promise of self-fulfillment:

> The voice of the sea is seductive; never ceasing, whispering, clamoring, murmuring, inviting the soul to wander for a spell in abysses of solitude; to lose itself in mazes of inward contemplation.
> The voice of the sea speaks to the soul. The touch of the sea is sensuous, enfolding the body in its soft, close embrace. (893)

Edna continually positions herself near the sea in the Grand Isle sequence so that the sea washes over her senses at all times; as occurs in the sense experiences of the solitary souls in the short stories, it functions both as a projection and reflection of her desire. What it reveals to her is that she cannot lead the dual life of Adèle, cannot be a true woman who willfully sublimates self-desire in self-effacing service to others: "In short, Mrs. Pontellier was beginning to realize her position in the universe as a human being, and to recognize her relations as an individual to the world within and about her" (893). Chopin also indicates that this movement of quickening consciousness cannot be anything but "vague, tangled, chaotic, and exceedingly disturbing" (893) and that, again, process instead of singular revelation is all.

That Edna has from early on been predisposed to pursuing the individual, or exceptional, rather than the socially determined, or sanctioned, life is shown in her childhood remembrances: "Even as a child she had lived her own small life all within herself. At a very early period she had apprehended instinctively the dual life—that outward existence which conforms, the inward life which questions" (893). In other words, she has always been both susceptible to the sensuous and intuitively aware of her circumscribed female existence. Her awakening, however, comes only after intellectual apprehension of what her feelings intimate. First, Edna's attraction to Adèle's beauty and Adèle's sympathetic response to Edna's tentative self-disclosures encourage Edna to explore the continuum of her existence, the past out of which comes her present and on which her future is predicated. Shortly after her confrontation with Léonce, Edna and Adèle sit alone by the sea. Edna stares into the water, and in answer to Adèle's question about her inwardness, she consciously explores the maze of her inner contemplation: "'I was really not conscious of thinking of anything; but perhaps I can retrace my thoughts'" (896). The sea has made her recall another "sea" of her childhood: she thinks of "a summer day in Kentucky, of a meadow that seemed as big as the ocean to the very little girl walking through the grass which was higher than her waist. She threw out her arms as if swimming when she walked, beating the tall grass as one strikes out in the water" (896). Edna further recalls her childhood awareness of self-limitation: "'My sun-bonnet obstructed the view. I could see only the stretch of green before me, and I felt as if I must walk on forever, without coming to the end of it'" (896). More importantly, she understands the connection of that self to her present, how her horizons are yet limited and her desire for unobstructed vision bewildering: "'sometimes I feel this summer as if I were walking through the green meadow again; idly, aimlessly, unthinking and unguided'" (897). Adèle's response is to enclasp Edna's hand, an affectionate but ultimately, futile sign of feminine empathy toward the womanhood condition. This first caress, however, serves to provoke Edna's further self-exploration; the sensuous, even in small ways, leads to self-realization and denial of blind, mechanical, or nonreflective behavior.

Edna begins then to analyze for the first time the past, the history of her self-constitution, and she perceives the bases for her self-alienation in her childhood's lacks—her motherlessness and her father's coldness—as well as in her propensity for romantic self-delusion. Her infatuation with unattainable men, most notably and ironically that with a famous tragedian, a man who acts out emotionally, and her business alliance with Léonce only furthered her sense of irrevocable duality: the split between inward and outward expression, her desires set in conflict with social expectations. She had, like so many women, effected the sublimation of her self-will and knowledge by rationalizing the unrealizability of passion, coming to believe that the most life could offer her was passive adoration. Like Désirée, she had settled herself securely in idolness: "As the devoted wife of a man who worshiped her, she felt she would take her place with a certain dignity in the world of reality, closing the portals forever behind her upon the realm of romance and dreams" (898). So too did she take on the role of mother, "a responsibility which she had blindly assumed and for which Fate had not fitted her" (899). It is only at the age of twenty-eight, with Adèle by the sea, that she admits to the dark side of such self-capitulation, that to be a wife and mother is, for some, only another denial of self-responsibility. She is, however, despite the concern and show of affection from Adèle and Robert, alone with this realization, and she cannot as yet take her intuitions a step further toward self-consciousness until inspirited once more by the sensuous embrace of the sea.

After her experience with Adèle, Edna couples the role of mother with the call of self, playing with her children by the sea. One might argue that she becomes a child herself again with them. So weeks pass, her reality unchanged. Then, at a dinner, the parrot again shrieks, music from *Zampa* echoes around her, and Edna experiences another quickening of consciousness. After dancing, she sits alone on the gallery, halfway between society and the sea, able to survey both. Mademoiselle Reisz, a consummate artist in the mold of Paula Von Stoltz, plays Chopin specifically for her. Since Edna is susceptible to aesthetic sensuousness, music speaks to her in a powerfully subjective way; she "sees" it and names it. For example, when Adèle played for her earlier on, Edna entitled the piece "Solitude" and envisioned a highly romanticized portrait of another solitary soul: "When she heard it there came before her imagination the figure of a man standing beside a desolate rock on the seashore. He was naked. His attitude was one of hopeless resignation as he looked toward a distant bird winging its flight away from him" (906). As Anna Shannon Elfenbein argues, Edna's vision is both one drawn from popular sentimental art and an indication of "her programming by her culture, a programming she shares with other women encouraged to visualize themselves as men in order to attain vicarious individuality and to adopt a negative view of the potential of women as well" (146). However, when Reisz plays, Edna does not see a discrete, displaced rendering of her sexual alienation or romantic fatalism; instead, because she is predisposed "to take an impress of the abiding truth" (906), she feels self-will and desire: "She saw no pictures of solitude, of hope, of longing, or of despair. But the very passions themselves were aroused within her soul, swaying it, lashing it, as the waves daily beat upon her splendid body" (906). This time Edna enclasps another woman's hand, and thus is created another female world, unlike Adèle's, which will inform and urge Edna forward in her quest for self. This show of deep sympathy and self-exposure readies Edna for the monstrous joy she embraces in her moonlight swim that night.

Up to this point, Edna, not surprisingly, cannot swim nor can anyone succeed in teaching her. It is the individual nature of the act and not its physicality which frightens her: "A certain ungovernable dread hung about her when in the water, unless there was a hand near by that might reach out and reassure her" (908). Those fears now leave her, and, indeed, she desires precisely the singularity that intimidated her before: "A feeling of exultation overtook her, as if some power of significant import had been given her to control the working of her body and her soul. She grew daring and reckless, overestimating her strength. She wanted to swim far out, where no woman had swum before" (908). She does swim out alone, searching for "space and solitude" (908) by gazing at the moonlit horizon, and, finally, she reaches "for the unlimited in which to lose herself" (908). That she does not seek physical annihilation is made clear by her momentary terror of death by drowning. Edna desires to embrace self and, simultaneously, to free herself from womanhood bonds. To that effect, she leaves the swimmers and walks home alone, claiming her experience as her own despite the private self-congratulation of the others. She also rejects Robert's myth-making, his romantic reading of her swim, determined instead to value and to reach an understanding of the "thousand emotions [that] have swept through [her]" (909). She does, however, allow Robert, her sometime psychic twin, to sit with her in the night and to become part of her self-desire.

That night, the second confrontation between Edna and Léonce occurs, but this time Edna is not oppressed by his possessiveness and stubbornness. She refuses to go to their bed, preferring to rest outside so that she can hear the sound of the sea. She is not asleep as in the first altercation; she is in fact intensely awake and alert to her dual life staring her in the face as Léonce commands her in:

> She perceived that her will had blazed up, stubborn and resistant. She could not at that moment have done other than denied and resisted. She wondered if her husband had ever spoken to her like that before, and if she had submitted to his command. Of course she had; she remembered that she had. But she could not realize why or how she should have yielded, feeling as she then did. (912)

This time she does not weep, and there are no mosquitoes. Instead, she experiences physical and mental fatigue coupled with the insistent and irritating presence of Léonce hovering about her:

Edna began to feel like one who awakens gradually out of a dream, a delicious, grotesque, impossible dream, to feel again the realities pressing into her soul. The physical need for sleep began to overtake her; the exuberance which had sustained and exalted her spirit left her helpless and yielding to the conditions which crowded her in. (912)

After this and in the face of seemingly insurmountable obstacles, Edna will attempt to make her fleeting vision of self-fulfillment a reality.

She begins by recapitulating her past, this time willfully forcing every experience to its ultimate conclusion. Edna has first been a babe in the sea, moving from childlike helplessness and submissiveness to a preconsciousness of her sensuality and self. She next relives her romantic adolescence, this time with a supposedly attainable man, Robert.

The day following her swim, Edna moves into another state of unreflective reaction and frenzied action: "She was blindly following whatever impulse moved her, as if she had placed herself in alien hands for direction, and freed her soul of responsibility" (913). She calls Robert to her for the first time, and together they leave for an out island, a lovers' haven. Edna now seems to accept Robert's romantic vision of herself and revels in their shared experience in near solitude: they are together outside the Creole society both seem to reject, in another world in which their coupled experience is nurtured. Edna, fatigued after her awakening in the sea the night before, reenacts a female version of the Sleeping Beauty tale: she goes to a pure white room within sound of "the voice of the sea" (917), lies in a virginally white bed, and perceives her own body "as if it were something she saw for the first time, the fine, firm quality and texture of her flesh" (918). She awakens herself. Robert tells her later that she has slept "precisely one hundred years" (919). Chopin indicates here, however, that Edna's romantic chatter is self-ironic and idle play; Robert is and remains the one true romantic. In fact, Edna is more radical than sentimental. While Robert would be her constant and unchanging prince-lover, Edna envisions massive social transformation which would leave them both behind: "'How many years have I slept?' she inquired. 'The whole island seems changed. A new race of beings must have sprung up, leaving only you and me as past relics'" (919).

Despite their different readings of their shared experience, Edna finds that this journey, this adventure, revitalizes her desire for a new self. After their return, she sees again that her singular though still limited insight has changed her forever:

she tried to discover wherein this summer had been different from any and every other summer of her life. She could only realize that she herself—her present self—was in some way different from the other self. That she was seeing with different eyes and making the acquaintance of new conditions in herself that colored and changed her environment, she did not yet suspect. (921)

Edna need not then realize in full her life's permanent alteration since her social relations, even her romantic attachment, at Grand Isle still reflect that society's expectations. It is only when the unusual occurs, when Robert abruptly departs for Mexico, that Edna faces how unconsciously she had expected him to remain a part of her immediate world, her key to her inner self. Edna must now define her feelings, although in doing so she senses self-inadequacy, as well as determine how inextricably bound her new self is to her relationship with Robert:

For the first time she recognized anew the symptoms of infatuation which she had felt incipiently as a child, as a girl in her earliest teens, and later as a young woman. The recognition did not lessen the reality, the poignancy of the revelation by any suggestion or promise of instability. The past was nothing to her; offered no lesson which she was willing to heed. The future was a mystery which she never attempted to penetrate. The present alone was significant; was hers, to torture her as it was doing then with the biting conviction that she had lost that which she had held, that she had been denied that which her impassioned, newly awakened being demanded. (927)

She is in the adolescence of her new life.

After Robert's abandonment, Edna returns to the primal scene, the originary setting of her new self, the sea which offers her now "the only real pleasurable moments that she knew" (927). She also grows increasingly obsessed with any traces of Robert—photos, letters, anecdotes—since this fetishism both keeps at bay her dull existence as Mrs. Pontellier and continuously reminds her by association of her rediscovered self-will and desire. In addition, she protects her inner self from violation and is virtually untouchable, especially with her husband and children. Only at the end of her vacation is she forced into a relationship with someone, Reisz, a relationship which becomes crucial later on since Reisz sees both Robert and Edna in a radically different way. In the meantime, however, Edna moves to another reenactment of her dual existence.

Edna next takes up again her roles as wife and mother as the Pontelliers return to New Orleans. The latter part is particularly shortlived since even at Grand Isle Edna made clear that she would not subsume self in motherhood:

> Edna had once told Madame Ratignolle that she would never sacrifice herself for her children, or for any one.... "I would give up the unessential; I would give my money, I would give my life for my children; but I wouldn't give myself. I can't make it more clear; it's only something which I am beginning to comprehend, which is revealing itself to me." (929)

Neither can she long sustain the illusion of herself as devoted wife. She rejects the simple social conventions of reception days, thus withdrawing her interest from her husband's business. The materialistic base of the Pontellier marriage is then exposed when Léonce attacks her both for hurting his business by neglecting hers and for mismanaging his familial establishment. As Brian Lee argues:

> The conspicuous consumption satirized by Veblen is the visible corollary of Edna's feelings of uselessness and futility. In order to maintain her husband's financial credibility, her role in their marriage is reduced to that of chief ornament in his display of wealth. The rules of their stylized existence permit her to take but not to make. Her creative instincts are stifled, and the need which Perkins [Gilman] argues is the distinguishing characteristic of humanity—to express one's inner thoughts in some outer form—is denied her. (66)

Despite the insensitivity of Léonce's responses to her actions, throughout their confrontations, Edna now deliberately tries to maintain her self-composure. However, after one such argument, she retires to her room and there attempts a reversal of her initial submissiveness: she tries to crush underfoot her wedding ring. Her failure to do so—the maid hands it back to her undamaged, and she puts it on—implicitly discloses that the individual cannot so easily erase the past, one's complicity with self-objectification. Although Edna does not yet conceive of an alternative to her society, she clearly sees the vacuity of the old ways.

Indeed, like Louise Mallard, Edna at first romanticizes her relationship to the real world beyond her window but instead of seeing it as a green world inviting her to it, she perceives it as the enemy in her quest for self-constitution: "She felt no interest in anything about her. The street, the children, the fruit vendor, the flowers growing there under her eyes, were all part and parcel of an alien world which had suddenly become antagonistic" (935). Even when she considers the seeming faultlessness of Adèle's marriage and domestic sphere, she cannot accept that ideological role and realm as holding for her the possibility of self-fulfillment. It is after her visit to Adèle that she gives up all pretense of social conformity and is then judged insane by Léonce though not by the narrator or resisting reader: "He could see plainly that she was not herself. That is, he could not see that she was becoming herself and daily casting aside that fictitious self which we assume like a garment with which to appear before the world" (939).

Edna's process of self-realization begins in earnest with yet another recapitulation of experience. She turns to her art for which she has a "natural aptitude" (891) but which before was mere "dabbling" (891). She now takes it up seriously in an attempt to articulate herself; as she tells Adèle, "'I believe I ought to work again. I feel as if I wanted to be doing something'" (937). Again, this action provokes Léonce into an attack on her. For him, her work should fall within prescribed womanhood roles; the artistic impulse can be icing on the cake but should never be the full repast. Edna, alienated from family and friends, then turns to Mademoiselle Reisz, and it is in this confrontation that Edna is offered the life possibilities available to her.

Edna tracks down Reisz through Madame Lebrun who also passes on inconsequential news of Robert. In sharp contrast to Lebrun, Reisz has only significant words for Edna. Theirs is not like the polite, reserved conversation between Edna and the Lebruns. They face each other without pretense of affection and are ultimately revealed to each other as kindred souls housed in arrestingly dissimilar bodies. Reisz in essence seduces Edna into self-recognition; she strokes her hand, nurtures her body, heart, and soul by feeding her, giving her a highly revealing letter from Robert, and playing again Chopin's "Impromptu," recalling for Edna the "one midnight at Grand Isle when strange, new voices awoke in her" (946). More importantly, Reisz speaks seriously with and to Edna of her "'becoming an artist'":

[Reisz says,] "To be an artist includes much; one must possess many gifts—absolute gifts—which have not been acquired by one's own effort. And, moreover, to succeed, the artist must possess the courageous soul."

"What do you mean by the courageous soul?"

"Courageous, *ma foi*! The brave soul. The soul that dares and defies." (946)

Because Reisz feels deeply for Edna, loves her for reasons left unexplored in the text, she feeds both Edna's desire and self-desire even as she herself feeds upon Edna's passion. Edna discovers through her the two paths from which she must choose: one is to surrender herself to romance with Robert and by that act to move away from self-fulfillment; the other is to rebel completely, following Reisz's example, to give up body and soul to the new life. The remainder of the novel focuses on these two alternatives and Edna's growing consciousness of how limited these life options are. Herein lies Chopin's most acute social criticism, that which shocked her contemporaries and still proves stunning today.

In essence, Chopin has Edna come to realize that there are no life options for her which afford her more than the illusion of satisfaction or the reality of self-compromise. To be a mother-woman is to abjure self for the sake of others; to be an artist-woman is to live celibate, to give all one's love to expression. Edna proves incapable of sustaining herself in such solitude, no matter how peaceful it seems for a while. Instead, she would be part of the world: "It was not despair, but it seemed to her as if life were passing by, leaving its promise broken and unfulfilled. Yet there were other days when she listened, was led on and deceived by fresh promises which her youth held out to her" (956). Edna's weakness, then, is her desire for action coupled with her own conditioned passivity, her desire for experience coupled with her ignorance of life. She hungers for "something to happen—something, anything; she did not know what" (958) but cannot herself initiate action to effect that occurrence. Instead, she is drawn repeatedly to the dynamic world of men seemingly unlike those she has known. Thus she becomes even more entrapped in a mire of self-deception.

Since both Robert and Léonce leave her, Edna is "free" to explore "the animalism" (961) awakened in her. She takes up with Alcée Arobin, a well-known libertine, and is drawn to him both because of his forceful sensualness and his extremely passionate nature. Early on she discovers his duelling scar, an insignificant mark itself save that it perhaps reflects her own love wounds and her duelling selves: "He stood close to her, and the effrontery in his eyes repelled the old, vanishing self in her, yet drew all her awakening sensuousness" (959). Even though Edna understands that he is "absolutely nothing to her" (960), he too acts as both reminder of and respite from her struggle with self-consciousness. Her naivety is such that she initially believes his presence will offer some sort of self-illumination; her affair does insofar as it makes her aware of her renunciation of "all the codes" through which she has identified herself (966). However, she also discovers, too late, that his is a world of deception and not compassion. She learns as well that her natural sensuality is not "devilishly wicked" (966) but that she has wasted her expression of self in the alienating experience of passion:

> She felt as if a mist had been lifted from her eyes, enabling her to look upon and comprehend the significance of life, that monster made up of beauty and brutality. But among the conflicting sensations which assailed her, there was neither shame nor remorse. There was a dull pang of regret because it was not the kiss of love which had inflamed her, because it was not love which had held this cup of life to her lips. (967)

After their first night together, then, Edna comprehends that this path, passion become entrapment, is another dead end. As Rosemary F. Franklin points out, "Chopin shrewdly designs the Alcée episode to present what will be Edna's greatest challenge: to understand that romantic love is born of the erotic longing within oneself for transcendence that cannot be fulfilled by union with another human being" (523). Though their relationship continues, Edna feels nothing, neither "despondency" nor "hope" (988). It is not the way for her to self.

Edna's other alternative, one which she actively pursues for some time, is to immerse herself in art, in her case notably a world made up of women, hoping to find the means to self-expression. This world is neatly divorced at times from that of men—she will not allow Arobin into her atelier—and it is based on ruthless honesty. Turning away from her lover, Edna finds the deepest satisfaction in her relationship with that other one who recalls her to true self: Reisz, "the woman, by her divine art, seemed to reach Edna's spirit and set it free" (961). While Edna philosophizes with Arobin about her self-discovery, she discusses pragmatics with Reisz. Edna speaks first to her of her resolution "never again to belong to another than herself" (963) and her decision to have rooms of her own, supporting herself with her mother's legacy and money earned from sale of her own art. She also openly admits to her love for Robert and is warned by Reisz that he is but another ordinary man, like Léonce, who wants to have her "'belong to him'" (964). Reisz speaks to Edna as well of her need for union with another, that which she has herself not been able to effect; she tells Edna to search for a man of "'some *grand esprit*; a man with lofty aims and ability to reach them; one who stood high enough to attract the notice of his fellow-men'" (964). Finally, Reisz forces Edna to contemplate anew a life of solitude—and, one surmises, celibacy—as an alternative. The true artist who gives voice to self is one who can stand alone; as Reisz tells Edna, "'The bird that would soar above the level plain of tradition and prejudice must have strong wings. It is a sad spectacle to see the weaklings bruised, exhausted, fluttering back to earth'" (966). Even though Chopin surrounds Edna with such deep sympathy, and though it is clear that Edna now desires self-expression and transcendence of the oppressive ordinary, the reader is also made aware that Edna is "devoid of ambition" (956), yet too passive to effect revolution.

Edna herself becomes fully conscious of this fact at her last dinner at the Pontellier home. She is feted by friends and lovers, is about to move to her own residence, is proving successful as an artist, seems, in short, to be beginning a new life on this her twenty-ninth birthday. However, she is also crowned by Léonce's jewels and toasted with a concoction made by her father especially for "the daughter whom he invented" (971). Furthermore, Arobin's dramatic self-presence suggests that she is yet still possessed. Even her closest friend, her confidante Reisz, is revealed as inadequate to the situation; as Susan Resneck Parr argues, Reisz's size and childlike seating at the table upon a pile of cushions indicate that Reisz also "has failed to achieve her maturity" (145). Edna sees her bacchanal for the "stupid" (976) debacle it is. Her "*coup d'état*" fails (969).

Despite a brief reunion with her children and Adèle, Edna moves herself after this into the solitary life, even though she knows herself incapable of maintaining such independence or self-possession. There is seemingly only one other path left open to her at this point: her reunion with Robert, whom she believes to be Reisz's man of grand esprit. They meet by accident at Reisz's apartment, and there begins Edna's final self-deception. Her idealistic visions of him and their relationship are first undercut by the awkward reality of chance encounter, trivial chatter, Robert's reticence and evasiveness. Once he accompanies her home, she finds him to be momentarily "like the old Robert" (983) but later admits to herself that in "some way he had seemed nearer to her off there in Mexico" (987). He, in turn, finds her "cruel" (984), a mimic of his romantic self. Their relationship is further complicated by mutual jealousy, his over Arobin and hers over his Vera Cruz woman. Robert also avoids her until she confronts him with his "selfishness" (990) and seduces him into giving her that which he has been saving for himself. Edna expects this "something" (990) to be a desire equal to her own; instead, as Reisz foresaw, Robert reveals his man-instinct of possession. He wishes to be her husband, and it is impossible for the reader not to recall that for Robert those who are married are never lovers (915). When Robert tells Edna he desires that she be given to him as wife, she then reveals herself as beyond his understanding: she says, "'You have been a very, very foolish boy, wasting your time dreaming of impossible things when you speak of Mr. Pontellier setting me free! I am no longer one of Mr. Pontellier's possessions to dispose of or not. I give myself where I choose'" (992). However, Edna's ability to articulate or to live out her superior sense of self is contingent upon Robert's reflecting that self to her. So that she might perhaps capture whole the truth of her singularity, she invests herself once more in achieving a relationship with him. In doing so, Edna misjudges or chooses not to recognize Robert's motives or his ability to "hold against her own passion" (987). That Robert does not prove equal to her desire is made obvious in his abandonment of her. One might also argue, as Rosemary F. Franklin does, that because Edna "has projected her awakening animus upon him and thus is unable to know him as an individual," he flees from her (515). His parting note to her, however, suggests another interpretation: that because she will not act as his mirror, will not reflect the primacy of his desire, he goes: "'I love you. Good-by— because I love you'" (997). Ironically, his desertion is "necessary" (999). It marks the end of the battle between Edna's "need for consciousness" and Robert's desire to maintain "the comfortable status quo" of unconsciousness (Franklin 514).

Edna comes then to realize that the world of womanhood is for her also a potentially deadly one. She sits by Adèle during her delivery and is deeply affected by what this reveals to her. During the birth of her own children, she had been put to sleep; she thus experiences the reality of childbearing for the first time, albeit from the distanced vantage point of spectator. This scene of suffering makes her apprehend at last what passion might effect: "Edna did not go. With an inward agony, with a flaming, outspoken revolt against the ways of Nature, she witnessed the scene of torture" (995). In this world, her body is her destiny, another means of entrapment. Chopin's description of Adèle's long hair lying "coiled like a golden serpent" (994) reminds the reader of woman's seduction in and expulsion from Paradise, the curse of childbirth given to her as her burden. The novel's structure also promotes such a reading: Edna's own nine-month gestation of self coupled with Adèle's pregnancy inextricably links woman's self-desire with self-accommodation.

After Adèle has given birth and even though Edna is deadened by fatigue, Edna comprehends that she can no longer amateurishly dabble at any of the womanhood roles available to her—martyr, beautiful object, social capital, the beloved; she also feels that such self-alienation is not too high a price to pay for self-knowledge if one thus be freed of the illusions that merely serve as "a decoy to secure mothers for the race": "'Yes,' she said. 'The years that are gone seem like dreams—if one might go on sleeping and dreaming—but to wake up and find—oh! well! perhaps it is better to wake up after all, even to suffer, rather than to remain a dupe to illusions all one's life'" (996). Robert's letter and second abandonment occasion her final moment of disillusionment, the experience of which sends her, depleted spiritually and physically, back to Grand Isle, almost nine months after her first awakening in the sea. Here in the Gulf, "the repository and graveyard of legend and dreams" (Taylor 177), she will at last deliver herself.

Edna thinks before she returns there, analyzing her search for subjectivity and her subjection, her sensuality and the dangers of sexuality. When she reaches Grand Isle, she is beyond contemplation and no longer duelling with incompatible selves. She has given up trying to communicate with those she loves or who love her. In this last chapter, she answers instead the voice of the sea which now calls her into eternal "abysses of solitude" (999), not of contemplation but of momentary self-possession followed by self-annihilation. Chopin's imagery expresses both Edna's alienation and singularity. She stands alone and defeated in her struggle to affirm her selfhood to others: "A bird with a broken wing was beating the air above, reeling, fluttering, circling disabled down, down to the water" (999). Yet Edna transcends despair, if only by embracing death.

Edna had said earlier that she "would give up the unessential" (929) but not herself. Now she throws aside her life as easily as she does her old bathing suit so that she might feel "like some new-born creature, opening its eyes in a familiar world that it had never known" (1000). Like Venus returning to her originary scene, she descends into the sea, re-experiencing for the last time her childhood motherlessness, adolescent infatuation, the terrors, and exhaustion of womanhood. She reaches then for a state of pure liminality, a prelapsarian world, one in which she might experience sensual transcendence, herself become one with nature, "the hum of bees, and the musky odor of pinks" (1000). Edna has only one experience that is not compromised, the fleeting moment of intense life force she embraces before drowning; that this experience necessarily leads to her death is Chopin's most radical statement about and to her civilized, genteel world.

Edna's defeat, her surrender of self to the abysses of solitude, is a profoundly despairing and desperate measure. Hers is not the beautiful death of romantic heroines, nor does Chopin write it as such; instead, Chopin focuses attention to the last line on Edna's desire for life, her fragmented, inexpressible desire for autonomy, and her inability to find subject position within a world in which a woman's life is deemed unessential even by herself. Yet one also sees in Edna's life, as one does in much of Chopin's fiction, intimations of alternatives to alienation and self-annihilation, a new "structure of feeling," as Raymond Williams called it, an embryonic social consciousness which cannot yet be fully articulated either by character or creator (131–132). Edna's death is unspeakable tragedy, yet one does hear in her story the constant murmur, whisper, clamor of another vision of life.

Through her work, Chopin invites the reader to imagine a world in which woman's experience and desire are no longer marginalized or effaced but have become critically central. In this way, as Judi Roller writes, *The Awakening* is "a fitting prelude to the twentieth-century's feminist novels" (28).

ELLEN PEEL

Semiotic Subversion in
"Désirée's Baby"

I

At first "Désirée's Baby," published in 1893 by Kate Chopin, seems no more than a poignant little story with a clever twist at the end.[1] Yet that does not fully explain why the tale is widely anthologized, why it haunts readers with the feeling that, the more it is observed, the more facets it will show. In "Désirée's Baby" Chopin, best known as the author of *The Awakening*, has created a small gem, whose complexity has not yet been fully appreciated. As I explore that complexity, my broader goal is a theoretical one: I plan to show not only that a semiotic and a political approach can be combined, but also that they must be combined in order to do justice to this story and to others like it, stories that lie at the nexus of concerns of sex, race, and class.

A semiotic approach to the work reveals that, despite its brevity, it offers a rich account of the disruption of meaning, and that the character largely responsible for the disruption is Désirée Aubigny, who might on a first reading seem unprepossessing.[2] She is a catalyst, however, for the subversion of meaning. When the semiotic approach is supplemented by a political approach, it can be seen that, in particular, Désirée casts doubt on the meaning of race, sex, and class.[3] In this drama of misinterpretations, she undermines smugness about the ability to read signs, such as skin color, as clear evidence about how to categorize people.

From *American Literature* Vol. 62, No. 2 (June, 1990), pp. 223–237. Copyright © 1990 Duke University Press. All rights reserved.

The disruption culminates when Désirée, whom everyone considers white, has a baby boy who looks partly black. When she is rejected by her husband, Armand, she takes the infant, disappears into the bayou, and does not return. Armand later finds out, however, that he himself is black, on his mother's side. Désirée, though unintentionally, has devastated him by means of these two surprises, one concerning her supposed race and one concerning his own.

Using a combined semiotic and political approach, my analysis consists of four steps: I trace how the surprises to Armand disrupt signification; question whether they are actually as subversive as they first appear; shift the focus more definitively to Désirée to show how the story associates her with certain enigmatic, subversive absences; and, finally, discuss how the story criticizes, yet sympathetically accounts for, the limitations of Désirée's subversiveness.

The story takes place in an antebellum Creole community ruled by institutions based on apparently clear dualities: master over slave, white over black, and man over woman. Complacently deciphering the unruffled surface of this symbolic system, the characters feel confident that they know who belongs in which category and what signifies membership in each category. Moreover, as Emily Toth has observed, in the story the three dualities parallel each other, as do critiques of their hierarchical structures.[4]

Within this system of race, sex, and class, the most complacent representative is Armand Aubigny. Confident that he is a white, a male, and a master, he feels in control of the system. In order to understand how his wife challenges signification, we must take a closer look at the surprises that Armand encounters.

The tale begins with a flashback about Désirée's childhood and courtship. She was a foundling adopted by childless Madame and Monsieur Valmondé. Like a queen and king in a fairy tale, they were delighted by her mysterious arrival and named her Désirée, "*the wished-for one*," "*the desired one*." She, like a fairy-tale princess, "grew to be beautiful and gentle, affectionate and sincere,—the idol of Valmondé." When she grew up, she was noticed by Armand, the dashing owner of a nearby plantation. He fell in love immediately and married her. She "loved him desperately. When he frowned she trembled, but loved him. When he smiled, she asked no greater blessing of God." They were not to live happily ever after.

Soon after the story proper opens, Armand meets with the first surprise. He, other people, and finally Désirée see something unusual in her infant son's appearance. She asks her husband what it means, and he replies, "It means ... that the child is not white; it means that you are not white." Désirée writes Madame Valmondé a letter pleading that her adoptive mother deny

Armand's accusation. The older woman cannot do so but asks Désirée to come home with her baby. When Armand tells his wife he wants her to go, she takes the child and disappears forever into the bayou.

Thus, Armand's first surprise comes when he interprets his baby's appearance to mean that the child and its mother are not white. What seemed white now seems black. Désirée, with the child she has brought Armand, has apparently uncovered a weakness in her husband's ability to decipher the symbols around him.

Ironically, Désirée's power comes from the fact that she seems malleable. Into an established, ostensibly secure system she came as a child apparently without a past. As a wild card, to those around her the girl appeared blank, or appeared to possess nonthreatening traits such as submissiveness. Désirée seemed to invite projection: Madame Valmondé wanted a child, Armand wanted a wife, and both deceived themselves into believing they could safely project their desires onto Désirée, the undifferentiated blank screen. Actually, however, her blankness should be read as a warning about the fragility of representation.

One aspect of Désirée's blankness is her pre-Oedipal namelessness. As a foundling, she has lost her original last name and has received one that is hers only by adoption. Even foundlings usually receive a first name of their own, but in a sense Désirée also lacks that, for her first name merely reflects others' "desires." In addition, namelessness has a particularly female cast in this society, since women, including Désirée, lose their last name at marriage. Namelessness connotes not only femaleness but also blackness in antebellum society, where white masters can deprive black slaves of their names. Although Désirée's namelessness literally results only from her status as a foundling and a married woman, her lack of a name could serve figuratively as a warning to Armand that she might be black.

But he sees only what he desires. Before the wedding he "was reminded that she was nameless. What did it matter about a name when he could give her one of the oldest and proudest in Louisiana?" On this virgin page Armand believes he can write his name, the name he inherited from his father or, more broadly, the patriarchal Name of the Father. In addition, as a father, Armand wants to pass on that name to his son. Before he turns against his wife and baby, she exclaims: "Oh, Armand is the proudest father in the parish, I believe, *chiefly because it is a boy, to bear his name*; though he says not,—that he would have loved a girl as well. But I know it isn't true. I know he says that to please me" (emphasis added).

The approaching downfall of Armand's wife, and hence of his plans for his name, is foreshadowed by the relationship between Désirée's blankness and another name, that of the slave La Blanche. The mulatta's name refers to the whiteness of her skin, but "*blanche*" can also mean "*pure*" or "*blank*," recalling Désirée's blankness. La Blanche is Désirée's double in several ways. Neither has a "proper" name, only a descriptive one. During the scene in which Armand rejects his wife, he explicitly points out the physical resemblance between the women:

> "Look at my hand; whiter than yours, Armand," [Désirée] laughed hysterically.
> "As white as La Blanche's," he returned cruelly....

The story also links the two women through their children, for the mistress first notices her son's race when she compares him to one of La Blanche's quadroon sons. And perhaps Armand is the father of La Blanche's son.[5] The two women—and even their sons—may have parallel ties to Armand because of the possible sexual connection between slave and master. So much doubling hints that the slave's racial mix has foreshadowed that of the mistress.

Because La Blanche's name refers to her in the visual but not the racial sense, her appearance illustrates the contradiction of a racial system that is based on color but does not consider visual evidence conclusive. In this discourse a person who looks white but has a "drop" of black "blood" is labeled black. As Joel Williamson says, the "one-drop rule" would seem definitive but in fact leads to the problem of "invisible blackness."[6]

Miscegenation, which lies at the heart of the contradiction, marks the point at which sexual politics most clearly intersect with racial politics. Theoretically either parent in an interracial union could belong to either race. Nonetheless, "by far the greatest incidence of miscegenation took place between white men and black female slaves."[7] Even when the white man did not technically rape the black woman, their relationship tended to result from, or at least be characterized by, an imbalance of power in race, sex, and sometimes class. Ironically, descendants of such a union, if their color was ambiguous, embodied a challenge to the very power differential that gave birth to them.

"Désirée's Baby" calls attention to the paradoxes that result from miscegenation and the one-drop rule. La Blanche and Désirée look white but are considered black, while "dark, handsome" Armand—whose hand looks darker than theirs—is considered white. Désirée's entry into the symbolic system forces Armand to confront the contradiction he ignored in La Blanche, another white-looking woman. A form of poetic justice ensures that the same one-drop rule that enables him to keep La Blanche as a slave causes him to lose Désirée as a wife. After the first surprise, Armand sees Désirée's blankness as blackness, not *blanche*-ness.

It is crucial to note that Désirée is disruptive, not because she *produces* flaws in the signifying system but because she *reveals* flaws that were already there. Long before her marriage, for instance, Armand was considered white and La Blanche was considered black. In a sense, Désirée acts as a mirror, revealing absurdities that were always already there in the institutions but repressed. Her blankness has reflective power.

In another sense, Désirée's potential as a mirror was one of her attractions for Armand, for he wanted her to bear a child that would replicate him—in a flattering way. Armand blames and smashes the mirror that has produced a black reflection. An outsider observing Armand's generally harsh treatment of slaves might, however, see his baby's darkness as another instance of poetic justice, the return of the oppressed.

Similarly, if the baby's darkness comes from his mother, whom Armand dominates, then the child's appearance represents the return of another oppressed group, women. To reproduce the father exactly, the child would have to inherit none of his mother's traits. In a metaphorical sense the first surprise means that Armand learns that his son is not all-male but half-female. The infant is an Aubigny but has inherited some of Désirée's namelessness as well, for we never learn his first name (nor that of his double). More generally, paternal power, the name of the father, seems to have failed to compensate for the mother's blackness or blankness.

To blame someone for the baby's troubling appearance, Armand has followed the exhortation, "*Cherchez la femme.*" In particular, he is looking for a black mother to blame. He is right to trace semiotic disruption to Désirée, but the trouble is more complex than he at first realizes.

The end of the story brings the second surprise—black genes come to the baby from Armand, through his own mother. Early on, readers have learned that old Monsieur Aubigny married a Frenchwoman in France and stayed there until his wife died, at which point he brought eight-year-old Armand to Louisiana. Only after Désirée and her baby have disappeared and her husband is burning their belongings, do he and the readers come across a letter from his mother to his father: "... I thank the good God for having so arranged our lives that our dear Armand will never know that his mother, who adores him, belongs to the race that is cursed with the brand of slavery." As Joseph Conrad suggested, the "heart of darkness" lies within the self: the letter unveils Armand's "dark, handsome face" to himself.

At this point, several shifts occur. One takes place between wife and husband. For Armand, his wife was originally a screen onto which he could project what he desired. When he found a black mark on the screen, he rejected it. Now he has learned that the mark was a reproduction of his own blackness. The mark, which he considers a taint, moves from her to him.

Another shift takes place between sons and fathers. As Robert D. Arner implies, Armand at first rejects his baby for being the child of a white man and a black woman but then finds that the description fits himself.[8] With blackness, the half-female nature attributed to the baby has also moved to Armand. An intergenerational shift occurs between women as well as men, for the role of black mother has gone from Armand's wife to his mother.

Thus two surprises have profoundly disturbed Armand. As in the Hegelian dialectic of master and slave, these two surprises have shaken the structure of white over black, male over female, and master over slave. Armand, the figure who seemed to belong to the dominant race, sex, and class, is shown to be heir to blackness and femaleness and to belong to the group "cursed with the brand of slavery." The repressed has returned and drained meaning from the established system of signification.

II

Nevertheless, these surprises are less subversive than they first appear. The fact that they shake Armand's concept of meaning and punish his arrogance does not mean that they actually change the inequality of power between the sexes, between the races, or between the classes, even on his plantation. Armand might be less sure of his ability to tell black from white, but he probably will not free his slaves. Moreover, through the traumas experienced by Armand, the story invites readers to pity the suffering caused by inequalities of power but not to wonder how those inequalities could change. In other words, the surprises are more disruptive in a *semiotic* than a *political* sense; they endanger the system of *signification* more than the system of *domination*.

The text directs sympathy less toward black characters than toward characters on the margin between black and white. The story urges us to consider it a pity that Désirée and Armand, brought up as white, must undergo the trauma of receiving the news that they are black. But we are hardly urged to pity the much larger number of people who have lived as enslaved blacks since birth. The implication is that being black might deserve no particular sympathy unless a person was once considered white. The broader effects of race and its relation to slavery remain unexamined.

The problem arises in part because Chopin is using the Tragic Mulatto convention, which appears repeatedly in American literature.[9] It is often easy for white readers to identify with the Tragic Mulatto, because she or he is typically raised as white and only later discovers the trace of blackness. Yet the invocation of "tragedy" introduces problems, partly because it implies resignation to the inevitable. The very idea of a Tragic Mulatto also suggests that mulattoes may be more tragic, more deserving of pity, than people of purely black ancestry.

Moreover, the very notion of pity is inadequate as a political response and can even have a conservative effect. The limitations of pity are best observed by looking at the traces of sexism that, like traces of racism, appear as a residue in the text. The parallel between racism and sexism in the story is complicated, because *insufficient* concern for blacks and slaves corresponds to *excessive* concern for women. Excessive concern can be debilitating for women by defining them solely as victims.

When Désirée walks away, apparently to her death, the tale most strongly urges readers to show such concern for women. This arises because of the sympathetic way in which the entire story has represented her. She is good: "beautiful and gentle, affectionate and sincere." She is appealing: "'Armand,' she called to him, in a voice which must have stabbed him, if he was human." She is vulnerable: "Her hair was uncovered and the sun's rays brought a golden gleam from its brown meshes.... She walked across a deserted field, where the stubble bruised her tender feet, so delicately shod, and tore her thin gown to shreds." This doe-like character joins a long line of women who, by dying at the end of a story or a novel, call forth readers' tears. In particular, Tragic Mulattoes tend to be *mulattas*.

But scrutiny of such endings raises the discomfiting possibility that they rely on feminine vulnerability in order to move readers. A strong, rebellious, surviving heroine might not provide such tidily tragic closure. I am not suggesting that Désirée's pain should be presented less sympathetically; rather, I am questioning the implication that a less vulnerable woman would deserve less concern.

The connection of pity with race, class, and sex is noteworthy in the double of Désirée's baby—La Blanche's quadroon son. In contrast to Désirée's bruised feet, his bare feet are described merely as coming in contact with a polished floor, for the story presents only Désirée as suffering from the lack of sturdy shoes. Here the stress on feminine vulnerability combines with the acceptance of black slavery, as if it were a pity for a person such as Désirée to suffer: a member of the weak sex, someone who at least used to belong to groups that do not deserve such treatment—the race with "a golden gleam" in their hair and the class with the right to "tender feet."

For these reasons, even though the meanings of race, sex, and class are threatened by Armand's surprises, those two events do not seriously disturb the system of power relations. The story invites sympathy for Désirée partly on the sexist grounds that feminine women are weak and on the racist grounds that white members of the master class do not deserve to be treated like black slaves.

Twentieth-century readers may be troubled to find that Armand's surprises have a less subversive effect than at first seemed possible. The ideologies behind them can be better understood if placed in historical context. Because the story is set in the era of slavery, its verisimilitude would falter if Armand suddenly reformed and freed his slaves. We must also consider the era in which the story was written and originally read, for the late nineteenth century in the United States was marked by a rebounding prejudice against blacks. Attitudes towards women also differed substantially from those of the late twentieth century: even the women's movement drew on notions of female purity and martyrdom that sound strange today but were part of nineteenth-century discourse. Thus it would be anachronistic to expect more subversiveness from the traumas experienced by Armand.

III

Some of these problems can be mitigated, however, by thinking more carefully about the text—or rather about what is missing from the text. Shifting the focus more definitively to Désirée discloses certain enigmatic, disruptive absences.

Almost everyone who has written on the story has mentioned, favorably or unfavorably, the concluding revelation about Armand's mother. This final twist recalls the surprise endings of Guy de Maupassant, who strongly influenced Chopin.[10] While evoking sympathy for Désirée, the twist essentially turns backward to tradition and male power: the very presence of a plot twist may reflect Chopin's inheritance from de Maupassant, a literary forefather; in the ending the focus of narrative point of view is Armand, upholder of conservative values; and the female character earns sympathy largely through a sentimental convention—through powerless, victimized innocence. In fact, my discussion itself has so far concentrated on surprises undergone by Armand, a figure of male conservatism. I agree with Cynthia Griffin Wolff that we should cease analyzing the surprise ending and look elsewhere.[11]

Instead of concentrating on the ending, with its conservative, male orientation, we should turn to Désirée, who is absent from the ending. Although submissive, the young woman does have some power. Her boldest action is disappearance, but she does act. While she neither desires nor anticipates the havoc she wreaks, she does catalyze the entire plot.[12]

Through Armand, we have already started to see how the meanings of race, class, and sex are crumbling. Désirée offers two greater challenges to meaning, because she may not be wholly white and because she may not die in the bayou. These are enigmas, in the sense used in *S/Z*,[13] and they remain inconspicuously unsolved, both for readers and, apparently, for other characters. The enigmas are silent, formless absences that cannot be found in any specific location.

To begin with, Désirée may be black—and thus a black mother—after all. If she is black, that mitigates some of the racism I discussed earlier. Instead of being a white character who deserves sympathy for unjust treatment that includes the accusation of being black, she is a black character whose unjust treatment, minus the accusation, on its own account deserves sympathy. Whether or not Désirée is black, the impossibility of knowing her race reveals the fragility of meaning more than Armand's knowable race does. The *presence* of a traditional, *male*-oriented twist *located* at the end of the story veils a troubling, *female*-oriented *absence*—of knowledge based on skin color or on writing—that has *no particular location*.

Désirée is troubling in another way as well. The tale says, "She disappeared among the reeds and willows that grew thick along the banks of the deep, sluggish bayou; and she did not come back again," but it never actually says she dies. Just as it is possible that she is partly black, so it is possible that she (with the baby) is alive. If so, that survival mitigates some of the sexism I discussed earlier. Désirée deserves sympathy even if she does not pay for it with her life. In addition, if she does not kill herself, she is saying in effect that life is worth living even if she is black and has lost Armand's love. Indeed, by escaping she has freed herself from those who once projected their desires on her. Even if she does kill herself and her child in the bayou, it is significant that the deaths are absent from the text, because in this way the work allows some hope, however slight, for the race, class, and sex the characters represent. Like the impossibility of knowing Désirée's race, the impossibility of knowing her death offers a challenge to complacency about knowledge.

As the two unsolved enigmas suggest, the challenge to meaning, like Désirée, tends to operate negatively, through non-sense. She sometimes cries out unconsciously and involuntarily or remains completely silent. These traits appear in the scene where she notices her baby is black:

> "Ah!" It was a cry that she could not help; which she was not conscious of having uttered....
>
> She tried to speak to the little quadroon boy; but no sound would come, at first. When he heard his name uttered, he looked up, and his mistress was pointing to the door.

She at first seemed no threat to the signifying structure she had entered, but the very inarticulateness of this blank card reveals that the system of signification sometimes breaks down.

By creating Désirée's enigmas—the possibility that she is black and the possibility that she and her baby are alive—Chopin to some extent resists the racism and sexism to which she was urged by much in her historical moment. It is important that the enigmas are not just difficult but decipherable puzzles that, when solved, would clearly state that Désirée was black and alive. Instead, the enigmas have the elusive indeterminacy typical of Désirée.

As we have seen, Armand first thinks his wife is white, but he decides he has misinterpreted her. He thinks his wife is black and solely responsible for their son's blackness, but again Armand finds he has misinterpreted. Although unsettling, both incidents leave intact the hope that knowledge can correct misinterpretations. Yet the absences associated with Désirée erode some of that semiotic hope. Because the readers—and probably the characters—never know whether she is partly black and whether she survives the bayou, the story throws into question the very possibility of knowledge, at least in some cases.

IV

It would be satisfying to end on that note, but I must add that Désirée still disrupts the practice of domination less than semiotic practice. While sympathetic to her, Chopin reveals the limitations of some of the character's values. Of course the author does not hold twentieth-century beliefs; yet she is far enough from Désirée's antebellum era to present a critique indicating that the young woman, as a product of her society, has internalized so many of its values that she can never fully attack it. Chopin subtly indicates that, in spite of the disruptiveness of Désirée's enigmas, her subversiveness remains limited, for three main reasons.

To begin with, Désirée is excessively dependent on the unconscious. She is "unconscious," in the sense that she is unaware. For example, Désirée is the last to realize that her child is not white, and it never occurs to her that her baby's blackness comes from her husband. On another level, she often seems unaware of herself, driven by her own unconscious. Her actions after discovering the baby's race seem trancelike, as if in a dream—or nightmare. And, as has been shown above, she sometimes cries out involuntarily. On still another level, Désirée's lack of political consciousness could also be seen as a kind of "unconsciousness." None of this detracts from her raw power, but uncontrollable power can be as dangerous to those who wield it as to others.

The second restriction on Désirée's subversiveness comes from a certain negative quality. Through her silence (and inarticulateness), through the story's silence about her enigmas, and through her final absence, she disrupts her society's signifying system by revealing its contradictions and meaninglessness. She does destroy complacency about knowledge. Yet all this is not enough. Destruction often must precede creation but cannot in itself suffice. Désirée creates nothing but a baby, whom she certainly takes away, and perhaps kills.

Even Désirée's destructiveness is limited, for she possesses another negative trait: she is "essentially passive."[14] She is discovered by Monsieur Valmondé, she is discovered by Armand, she is filled with joy or fear by her husband's volatile moods, and, while lying on a couch and recovering slowly from childbirth, she is visited by Madame Valmondé. Désirée is immersed in her husband's value system and never stands up to him, not even to interpret the meaning of his dark skin or the baby's, much less to criticize his racism, his sexism, or his treatment of slaves. When she finally acts, she pleads ineffectually with her husband, writes ineffectually to her mother, and then takes the most passive action possible—she disappears. Like the suicide of Edna Pontellier in *The Awakening*, Désirée's disappearance is hardly a triumph.

The third weakness lies in Désirée's lack of a sense of political solidarity. She acts only individually or as part of a nuclear family, never as part of a broader group. She fails to acknowledge ties with anyone outside the family who belongs to her sex or to her newly attributed race and class. Her similarity to La Blanche, for instance, fills her with horror. In fact, in Désirée's final efforts to win back Armand she is seeking someone she thinks is her diametric opposite—a white male, assured of his place as master. The only exception to Désirée's final solitude is her baby. But even he cannot represent any kind of political bonding. Even if she does not murder him, nothing indicates that she sees him as linked to her in shared oppression.

Désirée's individualism resembles that of other characters.[15] For instance, the general condition of blacks and slaves never really comes into question. Madame Valmondé, like Désirée, regrets that one individual, Armand, treats his slaves cruelly, but not that he or other people own slaves in the first place. Instead of recognizing the institutional nature of exploitation based on race, class, and sex, Désirée and others seem to feel that problems stem from the lack of certain personal qualities, such as pity or sympathy. "Young Aubigny's rule was a strict one ... and under it his negroes had forgotten how to be gay, as they had been during the old master's easy-going and indulgent lifetime." Indulgence rather than emancipation is presented as the alternative to Armand's harshness. In a similar vein, individualizing love is shown as the "antidote to the poison of Armand's racial abstraction."[16] His love for his wife and baby causes him to treat the slaves well for a while. This makes Désirée happy, but she does not question whether one man's moods should have such power over other people.

Chopin sympathetically but critically shows that her characters define problems in terms of the lack of individualistic qualities such as love and mercy, not in terms of the subordination of one group by another. I do not mean to say that individual virtues totally lack value, only that they may not suffice to solve certain problems. In short, though some characters feel pity for slaves, blacks, and women, the assumption that they are inferior goes unquestioned.

In this ideology, superiors should have a sense of *noblesse oblige*, but they remain superior. Concerning sex, race, and class, Désirée upsets systems of meaning but—by failing to connect the personal with the political—stops short of attacking hierarchical power structures. Disruption of meaning could lead to, and may be necessary for, political disruption, but Désirée does not take the political step.

Instead of attacking the meaningfulness of racial difference as a criterion for human rights, Désirée takes a more limited step: she reveals that racial difference is *more difficult to detect* than is commonly supposed. In this view, suffering can result if people classify each other too hastily or if, having finished the sorting process, people treat their inferiors cruelly. But the system of racial difference, with its built-in hierarchy, persists. In this system, superiority is still meaningful; the only difficulty lies in detecting it. It is no wonder that those viewed as inferior do not unite with each other.

Chopin presents these three reasons—unconsciousness, negativeness, and lack of solidarity—to help explain why Désirée does reveal her society's lack of knowledge but fails to change its ideological values, much less its actual power hierarchies.[17] She poses so little threat to the dominant power structures that she holds a relatively privileged position for most of her life. Yet subversiveness need not be bound so tightly to traits such as unconsciousness that make it self-limiting.

Désirée's semiotic subversiveness should be taken seriously. Her disruption of meaning may even be necessary, but Chopin skillfully suggests it is not sufficient.

NOTES

1. "Désirée's Baby," in *The Complete Works of Kate Chopin*, ed. Per Seyersted (Baton Rouge: Louisiana State Univ. Press, 1969), I, 240–45. I would like to thank Robert D. Arner, William Bush, Gillian C. Gill, Margaret Homans, and Gila Safran-Naveh for their comments on this paper.

2. I am using "semiotic" to refer to the study of signs in the broad sense, to the study of the systems by which we create signification, decipher meaning, and gain knowledge.

3. I am using "political" in the broad sense to refer to concern with societal power relations, not just electoral politics.

4. "Kate Chopin and Literary Convention: Désirée's Baby," *Southern Studies*, 20 (1981), 203; and see Robert D. Arner, "Kate Chopin," *Louisiana Studies*, 14 (1975), 47.

5. Cynthia Griffin Wolff, "Kate Chopin and the Fiction of Limits: 'Désirée's Baby,'" *Southern Literary Journal*, 10 (1978), 128.

6. *New People: Miscegenation and Mulattoes in the United States* (New York: Free Press–Macmillan, 1980), p. 98. To avoid confusion, I generally follow the terminology of the society shown in the story, using the one-drop rule in deciding how to refer to characters' race. I refer to "mulattoes" only when the context demands it. Important parallels exist between Chopin's story and *Pudd'nhead Wilson*, which Mark Twain published the next year. Eric Sundquist puts Twain's novel in historical context, explaining that the work both grows out of and protests against growing racism in the United States in the late nineteenth century, an era that sought to redefine "white" and "black" by concepts like the "one-drop rule" ("Mark Twain and Homer Plessy," *Representations*, No. 24 [1988], 102–28).

7. James Kinney, *Amalgamation! Race, Sex, and Rhetoric in the Nineteenth-Century American Novel* (Westport, Conn.: Greenwood, 1985), p. 19; see Winthrop D. Jordan, *White over Black: American Attitudes Toward the Negro, 1550–1812* (Chapel Hill: Univ. of North Carolina Press, 1968), p. 138; and Judith R. Berzon, *Neither White Nor Black: The Mulatto Character in American Fiction* (New York: New York Univ. Press, 1978), p. 9.

8. "Pride and Prejudice: Kate Chopin's 'Désirée's Baby,'" *Mississippi Quarterly*, 25 (1972), 133.

9. For more information on the Tragic Mulatto, see Berzon, pp. 99–116; Toth; Barbara Christian, *Black Feminist Criticism: Perspectives on Black Women Writers* (New York: Pergamon, 1985), pp. 3–4 and passim; and Jules Zanger, "The 'Tragic Octoroon' in Pre–Civil War Fiction," *American Quarterly*, 18 (1966), 63–70.

10. Per Seyersted, *Kate Chopin: A Critical Biography* (Oslo: Universitetsforlaget, 1969), p. 73; Wolff, p. 126.

11. Wolff, p. 125.

12. Arner makes a similar point ("Pride and Prejudice," p. 137).

13. Roland Barthes, *S/Z*, trans. Richard Miller (New York: Hill and Wang–Farrar, Straus and Giroux, 1974), pp. 209–10.

14. Barbara C. Ewell, *Kate Chopin* (New York: Ungar, 1986), p. 71.

15. Wolff makes a similar point (p. 127).

16. Arner, "Kate Chopin," p. 52.

17. The force of just one of the three influences can be seen by comparison with *Pudd'nhead Wilson*. Unlike Désirée, Roxana is conscious and takes positive action, but both characters lack unity with a group. Roxana, who suffers from only one of the three disadvantages I have explained, still cannot manage to bring about notable subversion.

BERT BENDER

The Teeth of Desire:
The Awakening *and* The Descent of Man

Kate Chopin's fiction is an extended and darkening meditation on the meaning of human life and love in the light of Darwinian thought. Like many other serious writers of her time, she was struck by *The Descent of Man and Selection in Relation to Sex* (1871). But she read Darwin more closely than did most of her contemporaries, and much more closely than her many interpreters have realized.[1] She did not find Darwin's "main conclusion ... distasteful" (as he "regret[ted] to think" many readers would).[2] Rather, in his main idea (that "man is descended from some lowly-organised form") and especially in his theory of sexual selection she found scientific support for the celebration of life that she knew and loved in Whitman's song of the "body electric." As she first viewed it, the theory of sexual selection offered a profoundly liberating sense of animal innocence in the realm of human courtship, especially for the Victorian woman.

In her first optimistic, if artless, presentation of the courtship drama, she created a heroine in *At Fault* (1890) who finally recognizes her "fault" of self-sacrifice for "what [had] seemed the only right."[3] Because of her commitment to conventional morality, she had denied the natural "electric" attraction she had felt for a divorced man (II, 762). But Chopin's announced purpose in the novel is to console the reader who she imagines is "driven by earthly needs to drag the pinioned spirit of your days through rut and mire" (II, 858).

From *American Literature* Vol. 63, No. 3 (Sept., 1991), pp. 459–473. Copyright © 1991 Duke University Press.

Thus she arranges for nature to intervene and provide a happy ending: the former wife drowns in a flood-swollen river, clearing the way for the lovers' "natural adjustment" to their predicament (II, 792). Chopin ended *At Fault* by bringing in a "highly gifted" new woman named Mrs. Griesmann to articulate the sense of reality that would support this first novel's happy ending. Mrs. Griesmann is a robust student of "Natural History" who collects "specimens" out west and promises that by "studying certain fundamental truths," we can attain a "restful" view "of life as it is" (II, 875).

Mrs. Griesmann also indicates the direction Chopin would take in her subsequent stories, and had she allowed us a closer view of Mrs. Griesmann, we might have seen her with a copy of *The Descent of Man*; for all of Chopin's courtship plots during the next ten years are studies in natural history according to the logic of sexual selection—the primary mechanism in "the whole process of that most important function, the reproduction of the species" (*Descent*, I, 13). Apparently rather simple in its general outlines, sexual selection "depends," as Darwin explains,

> on the success of certain individuals over others of the same sex in relation to the propagation of the species; whilst natural selection depends on the success of both sexes, at all ages, in relation to the general conditions of life. The sexual struggle is of two kinds; in the one it is between the individuals of the same sex, generally the male sex, in order to drive away or kill their rivals, the females remaining passive; whilst in the other, the struggle is likewise between the individuals of the same sex, in order to excite or charm those of the opposite sex, generally the females, which no longer remain passive, but select the more agreeable partners. (II, 398)

Despite the apparent simplicity of sexual selection, however, it took Darwin many pages to explain how it is actually "an extremely complex affair" (I, 296). And as Chopin pursued her own studies in the natural history of sex, she read *The Descent of Man* more and more closely until her references to it became most extensive and explicit in *The Awakening*. But her response to Darwin is complicated in this way: although she accepted his basic premises that evolution proceeds through the agencies of natural selection and sexual selection, she quarreled with his analysis of the female's role in sexual selection. And—throughout the 1890s—as she continued her meditations on sexual selection and its implications for the meaning of love, her initial optimism developed into ambivalence and finally into a sense of despair that Darwin had not expressed in *The Descent of Man*.

Many of her stories dramatize the "law of battle" that dictates "a struggle between the males for the possession of the female," but she also resisted its corollaries concerning the female's passive and modest role in sexual relations and the male's physical and mental superiority to the female.[4] Chopin's women often manage in various ways to deny Darwin's definitions of the female's inferiority. And Chopin was particularly interested in Darwin's interpretation of the evolutionary development among "savage" human beings, whereby the male had "gained the power of selection" by having kept the female in an "abject state of bondage."[5] Although Darwin wrote that "the civilized nations" were vastly improved in this regard (women now having "free or almost free choice" [II, 356]), Chopin still felt the bind. And—increasingly throughout the middle and late nineties—her women characters not only reclaim the power to select, but select for their own reasons. Eventually, especially in the case of Edna Pontellier in *The Awakening*, Chopin's women select on the basis of their own sexual desires rather than for the reasons Darwin attributed to civilized women, who "are largely influenced by the social position and wealth of the men" (II, 356).

Chopin's ambivalence toward the idea of sexual selection is apparent in two stories she wrote in 1894, five years after she had completed *At Fault* and four years before she began *The Awakening*. On one hand, Mrs. Baroda (in "A Respectable Woman") recognizes the sexual desire she feels for her husband's visiting friend and is at first repulsed by these feelings. She is a "respectable woman." But Mrs. Baroda will soon become one of the most daring women in American fiction during these years. For when she asks her husband to invite their friend for another visit, declaring that "I have overcome everything!" and promising that "this time I shall be very nice to him," it is clear that she is now determined to select the lover she desires. In creating this woman who not only threatens the institution of marriage but whose motive in sexual selection (her desire) is independent of the drive to propagate the species, Chopin modified Darwin's theory of sexual selection in a way that would have offended his Victorian sensibility. But Chopin did not at this stage in her development dare to depict a mother's desire (as she would in Edna Pontellier).

In Darwin's theory, civilization had evolved largely because woman's modesty curbs the male's eagerness to couple; and in this theory of the sexual reality, the male's eagerness is not only biologically innocent or red-blooded, but necessary. "In order that [the males] should become efficient seekers," Darwin concluded, "they would have to be endowed with strong passions. The acquirement of such passions would naturally follow from the more eager males leaving a larger number of offspring" (I, 274). The woman's role is of course different. As Ruth Bernard Yeazell has recently explained, in Darwin's description of "Nature's courtship," "females are at once less lustful and more discriminating" than males: "Like a respectable Victorian novel, *The Descent of Man, and Selection in Relation to Sex* implicitly defers the representation of sex in order to focus on the story of selection."[6] As Yeazell remarks, the "satisfying conclusion" to Darwin's story preserves the ideals of motherhood and the modest woman who knows nothing of appetite or sexual desire (p. 37). Clearly, Chopin had freed the "respectable" Mrs. Baroda from the restrictive definitions of womanhood provided by both *The Descent of Man* and the respectable Victorian novel.

In "The Story of an Hour," on the other hand, Mrs. Mallard feels the ecstasy of being liberated from what seems an agreeable marriage after the apparent accidental death of her husband. But then she comes to question the meaning of love. At first she realizes that there would no longer be a "powerful will bending hers in that blind persistence with which men *and* women believe they have a right to impose a private will upon a fellow-creature" (my emphasis). Then, thinking that "she had loved him—sometimes," she wonders, "what could love, the unsolved mystery, count for in the face of this possession of self-assertion which she suddenly recognized as the strongest impulse of her being!" A few years later, Edna Pontellier's conflict will develop from feelings like these in Mrs. Baroda and Mrs. Mallard. Like Mrs. Baroda, Edna will be determined to select the lover she desires; and like Mrs. Baroda, her desire will develop to the accompaniment of an explicitly Whitmanesque celebration of sexual innocence.[7] But also, after she has acted in response to her desire, Edna will realize that "it was not love which had held this cup of life to her lips" (chap. 28). She will become depressed by what had only puzzled Mrs. Mallard: the meaninglessness of love in natural history. Realizing by 1897 that love has no claim to constancy, that it beats in self-assertion to the evolutionary time of sexual selection, Chopin had come to feel that the human spirit had been denied its place not only in a Christian universe but also in the more limited sphere of human courtship and love.

Chopin's darkening response to *The Descent of Man* is reflected in her translations of Maupassant. In "A Divorce Case," for example, a young man with "a noble and exalted soul" falls "in love." But his love turns to despair, his "dream" to "miserable dust," when he becomes obsessed with the inescapable "bestial instinct" to "couple": "Two beasts, two dogs, two wolves, two foxes, roaming the woods, encounter each other. One is male, the other female," and they couple because the "bestial instinct ... forces them to continue the race." He realizes that "all beasts are the same, without knowing why.... We also."[8] And in "It," another of Maupassant's maddened narrators confesses that he cannot stop himself from marrying repeatedly, even though he considers "legal mating a folly." He is "incapable of confining [his] love to one woman" and marries again and again only "in order not to be alone!" (p. 189).

The solitude of Maupassant's characters—like that of Chopin's "solitary soul," Edna Pontellier—follows their shattering realizations that human sexuality as presented in *The Descent of Man* denies the myth of constant love. This is not to suggest that Chopin merely rewrote Maupassant; rather, that writing from the female point of view, she addressed the same troubling question that she saw in Darwin and Maupassant. When Edna finally realizes "that the day would come when [Robert], too, and the thought of him would melt out of her existence, leaving her alone," she enters the "abysses of solitude" (chap. 39); and Maupassant's narrator in "Solitude" (again, as translated by Chopin), feels that he is "sinking ... into some boundless subterranean depths." Sexual intercourse merely intensifies his solitude, for then he is momentarily "deceived ... with the illusion that [he is] not alone"; "the rapturous union which must, it would seem, blend two souls into one being" ends in "hideous solitude" (pp. 196–97).

Edna Pontellier is a "solitary soul" in this modern sense. We cannot appreciate Chopin's understanding of life if we imagine Edna as the goddess of love reincarnated. For the sea with which Edna is repeatedly associated and in which she dies is millions of years older than that which had given birth to Venus in classic mythology: Edna is a post-Darwinian woman-animal who had evolved from the sea in a world without gods. Nor can we justly evaluate Chopin's work if we fail to see that beyond her unquestionable exploration of the female "self and society"—an exploration which has been so profoundly resonant in the feminist movement of the last quarter century—she explored the larger question of the female (and male) self in *life*.[9]

As a meditation on the Darwinian reality of Edna's life, *The Awakening* begins and ends with the essential fact of motherhood. Edna is of course a mother, but she cannot be like the "mother-women" she sees at Grand Isle, whose "wings as ministering angels" identify them as "the bygone heroine[s] of romance" (chap. 4). By the end of the novel Dr. Mandelet will refer to this "illusion" of angelic love as "Nature['s] ... decoy to secure mothers for the race," but this cannot console Edna (chap. 38). Attending the birth of her friend's child, she had seen this "little new life" as merely another in the grotesque "multitude of souls that come and go"; thus she revolts "against the ways of nature" and finally sees her own children as "antagonists" (chaps. 37 and 39).

Twenty-eight years old at the beginning of the novel, Edna was ready to become a woman like the one Chopin knew in Whitman's "Song of Myself"—whose "Twenty-eight years of womanly life and all so lonesome" end in the vision of her bathing with the twenty-eight young men (section

11). In her twenty-eighth year, Edna, too, will discover the watery, erotic innocence that Whitman had dreamt for his woman. She will soon be ready to love "young men," to let her hand "descend tremblingly from their temples and ribs" (section 11). And she will know "the first-felt throbbings of desire" on August twenty-eighth, after her midnight swim with Robert (chap. 10). Chopin's emphasis on Edna's twenty-eight years is only one of her many references to Whitman; but Chopin's critics have never grasped the relevance of these references in *The Awakening*. Harold Bloom, for example, has recently concluded that "Chopin's representation of Edna's psychic self-gratification is not essentially altered from Whitman's solitary bliss"; Emerson is her "literary grandfather."[10] But Chopin could scarcely indicate her rejection of Emersonian thought more emphatically than she does in noting that Edna cannot read Emerson without growing "sleepy" (chap. 24). Edna awakens to a new reality. True, she begins her career as a conventional Victorian woman and then awakens in her twenty-eighth year to the joy of Whitman's transcendental eroticism. But as Chopin frees Edna to satisfy her desire for a lover, she will cause her to awaken more fully (in the pivotal twenty-eighth chapter of her story) to realize that desire had not brought her "love." And in the ritual celebration of her twenty-ninth birthday, Edna will know the strife and struggle for self-assertion that Darwin had uncovered in *The Descent of Man*: she will confront the "graven image of Desire" in the face of Victor, with his smile and gleaming "white teeth"—Victor, Robert's brother and antagonist in sexual competition first for Mariequita and now for Edna.[11]

In tracing the story of Edna's development from her twenty-eighth to her twenty-ninth year, Chopin begins where she must—"by the shore," as Whitman did in section 11 of "Song of Myself." But her logic in choosing this setting is not to affirm but to revise Whitman's view of the self in life. Beginning where she knew that life itself had begun according to *On the Origin of Species*, Chopin first presents Edna "advancing at snail's pace from the beach" with Robert. We will last see these creatures of evolution together in chapter 36, which opens in a scarcely Edenic "garden" (where they have met as though "destined to see [each other] only by accident") and which ends in Edna's "pigeon house." Here Chopin will describe the lovers' relationship with explicit references to *The Descent of Man*.

Chopin's first pointed reference to the role of sexual selection in Edna's life occurs in chapter 9. She has already responded to "the seductive odor of the sea," but now she will know the "wonderful power" of music as Darwin described it in both *The Descent of Man* and *The Expression of Emotions in Man and Animals*. Edna's response to Mademoiselle Reisz's piano performance of a piece by Frédéric Chopin is clearly based on a passage from Darwin, the point of which is that music was originally the means by which our "half-human ancestors aroused each other's ardent passions" (*Descent*, II, 337).

Edna had responded to music before, but never as she will during this performance. Before, music had sometimes evoked in her a picture of "solitude" that is again a measure of Chopin's passage beyond Whitman's mid-nineteenth-century view of life. She had imagined "the figure of a man standing beside a desolate rock on the seashore. He was naked. His attitude was one of hopeless resignation as he looked toward a distant bird winging its flight away from him" (chap. 9). Even in this echo from "Out of the Cradle Endlessly Rocking," the "hopeless resignation" of Chopin's man presents a considerably darker view of life and solitude than that projected by Whitman. Still, in this image of a "distant bird winging its flight away," there is a suggestion of the consoling thought which Whitman had imagined in the surviving he-bird's song, or in the solitary thrush's in "When Lilacs Last in the Dooryard Bloom'd." But this image had come to Whitman's "awaken[ed]" imagination in "Out of the Cradle" (in 1859), and when Edna fully awakens to Chopin's view of the Darwinian reality by the end of the novel, the bird will reappear as the image of the spirit defeated—"with a broken wing ... beating the air above, reeling, fluttering, circling disabled down, down to the water" (chap. 39).

The musical performance on August twenty-eighth is crucial in propelling Edna toward her final bleak awakening, for here her response to the music is as Darwin explained in *The Expression of Emotions*: music can cause a person to "tremble," to feel "the thrill or slight shiver which runs down the backbone and limbs," or to experience "a slight suffusion of tears" that resembles "weeping" caused by other emotions.[12] Thus, during this musical performance in *The Awakening*, "the very first chords which Mademoiselle Reisz struck upon the piano sent a keen tremor down Mrs. Pontellier's spinal column." And because "her being was tempered to take an impress of the abiding truth," she finds that "the very passions themselves were aroused within her soul, swaying it, lashing it, as the waves daily beat upon her splendid body. She trembled, she was choking, and the tears blinded her" (chap. 9). The musical performance moves others, too: "What passion!" one exclaims—"It shakes a man!" Immediately following the performance the group decides to take a midnight swim; and now, like a joyful child taking her first steps, Edna realizes that she can swim. Feeling that "some power of significant import had been given her to control the workings of her body and her soul," she wants to "swim far out, where no woman had swum before" (chap. 10). Later, alone with Robert, she tells him of the "thousand emotions" that had swept through her as a result of Mademoiselle Reisz's playing, and before they part she is "pregnant with the first-felt throbbings of desire."

Chopin indicates at once that Edna's developing desire will eventually lead her into the "abysses of solitude." When she enters the water on this night, she gathers "in an impression of space and solitude" from "the vast expanse of water"; and in her solitary swim she realizes that she might perish "out there alone." Moreover, the simultaneous development of her desire and her sense of solitude will eventually lead her to a clearer understanding of her "position in the universe" as an animal and therefore as a creature empowered to participate fully in the sexual reality as a self-conscious selector (chap. 6). Her development toward claiming the power to select is gradual, but she takes a first crucial step immediately after her swim by refusing to yield to Mr. Pontellier's "desire." And a few days later she awakens more fully to her animal nature after fleeing from an oppressive church service to Madame Antoine's seaside home. Here, awakened from a nap, "very hungry," she "bit a piece" from a loaf of brown bread, "tearing it with her strong, white teeth" (chap. 13).

In his remarks on the canine tooth in human beings, Darwin notes that it "no longer serves man as a special weapon for tearing his enemies or prey." But he sharpens his main point here by adding: "He who rejects with scorn the belief that the shape of his own canines, and their occasional great development in other men, are due to our early forefathers having been provided with these formidable weapons, will probably reveal, by sneering, the line of his descent. For though he no longer intends, nor has the power to use these teeth as weapons, he will unconsciously retract his 'snarling muscles'...."[13] Clearly, Edna's strong teeth indicate her kinship with our "half-human ancestors" in *The Descent of Man*, for she tells Robert that the "whole island seems changed" now: "a new race of beings must have sprung up, leaving only you and me as past relics" (chap. 13).

But now Chopin will force the awakening Edna to endure the frustrations of civilized life, first by having to contend with Robert's sudden departure and the jealousy she feels when Robert writes only to others; and then when she suffers more consciously from the restrictions in her marriage. She rebels against her husband's and society's covenants, refuses to be one of his "valued ... possessions," and stamps on her wedding ring (chap. 17). And when she obstinately withdraws her normal "tacit submissiveness" in her marriage (chap. 19), she takes another of her crucial steps toward claiming her place in the arena of sexual selection. Before she selects a lover, she rejects her husband's sexual advances, leaving him "nervously" to explain to Dr. Mandelet that her "notion ... concerning the eternal rights of women" means that "we meet in the morning at the breakfast table" (chap. 22).

Dr. Mandelet counsels Mr. Pontellier to be patient with Edna, for "woman ... is a very peculiar and delicate organism." But it would seem that even the doctor does not understand the "new set of sensations" Edna experiences in response to her father's visit (chaps. 22, 23). That is, he knows "the inner life" of his "fellow creatures" better than most men; and, seeing the subtle change in Edna after her father's visit ("palpitant with the forces of life ... she reminded him of some beautiful, sleek animal waking up in the sun"), he guesses that she has taken Arobin as her lover (chap. 23). But he does not theorize, as Chopin does, on how the "laws of inheritance" (as Darwin understood them before Mendel) might have enabled Edna to acquire some of her father's masculine authority and passion. Her father has the essential male qualities that are "accumulated by sexual selection"—"ardour in love" and "courage" (*Descent*, I, 296). An aging Confederate colonel, he still has the power to arouse Madame Ratignolle at a *soirée musicale* (here again Chopin indicates her understanding of the sexual meaning of music): she "coquetted with him in the most captivating and naïve manner," and she invites him to dinner with her on "any day ... he might select" (chap. 23). The Colonel plays an essential role in Chopin's effort to validate Edna's developing power to select, and in this scene at the *soirée musicale* "her fancy selected" one or two men.

This is perhaps the most intricate part of Chopin's quarrel with Darwin, for in referring to his theory on the laws of inheritance, she exploits a possibility that he allows the female but does not himself develop: to do so would have contradicted his image of the modest woman with "powers of perception" and "taste" (*Descent*, I, 296). In this way, Chopin used Darwin's own theory in order to modify his definition of the sexual reality among humans: building on his "hypothesis of pangenesis," whereby "gemmules ... are transmitted to the offspring of both sexes," she suggests that Edna is an example of how "both sexes" can be "modified in the same manner" (I, 280, 299). Chopin's point seems clear when she has the Colonel imagine that "he had bequeathed to all of his daughters the germs of a masterful capability" (chap. 23). And, in arranging for Edna's lover, Arobin, to toast the Colonel for having "invented" Edna (chap. 30), Chopin underscores the irony of her quarrel with Darwin. After the Colonel's visit, Edna will attend the horse races; and there, her "blood" and "brain" inflamed, she talks "like her father," causing nearby people to turn "their heads" and Arobin to feel her magnetic force (chap. 25). Later that evening, when Arobin is moved by an impulse to show her the scar on his wrist which he had received—according to Darwin's law of battle for possession of the female—"from a saber cut ... in a duel ... when he was nineteen," Edna is agitated and sickened; but Arobin "drew all her awakening sensuousness" (chap. 23). Within days, she will respond to his effrontery not with a "crimson" blush of modesty, as Darwin might have imagined,[14] but with pleasure because it "appeal[ed] to the animalism that stirred impatiently within her" (chap. 26).

By now Edna has awakened enough to her own sexual reality to articulate the main point in Chopin's quarrel with Darwin. In a discussion with Mademoiselle Reisz about the meaning of love, Edna exhibits a wisdom that Chopin will not grant Mademoiselle Reisz, whose "avoidance of the water" is not only amusing (some of the bathers imagined that "it was on account of her false hair") but indicative of her essential sexlessness (chap. 16). Accusing Mademoiselle Reisz of either lying or having "never been in love," Edna proclaims, "do you suppose a woman knows why she loves? Does she select? Does she say to herself. 'Go to! Here is a distinguished statesman with presidential possibilities. I shall proceed to fall in love with him ... [or with] this financier?'" She admits that she loves Robert when she "ought not to," but Chopin's "ought" refers more to Darwin's theory about why civilized women select (modestly and discriminately, for wealth, etc.) than to the more obvious social prohibition against extramarital love. Edna loves Robert for the same reason that Whitman's imagined woman let her hand descend "tremblingly from [the young men's] temples": "Because his hair is brown and grows away from his temples, because he opens and shuts his eyes," because she likes his "nose," "two lips," and "square chin"—in short, because she is "happy to be alive" (chap. 26).

In her next meeting with Arobin, then, Edna's "nature" responds fully and for the first time to a kiss—"a flaming torch that kindled [her] desire" (chap. 27). And she will awaken next morning—in the pivotal twenty-eighth chapter—to her post-Whitmanian sense of the "significance of life, that monster made up of beauty and brutality." Comprehending life in this new way—"as if a mist had been lifted from her eyes"—she feels neither shame nor remorse, only "regret" that "it was not the kiss of love which had inflamed her, because it was not love which had held this cup of life to her lips" (chap. 28).

But far from denying this regrettable reality, Edna enters bravely and immediately into her new sexual independence by moving out of the family home into her own "pigeon house." In creating Edna's pigeon house, Chopin refers to Darwin's theories of sexual selection as explicitly as she had in her earlier references to the law of battle, the role of music in sexual selection, the relevance of our canine teeth, or the laws of inheritance. Scarcely a merely eccentric name for Edna's new dwelling after the *coup d'état*, "pigeon house" is an emphatic reference to the triumphant female pigeons Darwin describes in *The Descent of Man*—creatures who, like Edna, "occasionally feel a strong antipathy towards certain males [and preference *for* certain other males] without any assignable cause" (II, 118). Quoting a French study, Darwin tells how, when a female pigeon experiences an antipathy for a male, nothing can cause her to submit to him—neither the male's flaming desire nor any inducements a breeder might give her. She constantly refuses his caresses, even if confined with him for a year, sulking in a corner of her "prison," and coming out only to eat or drink; and if he forces his affections, she will repel him in a rage.[15] "On the other hand," Darwin notes, some females will desert their mates if they take "a strong fancy" for another; and some are even so "profligate" that they "prefer almost any stranger to their own mate" (II, 119).

Edna's birthday party is a ritual celebration of her entry into the modern sexual reality that Whitman's woman could not have known when he created her in 1855. Edna "selected [her guests] with discrimination," and Victor, "a graven image of Desire," is among them. When she tries to stop him from singing Robert's love song ("*Ah! si tu savais!*"), placing her hand over his mouth, "the touch of his lips was like a pleasing sting" (chap. 30). Thus, when Robert returns unexpectedly, she will quickly see that the love she had imagined is now impossibly complicated with all the strife even pigeons know in the arena of sexual selection. Robert is jealous of Arobin; she is jealous of the Mexican woman who gave Robert his embroidered tobacco pouch. And when she sleeps with Arobin again—to satisfy "her nature's requirements"— she enters into the hopelessness that will lead her back to the sea (chap. 35). After her accidental meeting with Robert (in a garden), they return to her "pigeon house" and define their irreconcilable differences as would-be lovers: he explains that he had left her because she belonged to Mr. Pontellier and that it was impossible to imagine him setting Edna "free." For Edna, of course, this would be absurdly "impossible," for she is "no longer one of Mr. Pontellier's possessions.... I give myself where I choose" (chap. 36). Although Robert is shocked by Edna's assertion of her absolute liberation, his only impulse at last is still "to hold her and keep her." Then—even after Edna revolts against nature when she helps her friend give birth, and even after she hears Dr. Mandelet's explanation about nature's "decoy" for securing "mothers for the race"—she returns to Robert, imagining "no greater bliss on earth than possession of the beloved one" (chap. 38). Even now she, too, would impose her "private will upon a fellow creature" and call it love, as Mrs. Mallard had imagined. And she will follow the illusion of love, nature's decoy, until she returns to her empty "pigeon house" and finds Robert's note.

Edna is now fully awake to her new reality: "Today it is Arobin," she tells herself, and "tomorrow it will be someone else" (chap. 39). Her desire (like the passion she had felt at the musical performance that night when she was twenty-eight) will rise and fall, "lashing" her soul "as the waves daily beat upon her splendid body" (chap. 9). She knows that the sense of her absolute isolation as a solitary soul will descend inevitably when she forgets even Robert. She will find no peace until she feels the "soft, close embrace" of the sea, her true element. And in this despair she sees her children as "antagonists," for *they* are nature's cause in natural and sexual selection—the force within herself by which love's wing was broken.

Notes

1. In his 1894 portrait of Chopin, William Schuyler reported that "the subjects which ... attracted her were almost entirely scientific, the departments of Biology and Anthropology having a special interest for her. The works of Darwin, Huxley, and Spencer were her daily companions; for the study of the human species ... has always been her constant delight" (in *A Kate Chopin Miscellany*, ed. Per Seyersted [Natchitoches, La.: Northwestern State Univ. Press, 1979], p. 117). But no critic to date has looked closely at Chopin's response to Darwin. Per Seyersted provided the most reliable insight in his general but undeveloped remark that she "wanted ... nothing less than to describe post-Darwinian man with the openness of the modern French writers" (*Kate Chopin* [Baton Rouge: Louisiana State Univ. Press, 1969], p. 90). See also Seyersted's "Introduction" to *The Storm and Other Stories by Kate Chopin with The Awakening* (Old Westbury, N.Y.: Feminist Press, 1974), p. 15; and his remarks on Edna's realization "that sex is largely independent of our volition" in his edition of *The Complete Works of Kate Chopin*, 2 vols. (Baton Rouge: Louisiana State Univ. Press, 1969), I, 28. Two other critics have written on naturalism in *The Awakening*, but without examining Darwin's presence in that book: Jerome Klinkowitz, in his chapter, "Kate Chopin's Awakening to Naturalism," *The Practice of Fiction in America: Writers from Hawthorne to the Present* (Ames: Iowa State Univ. Press, 1980); and Nancy Walker, in "Feminist or Naturalist: The Social Context of Kate Chopin's *The Awakening*," *Southern Quarterly*, 17, No. 2 (1979), 95–103.

2. *The Descent of Man and Selection in Relation to Sex*, 2 vols. in 1 (1871; rpt. Princeton: Princeton Univ. Press, 1981), II, 404. Unless otherwise noted, further references to *The Descent* are from this edition and this text, and are cited parenthetically by volume and page.

3. *The Complete Works of Kate Chopin*, II, 872. Subsequent references to *At Fault* will be to this text, cited parenthetically by page. In subsequent references to *The Awakening*, however—because there are now so many reliable editions of that book—I cite chapter numbers only. Also, since the two stories I discuss here ("A Respectable Woman," and "The Story of an Hour") are so short and so widely collected, I have not cited page numbers.

4. *The Descent of Man*, I, 259; for Darwin's understanding of the female's inferiority, see, for example, his remark that "man is more powerful in body and mind than woman" (II, 371). Cynthia Eagle Russett's *Sexual Science: The Victorian Construction of Womanhood* (Cambridge: Harvard Univ. Press, 1989) is an indispensable guide to the implications of Darwinian thought for the Victorian woman.

5. *The Descent of Man*, II, 371. Among most animals (birds, especially), in Darwin's analysis, the female selects the victorious male or the most attractive one—i.e., the most colorful or highly ornamented one.

6. "Nature's Courtship Plot in Darwin and Ellis," *Yale Journal of Criticism*, 2 (1989), 36–37.

7. Sitting under a live oak alone with Mrs. Baroda, the Barodas' friend, Gouvernail, murmurs these lines from "Song of Myself": "Night of south winds—night of the large few stars! / Still nodding night"; these lines are contained in Whitman's sentence, "Press

close bare bosom'd night ... mad naked summer night," in section 21, which ends, "O unspeakable passionate love."

8. Thomas Bonner, Jr., *The Kate Chopin Companion, with Chopin's Translations from French Fiction* (New York: Greenwood, 1988), pp. 179, 181. Further references to Chopin's translations of Maupassant are cited parenthetically by page from this text.

9. The distinctions I suggest here in my remarks about Aphrodite and the "self and society" refer to two of the very best essays on *The Awakening*—Sandra M. Gilbert's "The Second Coming of Aphrodite: Kate Chopin's Fantasy of Desire," *Kenyon Review*, 5 (1983), 42–56; and Nina Baym's "Introduction" to *The Awakening and Selected Stories* (New York: Random House, 1981), p. xxxiv.

10. *Kate Chopin*, ed. Harold Bloom (New York: Chelsea House, 1987), pp. 3, 2, 1.

11. Chap. 30; in chap. 16 Edna hears that Robert had once "thrashed" Victor for thinking "he had some sort of claim upon" Mariequita. In chap. 39 Mariequita senses that Victor is "in love with Mrs. Pontellier"; and Victor, jealous of one of Mariequita's lovers, threatens "to hammer his head into a jelly."

12. *The Expression of Emotions in Man and Animals* (1872; rpt. New York: Appleton, 1924), p. 217.

13. *The Descent of Man and Selection in Relation to Sex*, 2nd ed. (New York: Wheeler, n.d.), pp. 40–41. In the second edition, Darwin added this new chap. 2; and Chopin's apparent reference to it is one of several suggestions in her work that her text was the second edition.

14. See, for example, Darwin's discussion of blushing in *The Expression of Emotions* (p. 334). Many of Chopin's characters blush or flush in ways that indicate their animal emotions.

15. The quoted passage (from Boitard and Corbié, "Les Pigeons" [1824]) reads: "Quand une femelle éprouve de l'antipathie pour un mâle avec lequel on veut l'accoupler, malgré tous les feux de l'amour, malgré l'alpiste et le chènevis dont on la nourrit pour augmenter son ardeur, malgré un emprisonnement de six mois et même d'un an, elle refuse constamment ses caresses; les avances empressées, les agaceries, les tournoiemens, les tendres roucoulemens, rien ne peut lui plaire ni l'émouvoir; gonflée, boudeuse, blottie dans un coin de sa prison, elle n'en sort que pour boire et manger, ou pour repousser avec une espèce de rage des caresses devenues trop pressantes" (II, 118–119).

MARTHA FODASKI BLACK

The Quintessence of Chopinism

At the 1988 Modern Language Association conference, Elizabeth Fox-Genovese asserted that Kate Chopin had "little patience with the woman question." In underscoring this argument by writing that Chopin had "scant interest in social problems," she misleads us. Her argument that Chopin tried "to treat sexuality independent of gender relations" overlooks the textual evidence in *The Awakening*.[1] Close analysis of the novel reveals that Chopin examines the interdependence of female sexuality and gender roles to challenge cultural assumptions about women. Even though she was not an advocate or unequivocal reformer, *The Awakening* reveals the influence of late-nineteenth-century feminists and their search for a new kind of heroine on whom women could model their lives.

Internal evidence and references in Chopin's other writings reveal that she was well aware of writers such as Henrik Ibsen, George Bernard Shaw, and Elizabeth Cady Stanton. Although her biographers—even her most recent, Emily Toth—have found no direct evidence of her having read Shaw, Chopin's symbolic framework and conception of her main characters were probably influenced by Shaw's essay "The Womanly Woman" in *The Quintessence of Ibsenism*. In the 1890s, when Chopin's novel was germinating, Shaw's controversial essays in defense of Ibsen were circulating. The essay in which he defined and defended the feminist heroine by wryly comparing

From *Kate Chopin Reconsidered: Beyond the Bayou*, Lynda S. Boren and Sara deSaussure Davis, eds., pp. 95–113. © 1992 by Louisiana State University Press.

103

married women to caged parrots could hardly have escaped Chopin's attention.

The Awakening opens with a description of a parrot and a mockingbird—as Per Seyersted notes in his critical biography, "caged imitators," one of whom is "repeating its master's words, the other echoing the voice of other species" (*CB*, 159). This initial scene has, however, even more importance than Seyersted attributes to it. The parrot screams, "'*Allez vous-en! Allez vous-en! Sapristi!*'" The talking birds annoy Mr. Pontellier, who can do exactly what the parrot advises—go away. He has the "privilege of quitting their society when they cease to be entertaining" (*KCA*, 3). This opening is integral to Chopin's novel, whose descriptive details imply her theme. Without stating a message, the carefully self-effacing author suggests through strategically selected particulars the domestic relationships that her novel will explore. Her references to birds become a commentary on the action. The colorful, noisy imitators, like women, entertain men until they depart for spheres of more compelling interest—business and entertainment in a man's world.

In the opening episode, Edna Pontellier's husband, who is spending a summer weekend at Grand Isle where his wife and two small sons are vacationing, displays his male prerogative. When his wife's chatter with Robert Lebrun—resident swain, a Creole version of the courtly lover, and son of the resort's proprietress—becomes as annoying and boring as the birds' prattle, Léonce "yawns, stretches," and leaves for the local hotel to play billiards with his male friends. His freedom is so complete that his wife does not even require an answer to her perfunctory question whether he will return for dinner, and he does not feel obligated to give one. Nor does he come home until he feels like it.

The source of the opening description with its combative tone is probably Shaw, in spite of the fact that he did not originate the comparison of wives to caged birds. In 1772 Mary Wollstonecraft wrote of women: "Confined then in cages like the feathered race, they have nothing to do but to plume themselves, and walk from perch to perch. It is true they are provided with food and raiment, for which they neither toil nor spin; but health, liberty and virtue, are given in exchange." Nearly a century later, Nietzsche wrote, "Men have so far treated women like birds who had strayed to them from some height; as something more refined and vulnerable, wilder, stranger, sweeter, and more soulful—but as something one has to lock up lest it fly away."[2] Whereas Nietzsche asserted that the cage was the right place for woman, the feminist Shaw insisted that woman had the right to be free. Others, such as George Eliot in *Middlemarch*, had taken Wollstonecraft's cue to liken wives to pet birds, but Shaw's comparison directly anticipates Chopin's treatment of women in *The Awakening*.

Although what Richard Ohmann terms Shaw's "pugilistic stance" was not congenial to Chopin, in her novel she deliberately set out to enlarge upon Shaw's analogy to test it. Woman's freedom is one of Chopin's persistent themes. As Joan Zlotnick has pointed out, her women, "young and old, are often faced with rejecting or fleeing from marriage." Chopin's latest biographer, Emily Toth, confirms that Chopin "drew on real life for most of her inspirations." Whereas Toth has found no written indication of Chopin's interest in Shaw, evidence of her reading is implicit in *The Awakening*. Even the fact that Chopin's father, Thomas O'Flaherty, was, like Shaw, an Irish expatriate would have piqued Chopin's interest. Her literary and cultural interests—interests, according to Nancy Walker, not stifled among women in the New Orleans subculture—would have spurred her. In St. Louis her home was a meeting place for intellectuals who surely would have buzzed about Shaw's stinging defense of Ibsen. As the central figure of a "vigorous intellectual" circle, Chopin, who delighted in attending "concerts and plays," would surely have been in on the great Shavian debate.[3] A literate, cultured woman aware of the intellectual temper of her times, Chopin had read and probably attended Ibsen plays and could hardly have overlooked Shaw's controversial work on Ibsen; after all, by the 1890s, it had created a stir in literary and intellectual circles all over the western world.

Nevertheless, in reviewing Hamlin Garland's *Crumbling Idols* (1894), Chopin dissociated herself from writers whose avowed aim was social reform (even though Garland's Ida Wilbur could be a model for Edna Pontellier; both rejected the conventional and arbitrarily restricted roles society prescribed for women). Impressed by Garland's "veritism," a style she emulated, Chopin defended fiction as a craft. Without anticipating late-twentieth-century reassessments, she wrote of Ibsen that he "will not be true in some remote tomorrow, however forcible and representative he may be for the hour, because he takes as his themes social problems which by their very nature are mutable" (*CW*, 693).

Chopin's heroines are nonetheless drawn in marital settings like Ibsen's, even though the bleak Norwegian atmosphere differs sharply from the lush New Orleans region that lulls or awakens her women. In her story "A Shameful Affair," the heroine is indeed reading Ibsen (*CW*, 131). Readers can assume, therefore, that in spite of her objection to a writer like Zola who communicates "the disagreeable fact that his design is to instruct us," Chopin was well aware of Ibsen's domestic dramas and of the two so salient for her inspiration—*Hedda Gabler* (1890) and *A Doll's House* (1879), the latter of which, after its first performance in English with Shaw in the role of the blackmailer, played in almost every Western country (*CW*, 698). William P. Warnken has examined the parallels between *The Awakening* and *A Doll's House*, whose ideas about the "infantilization of women in marriage provoked extensive discussion and analysis in print." Among the most important contributions to the controversy was *The Quintessence of Ibsenism*, whose section on women presages Chopin's central fictional theme.[4]

Thus, despite her objection to "zeal for reform," the St. Louis Creole no doubt co-opted the parrot for the purposes of her art (*CW*, 24). Her novel about the womanly woman and female alternatives is diagnostic, treating characters within the fictive system that the realistic story demands. Although she first wants to tell her tale plausibly and effectively, the story is nonetheless a "problem" in the same way that Ibsen's plays are, despite the pronouncements of critics like Edmund Wilson and Lewis Leary, who prefer to consider *The Awakening*'s aesthetic apart from its social merits, or Fox-Genovese, who argues that Chopin "viewed woman's independence as a personal more than a social matter."[5] Firmly locating the personal in a social milieu that implies the relationship between the two, *The Awakening* is as much "problem" literature as an Ibsen play or a Shaw polemic. Readers at the time of *The Awakening* were so aware of its challenge to middle-class mores that it was damned by critics for its immoral subject matter (but praised for its style) and banned in St. Louis, Mrs. Chopin's hometown. Outraged moralists wanted to make its supposedly wicked author suffer for her heroine's shocking sexuality and her suicide, almost vindicated as ecstatic release.

Puritanical Americans were even more offended in the age of Comstockery than the French in 1857 when Flaubert was tried for alleged obscenity in *Madame Bovary*. Whereas conventional French Catholics were scandalized by Emma, driven by lust and greed to subvert the conventional role of wife and mother, her gruesome death saved Flaubert from persecution because the hysterical adultress got what moralists thought she deserved. Chopin's heroine, a sensuous, intelligent American refinement on Emma, was perhaps even more disturbing because she more clearly chose her fate, thus raising the issue of a person's right to control her own life and even choose her own death.

Chopin's novel is therefore clearly a "problem" work whose reception prompted Chopin to write a tongue-in-cheek apologia: "Having a group of people at my disposal, I thought it might be entertaining (to myself) to throw them together and see what would happen. I never dreamed of Mrs. Pontellier making such a mess of things and working out her own damnation as she did. If I had had the slightest intimation of such a thing I would have excluded her from the company. But when I found out what she was up to, the play was half over and it was then too late."[6] Significantly comparing her novel to a drama and arguing that her realistic characters have their own rationale, Chopin tried to dismiss her indignant critics.

Shaw's witty attack on Philistine hypocrisy would have struck a responsive chord in Chopin, who was, even as a young woman in St. Louis, noted for her sharp, cynical social observations.[7] Shaw's description of the caged wife states Chopin's fears of bondage, fears expressed in an early "fable" she called "Emancipation," a parable that celebrates the animal instinct for freedom. Chopin describes a captive animal escaping its cage in spite of "limbs ... weighted" to reach "the water that is good to his thirsting throat.... So does he live, seeking, finding, joying, suffering. The door which accident had opened is open still, but the cage remains empty forever!" (*CW*, 38–39). It seems no mere coincidence that the self-conscious artist (who had been forced into freedom by her husband's premature death) drew on her own parable, using the water symbol for sexual freedom and fruition in conjunction with the bird motif of Shaw, with whose parrot she begins her novel.

Shaw compares the self-sacrificing "womanly-woman" to a pet whose natural sphere is thought to be a cage because it has never been seen anywhere else. Man, for his own advantage, relegates woman to the role of pretty entertainer and breeder, and then concludes that her unnatural confinement is natural. Shaw's extension of the analogy is a good gloss of the sort of woman Chopin depicts as the main foil for her heroine. Adèle Ratignolle, the beautiful matron, is like Shaw's "idealistic parrots who persuade themselves that the mission of a parrot is to minister to the happiness of a private family by whistling and saying Pretty Polly, and that it is in the sacrifice of its liberty to this altruistic pursuit that a true parrot finds the supreme satisfaction of its soul."[8] Shaw's analysis could be a summary of Adèle's raison d'être, for she accepts the role of wife-mother and complacently enjoys her conventional, comfortable marriage. She accedes to the adage that women often take as a prescription rather than description—woman's place is in the home.[9] She is what Betty Friedan later called a happy-housewife heroine, dependent upon her husband and children for definition.[10]

Kate Chopin describes Adèle as a "faultless Madonna" (*KCA*, 12), confident, as her name suggests, in her noble role. Only slightly plumper than Petrarch's Laura, she has the standard features of the beloved of the love-sonnet tradition—golden hair, blue eyes, and rosy lips. Echoing Shaw, Chopin calls her a "mother-woman." From her maternal pedestal, she makes herself the central figure in the bourgeois drama of domesticity—a nurturing, selfless, self-sacrificing mother-goddess par excellence, exacting from her exalted position the adoration of others.

Chopin's initial description is, however, somewhat ironic, for this "heroine of romance and the fair lady of our dreams ... sewed away on the little night-drawers or fashioned a bodice or a bib," anticipating her children's winter needs and advertising her maternal care. She draws attention to herself by "always talking about her 'condition,'" even though her pregnancy isn't apparent early in the novel (*KCA*, 10–11). Enjoying the role of a weak, helpless dependent who faints easily and must be pampered because of her delicate condition, she is the epitome of the womanly women who "seemed to prevail that summer at Grand Isle. It was easy to know them, fluttering about with extended wings when any harm, real or imaginary, threatened their precious brood" (*KCA*, 10).

This not so rara avis makes the most of her position as decorative but fragile mother-Madonna. Because of her vested interest in the holy bonds of matrimony and maternity, she basks in the privileges of a mother hen who idealizes her domestic captivity. She smother-loves her children, although everyone knows that "the doctor had forbidden her to lift so much as a pin!" (*KCA*, 14). In dramatizing her dependence, she seeks masculine applause and support, achieving power through weakness. After complaining of various minor ailments, Adèle "begged Robert to accompany her to the house" and "leaned draggingly upon his arm as they walked" (*KCA*, 20).

To prove her total devotion to the ideal that she represents, Adèle rationalizes all of her behavior as good for her husband and children. Unlike Edna, she has, as Peggy Skaggs has noted, a "lack of aesthetic sensitivity ... another limitation of her total immersion in her role."[11] Chopin writes, "She was keeping up her music on account of the children, she said; because she and her husband both considered it a means of brightening the home and making it attractive" (*KCA*, 25). Her husband's wish is her command. When Edna returns from a day at the Chênière Caminada with Robert, Adèle will not stay with her (although Léonce has gone to Klein's to look up a cotton broker to discuss business) because M. Ratignolle "detested above all things to be left alone" (*KCA*, 40). Although Edna pities "that colorless existence which never uplifted its possessor beyond the region of blind contentment," Adèle and her husband, understanding "each other perfectly," are united in "domestic harmony" (*KCA*, 56), for Adèle sings her husband's song. They represent the social majority, which according to Shaw accepts illusions about the beauty of the family as a "holy natural institution."[12]

To live up to this bourgeois ideal, Adèle remains confined at home. Entertainments are house music or "a languid walk around the block with her husband after nightfall" (*KCA*, 76). Nevertheless, although she is a carefully realized portrait of Shaw's colorful musical pet in a cage, gratified by the attention she gets and living her life for others, reality muddles the pretty picture: The price of Adèle's life is the scene of "torture" near the end of the novel when her role is vividly clarified. While she is in labor—the "work" expected of proper Victorian women—the wife-mother who depends on the attention of others cries, "'This is too much! ... Where is Alphonse? Is

it possible that I am to be abandoned like this—neglected by everyone?!'"
(*KCA*, 108). Her entrapment, clear in this scene, is counterpointed by Edna's
final solitary act of self-assertion. The action of the novel is paralleled by
Adèle's pregnancy. While yearning for new life quickens in Edna, the new life
in Adèle results in her literal confinement, for she remains deaf to the angry
voice of the parrot whose refrain, like an inner voice for Edna, is a command
to "Go away! Leave!"

The parrot belongs to Mme. Lebrun, whose husband is departed,
whose sons are expected to go away to seek their fortunes and fulfillment.
Even the imprimatur of patriarchal tradition that sanctions Léonce's
behavior is obliquely suggested in the parrot's epithet "'By Jove' ('*Sapristi*')."
For Edna, an outsider in Creole society who takes its badinage seriously,
the bird's imperative becomes a directive to escape from the restrictions
of motherhood and marriage. She discovers that she wants to be the sort
of bird that Shaw describes as the only kind "a free souled person can
sympathize with ... the one that insists on being let out of the cage as the
first condition of making itself agreeable. A selfish bird, you may say: one
that puts its own gratification before that of the family which is so fond of
it—before even the greatest happiness of the greatest number; one, that in
aping the independent spirit of a man, has unparroted itself and become a
creature that has neither the home-loving nature of a bird nor the strength
and enterprise of a mastiff."[13]

In her quest to be a free-souled person, Edna tries to achieve
emancipation in the manner Shaw prescribed: "The sum of the matter is
that unless Woman repudiates her womanliness, her duty to her husband, to
her children, to society, to the law, and to everyone but herself, she cannot
emancipate herself.... Woman has to repudiate duty altogether. In that
repudiation lies her freedom; for it is false to say that Woman is now directly
the slave of Man: she is the immediate slave of duty; and as man's path to
freedom is strewn with the wreckage of the duties and ideals he has trampled
on, so must hers be."[14] Although Edna does not admit to herself that she is
a slave to man, she resolves "never again to belong to another than herself,"
knowing that the world will think her selfish.

The most severe test of her freedom, however, is her sense of duty to
her children. Even though Adèle's accouchement is to Edna a scene of horror,
she cannot escape, except through death, Adèle's admonition to remember
her obligations to her sons. During the summer at Grand Isle, Edna tells
Adèle, "'I would give up the unessential; I would give my money, I would give
my life for my children; but I wouldn't give myself'" (*KCA*, 80). Before her
suicide, Edna's children appear to her as "antagonists" seeking to enslave her
soul forever (*KCA*, 113).

Her husband assumes that she should dedicate her life to serving her sons. Her failure to watch over them in the night while he is out enjoying himself is disquieting to him. After a week of agreeable freedom in New Orleans, the model husband expects to buy favor and forgiveness from his wife and children with bonbons. From the start, he regards Edna as "a valuable piece of property" (*KCA*, 4). As Shaw put it in outlining the position of women in marriage, Edna "finds that her husband is neglecting her for business" and that his real life "lies away from home" where he is "thinking of stocks and shares." Even down to his professional interests, Léonce is the type of husband Shaw depicts. And Edna had as a girl the same idealistic illusions that Shaw says "youthful imagination weaves so wonderfully under the stimulus of desire" to delude women into accepting, indeed relishing, a submissive, nurturing role.[15]

But when Edna learns to swim and recognizes her desire for a man other than her husband, she awakens to the fact that she married only to comply with society's expectations. After her awakening, Edna yearns for the liberation sought by insurgent females of Chopin's time. As she begins to take pleasure in self-reliance, she turns to books and, significantly, chooses Emerson. Like that other transcendentalist Margaret Fuller, she determines to throw down "every arbitrary barrier to development" and to isolate herself to meditate on the meaning of her life.[16] Personal experience raises Edna's consciousness of her entrapment and her servitude as a woman of the nineteenth century.

Her declaration of independence to choose whom she will love suggests the influence of the outspoken Victoria Woodhull (née Claflin), who in 1873 broadcast her belief in free love and the need for women to revolt against sexual slavery in marriage. On her wedding trip, Kate Chopin had met one of the infamous Claflin sisters, probably Victoria, who shocked Americans by insisting, like Edna, on woman's sexual freedom (*CB*, 33–34). However, Edna's decent but paternalistic husband is perhaps not so blatantly sexist as the stereotype Elizabeth Cady Stanton described in an address on "Womanliness"—the male who prefers a woman "quiet, deferential, submissive, approaching him as a subject does a master."[17] Stanton considered marriage a tyranny in which "women have simply echoed" (like parrots?) male thought.

In *The Awakening* Adèle parrots patriarchal attitudes, whereas Edna rebels against them. Although her husband is not overtly despotic, Edna's Creole lover, Arobin, surmises that for Edna, marriage is nevertheless a despotism to be overthrown. When she gives her farewell dinner before moving out of the family house, Edna, having ironically exchanged male for female monarchy, is now "the regal woman," who in her obvious superiority "stands alone" (*KCA*, 88). In playfully calling the dinner party her "*coup d'état*," Arobin is partially right, for she is symbolically overthrowing the institution of marriage. Earlier she took off her wedding ring, having recognized it as a miniature fetter. She threw it on the carpet and stamped on it, "striving to crush it. But her small boot heel did not make an indenture, not a mark upon the little glittering circle" (*KCA*, 53).

Her attempt to destroy the sign of her bondage foreshadows her ineffectual struggle for freedom. She refuses to attend her sister's wedding, an occasion that she derides as "most lamentable" (*KCA*, 66), thus thwarting her authoritarian father, a former colonel in the Confederate army. Having "coerced" his wife into the grave, this rigid gentleman gravely advises Léonce to rule Edna, if necessary, through male compulsion (*KCA*, 71). In rejecting paternalistic dominance, Edna becomes without knowing it an isolated Shavian rebel trying to fly the coop society built for her.

Ironically, she moves to what her maid calls "the pigeon house." As a revolutionary act, such a move is indeed tame, for the pigeon is a domestic bird, usually monogamous, that we associate with a coop or wobbling parasitically on the ground, hoping to be fed. Even pigeons capable of sustained flight are called homing pigeons. Thus when Edna nests in the little house, the reader, wondering whether it is merely a microcosm of the family mansion, cannot feel reassured that she will have the strength to soar and fly away. Nevertheless, having "escaped" and accepted Arobin as her lover, Edna feels briefly some of the power that Shaw believed the free woman would experience. Chopin writes, "Every step which she took toward relieving herself from obligations added to her strength and expansion as an individual. She began to look with her own eyes, to see and to apprehend the deeper undercurrents of life. No longer was she content to 'feed upon opinion' when her soul invited her" (*KCA*, 93).

During the summer at Grand Isle, Edna had heard Adèle playing a piece on the piano that Edna named "Solitude." When she heard it, she imagined the figure of a naked man standing beside a desolate rock on the seashore in an attitude of "hopeless resignation as he looked toward a distant bird winging its flight away from him" (*KCA*, 26–27). Although, as Larzer Ziff suggests, the fantasy may be erotic, this Whitmanesque daydream embodies Edna's frustrated desire for masculine freedom and autonomy and presages the tragic denouement of the novel.[18] Divested of the raiments of sexual stereotyping, Edna longs for a heightened experience that would transcend sex roles.

Edna's longing for solitude reflects attitudes that Chopin no doubt found in Elizabeth Cady Stanton's 1890 address, "Solitude of Self." Indeed, Chopin's first choice of a title for her novel alludes to Stanton's feminist tract;

she called *The Awakening* "A Solitary Soul." Stanton had argued that "self-sovereignty" is a prerequisite for individual fulfillment, a prescription that Shaw, a year later, advocated for women. Stanton stressed that "the isolation of every human soul and the necessity of self-dependence must give each individual the right to choose his own surroundings." But a Presbyterian with strong fatalistic tendencies who reads Emerson and demonstrates self-reliance by moving around the corner with a servant is no doubt being treated with tolerant irony. Edna clearly wants, however, to be the kind of person Stanton describes as "an individual, in a world of her own, the arbiter of her own destiny, an imaginary Robinson Crusoe with her woman Friday on a solitary island."[19]

Twice Edna goes to a solitary island, once to a real one and once to her pigeon house (not to mention her crucial summer vacation and final trip to Grand Isle) where she is tended by a "woman Friday" while she experiences an awakening. At the Chênière, all of her dreams of erotic fulfillment are aroused, and in the pigeon house her illusions are shattered. Edna's trip to the island with Robert makes her feel that she has escaped an "anchor" and become her own navigator. As Stanton wrote, "No matter how much women prefer to lean, to be protected and supported, nor how much men desire to have them do so, they must make the voyage of life alone and for safety in emergency they must know something of the laws of navigation."[20] Although Edna feels that she is gaining control, ironically she relies heavily on Robert. In playfully saying that she'll give him the pirate's gold and treasure they might find together, she innocently suggests the illicit love and sexuality she may offer him. Although she sleeps and awakens on the island, like Rip Van Winkle, into a brave new world, it is not, despite her assertions, one for which she is fully prepared.

At the pigeon house, romance encounters reality, for Edna discovers that Robert is not the dashing romantic lover created by her overactive imagination, stimulated as it had been by the colors and textures of Grand Isle whose sensuous promises created a grand illusion. A charming but superfluous young man, Robert nevertheless shares Léonce's assumptions about women. Edna wakes to the fact that Robert assumes that Léonce owns her, that he must ask her husband's permission to love her. An impecunious variant of the male stereotype and an ineffectual Tristan to Edna's Isolde, he smokes cigarettes, whereas the wealthy, successful Léonce smokes cigars, denoting his masculine power and status. In light of Sara de Saussure Davis' theory that Edna is seeking the "delirium" associated with cigarettes laced with narcotics, Robert's switch from cigarettes to cigars might have provided another rude awakening for Edna.[21] It establishes him as the Philistine male who encages women. Edna realizes that Robert, who has finally indulged

himself with a box of cigars, is as much a conformist as her husband. As if
to confirm her discovery, her beloved makes a cowardly exit, destroying her
dream of love.

Her awakening to the fact that she cannot consummate her romance
with him fatally wounds her. Her friend Mlle. Reisz had warned her, "'The
bird that would soar above the level plain of tradition and prejudice must have
strong wings. It is a sad spectacle to see the weaklings, bruised, exhausted,
fluttering back to earth'" (*KCA*, 82). Edna's failure with Robert brings her
back to earth and to her limited options. She can, but will not, return to
domestic captivity, or she can suffer social and self-castigation if she denies
her duty to her children and becomes a free-lover.

Edna's repressive Protestant training and romantic illusions create a
dilemma that leads to her tragic death, a final act of existential independence
that is also an act of desperation. Like the uncaged domesticated bird unfit
for survival alone, Edna must be recaptured if she is not to be killed. Aroused
by her newly found animal instincts, she has not developed the "strength and
enterprise" of Shaw's mastiff. The exigencies of art and character portrayal
demand that Chopin "kill" Edna, whose swim into the sea's sensuous embrace
is nonetheless ecstatic and courageously defiant. Her death by water is a
declaration of both freedom and despair.

Among the last images that flash through her mind as she is swimming
out to drown are her military father, her married sister, and the young officer
whom she desired from a fanciful distance. Even in death she cannot escape
reminders of the cultural patterns that formed her—patriarchy, marriage,
and promises of romantic love—illusions Shaw targeted in *The Quintessence
of Ibsenism*. Although Edna is suited neither for marriage nor for the role
of mother-woman, she is unprepared for freedom. The bird that she had
fantasized earlier as winging away and about which Mlle. Reisz had warned
her is, when she finally stands alone on the beach, wounded, "with a broken
wing ... reeling, fluttering, circling disabled down, down to the water"
(*KCA*, 113).

In *The Sanity of Art* (1891) Shaw wrote that life is "not the fulfillment
of a moral law or of the deductions of reason but the satisfaction of a passion
in us of which we can give no account whatsoever." Edna wants to satisfy the
unaccountable passion, the life force within her that longs for aesthetic and
sensual fulfillment. Like Shaw (and Ibsen as Shaw interprets him), Chopin's
heroine comes to believe in the individualism of obeying her senses, even
though passions are dangerous. But in spite of her liberation, at bottom she has
not fully forgone the notion, which Shaw disavows, that love is self-surrender
or self-abandonment. "Love," he writes, "loses its charm when it is not free."

Shaw would urge "a young woman in a mood of strong reaction against the preaching of duty and self-sacrifice ... not to murder her own instincts and throw away her life in obedience to a mouthful of empty phrases." Although Edna's last interview with Robert would seem to illustrate her agreement, she commits suicide in literal self-abandonment and surrender to the sea. Chopin's description of her death, however, can be construed, like Shaw's feminist writings, as an attack on "the compulsory character of the legalized conjugal relation."[22]

Shaw distinguishes love as we idealize it from "the practical factor in society that is still more appetite." In her infatuation with Robert and her affair with Arobin, Edna learns the difference between romantic love and sexual appetite, and before her final dilemma decides that she will love without concern for society's demands. Nonetheless, having absorbed all too well her repressive Protestant training, she feels guilty for desires that do not conform to her notions of romantic love. Her confusion of "romance and passion" is a disorder that Shaw blamed on the social milieu of the times.[23] In trying to talk to Edna about things she "never dreamt of before" (KCA, 110), Dr. Mandelet voices Shavian ideas. A surrogate for Shaw (and Ibsen) who exposed the life lies upon which phallocentric culture depended in socializing women, the doctor tries to cure Edna by explaining the romantic "illusions" of youth that nature provides to serve as "a decoy to secure mothers for the race" (KCA, 109–110). He is too late to save her from electing a fate that demonstrates rebellion against two of Shaw's bêtes noire—the majority view that "the domestic career" is natural for all women and the "idealist illusion" that deludes women into accepting the marriage cage.

Whereas womanly-women gain self-esteem in motherhood and foster "the idealist illusion that a vocation for domestic management and the care of children is natural for women," the idealists, according to Shaw, attack women who lack the domestic vocation, calling them "not women at all, but members of the third, or Bashkirtseff sex." Shaw's essay on the womanly-woman was inspired by male response to this type of female—Marie Bashkirtseff, the literary sensation of 1890 whose diary was criticized by the editor of the Review of Reviews for being the shameless revelations of an "'artist, musician, wit, philosopher, student, anything you like but a natural woman with a heart to love, and a soul to find its supreme satisfaction in sacrifice for lover or for child.'"[24] Finding this attitude "pestiferous," Shaw assailed the editor for insisting upon the feminine ideal. Chopin created Mlle. Reisz to represent the Bashkirtseff sex and a social microcosm to reveal the conventional response to such an emancipated woman.

Most of the vacationers at Grand Isle consider the eccentric pianist self-absorbed, arrogant, and unpleasant. Edna's initial response to her is mixed, but as she grows in self-awareness and in desire to love where she chooses and develop as she will, she is drawn to Mlle. Reisz, who lives alone in bohemian squalor and devotes herself to the high calling of her art. Her wizened ugliness may, however, have more than a little to do with her biological destiny, just as Adèle's conventional beauty may have much to do with hers. The pianist warns Edna that "'to succeed, the artist must possess the courageous soul ... The soul that dares and defies'" (*KCA*, 63). Apparently having sacrificed much in her quest for artistic success, she has defied society's rules by remaining single. In contrast to the womanly women, the New Woman cares nothing for children. She tells Edna that the summer would have been "'rather pleasant, if it hadn't been for the mosquitoes and the Farival twins'" (*KCA*, 49), who play kitsch piano duets that perhaps offend her more than their childhood.

However, Chopin treats Mlle. Reisz with the same indulgent irony she uses in depicting Adèle. The emancipated woman who has cut herself off (or been cut off?) from romantic fulfillment enjoys Edna's visit somewhat voyeuristically. No matter what the season, Mlle. Reisz wears the same "shabby lace" and artificial bunch of violets on the side of her head" (*KCA*, 62), tokens of frustrated and blighted erotic fantasy. She titillates Edna with amorous music that moves the younger woman to tears. In describing Mlle. Reisz playing Chopin, Chopin is no doubt wryly reminding her educated readers of writer George Sand, Frédéric Chopin's lover, a woman who successfully combined all three of the female roles examined in *The Awakening*. Identifying Edna as a femme fatale by referring to Keats's "La Belle Dame Sans Merci," Mlle. Reisz plays Isolde's song from Wagner's *Tristan and Isolde*, associating Edna with romantic agony and Wagner's tragic love-death motif. In spite of Mlle. Reisz's snobbish but serious preoccupation with her art, she gets a sterile emotional satisfaction vicariously, as Lynda Boren has indicated, through manipulating and sharing Edna's turbulent, newly awakened emotions. Like Shaw, whose *The Perfect Wagnerite* (1898) Chopin could have read while writing *The Awakening*, the pianist no doubt admires Wagner's artistic daring.[25] She has wings to defy convention, but she lacks the sensuality that is even more a threat to society than her "third" sex.

Although aroused by the older woman's music and envious of her freedom to pursue her artistic interests, Edna does not want to emulate Mlle. Reisz's lonely life any more than she wants to accept a life like Adèle's as a brood hen. Wishing for full self-realization, Edna longs to design herself as a New Woman without being condemned to the role of the Victorian feminine. As Per Seyersted notes, Chopin's stories deal with "what we might call the three main types of women: the 'feminine,' the 'emancipated,' and the 'modern' (to use the terminology of Simone de Beauvoir's *The Second Sex*)," types that Shaw anticipated, without emphasizing erotic satisfaction as an end in itself.[26] Chopin's Edna is aware of all three claims—the subservient role that she tries to escape, the "active taker" who puts "flesh above the spirit," and the "modern" woman who "prides herself on thinking, taking action, working, creating."[27] Edna rejects her subjugation as wife and mother, but having been socialized by a rigid puritan ethic, she cannot with impunity and without guilt achieve full emancipation and sexual liberation.

Because romantic ideals deluded her into desiring "the acme of bliss" that equates love with sexual desires, and because reality taught her that erotic satisfaction can be divorced from love, Edna is trapped by her delusion that without a man, she is incomplete. She wants Robert but knows that she will have to content herself with Arobin. Despite her talent as a painter, she recognizes that in her time and place the third option—what Shaw calls "emancipated" and de Beauvoir "modern"—is an inadequate model for her longings for completeness, for Mlle. Reisz's narrow life belies her brave talk of artistic daring. Aware of all of her choices, Edna realizes that none will satisfy her unaccountable passion for life. Having discovered the desire but not the sufficient will for self-actualization, Edna is ensnared by her romantic yearnings and the preset springs of polite society.[28]

To underscore her treatment of the three pigeonholes available to Edna, Chopin creates variations on her theme. Adèle, the womanly woman, is paralleled by the widow Mme. Lebrun, who dominates one son and dotes on the other, still living through her offspring. Mlle. Reisz, the unsexed voyeuristic woman with a profession, is paralleled ironically by the woman in black, probably a nun saying her beads, who is following a pair of young lovers. Edna, the sensuous woman who would fly from the cage of her conditioning, is confronted with representatives of her three sexual options— the young lovers, who exemplify romantic escape; the barefoot Spanish girl Mariequita, who stands for direct, earthy sexuality; and Mrs. Highcamp, who represents the possibility of sophisticated extramarital affairs. Edna dreams of lovers escaping the world in a pirogue; she frankly recognizes that she shares Mariequita's bold sensuality; and she fears that she could become a Mrs. Highcamp involved in a succession of affairs with younger men. She rejects the role of Adèle and because of her aroused sensuality cannot, despite artistic talent, accept or aspire to the sterile independence of Reisz. When she faces the sea alone, she has run out of choices.

Thus with sensuous imagination, irony, and acute sensitivity to the climate of thought about women in her time, Chopin patterns a medium fully appropriate to her realistic, insightful message. She does not warn women to conform, but implicit in her imagery and her story is the idea that without fulfilling work and the collaboration of men, female freedom may be destined to frustration. Edna's broken wing is caused by the snare of her illusions and by the winds of social expectations. Although, as Léonce says, she does have "some sort of notion in her head concerning the eternal rights of women" (*KCA*, 65), she falls short of daring Shavian liberation. A diagnostic and a cautionary tale, Chopin's narrative subjects Shavian argument and feminist thought to the corrective of her imagination. Without compromising her aesthetic principles, Chopin created a work of "destruction," like Ibsen's problem plays, one that exposes the domestic lies people live by. According to Shaw, "Every step in morals is made by challenging the validity of the existing concept of perfect propriety of conduct."[29]

Chopin's novel is such a challenge. It illustrates Shaw's belief in works of "destruction," for "the advantage of the work of destruction is that every new ideal is less of an illusion than the one it has supplanted; so that the destroyer of ideals, though denounced as an enemy of society, is in fact sweeping the world clear of lies."[30] In questioning the conventional lies about women, *The Awakening* is quintessential Chopinism. With uncompromising realism, wry irony that exposes the gulf between the illusions and realities of her characters, and sensuous symbolic detail that communicates theme without presenting it, the novel tests society's assumptions about women. It effectively gives Shavian argument fictional form.

NOTES

1. Elizabeth Fox-Genovese, "Edna's Suicide," paper delivered at MLA convention, New Orleans, December 27, 1988; Elizabeth Fox-Genovese, "*The Awakening* in the Context of the Experience, Culture, and Values of Southern Women," in *ATA*, 34, 39.

2. Mary Wollstonecraft, *A Vindication of the Rights of Women*, Scott Library edition (N.p., 1891), 70; Friedrich Nietzsche, *Beyond Good and Evil*, trans. Walter Kaufman (New York, 1966), 235.

3. Richard M. Ohmann, *G. B. Shaw, the Style and the Man* (Middletown, Conn., 1965), 235; Joan Zlotnick, "A Woman's Will: Kate Chopin on Selfhood, Wifehood, and Motherhood," *Markham Review*, III (1968), 2; Emily Toth, "A New Biographical Approach," in *ATA*, 60. Nancy Walker, "The Historical and Cultural Setting," in *ATA*, 67; Peggy Skaggs, *Kate Chopin* (Boston, 1985), 23.

4. Warnken quotation from Miriam Schneir, ed., Preface to *A Doll's House*, in *Feminism: The Essential Historical Writings* (New York, 1972), 179; George Bernard Shaw, *The Quintessence of Ibsenism* (New York, 1958).

5. Edmund Wilson, *Patriotic Gore* (New York, 1962), 591; Lewis Leary, Introduction to *The Awakening and Other Stories by Kate Chopin* (New York, 1970); *ATA*, 35.

6. *Book News*, XVII (July, 1899), 612.

7. Toth, "New Biographical Approach," 62.

8. Shaw, *Ibsenism*, 23.

9. See Elizabeth Janeway, *Man's World, Woman's Place* (New York, 1971), for a discussion of this phenomenon.

10. Betty Friedan, *The Feminine Mystique* (New York, 1963).

11. Skaggs, *Chopin*, 92.

12. Shaw, *Ibsenism*, 56.

13. *Ibid.*

14. *Ibid.*, 53–54.

15. *Ibid.*, 52.

16. Margaret (Ossoli) Fuller, *Woman in the Nineteenth Century* (Boston, 1855), 36.

17. Elizabeth Cady Stanton, "'Womanliness,' an Address to the N.Y. State Legislature, 1880," in *History of Woman's Suffrage*, ed. Mari Jo and Paul Buhle (Urbana, 1978), 25.

18. Larzer Ziff, *The American 1890's: Life and Times of a Lost Generation* (New York, 1966), 302.

19. Elizabeth Cady Stanton, "'Solitude of Self,' an Address Before the U.S. Senate Committee on Woman's Suffrage, 1892," in *History of Woman's Suffrage*, 326, 325.

20. *Ibid.*, 327.

21. Sara de Saussure Davis, "Chopin's *A Vocation and a Voice*: Its Relevance to *The Awakening*," paper delivered at MLA convention, New Orleans, December 28, 1988.

22. George Bernard Shaw, *The Sanity of Art* (New York, 1908), 50; Shaw, *Ibsenism*, 39, 40.

23. Shaw, *Ibsenism*, 50. See Barbara C. Ewell, *Kate Chopin* (New York, 1986), 140, for a discussion of Edna's confusion.

24. Shaw, *Ibsenism*, 51, 50.

25. Lynda S. Boren, "The Music of Passion: Kate Chopin's Experimental Keyboard," paper delivered at MLA convention, New Orleans, December 28, 1988; George Bernard Shaw, *The Perfect Wagnerite* (London, 1923).

26. *CB*, 103; see also Simone de Beauvoir, *The Second Sex* (1952; rpr. New York, 1974).

27. De Beauvoir, *Second Sex*, 798.

28. See Jo Ellen Jacobs, "*The Awakening* in a Course on Philosophical Ideas in Literature," in *ATA*, for a discussion of this dilemma.

29. Shaw, *The Sanity of Art*, 44.

30. Shaw, *Ibsenism*, 57.

KATHLEEN WHEELER

Kate Chopin: Ironist of Realism

Katherine Chopin (née O'Flaherty) was born in 1851, in St Louis, Missouri, of a French Creole mother and an Irish immigrant father. She died in 1904, in St Louis, of a brain haemorrhage. Chopin received a strict Catholic education, was an excellent pianist, and was fluent in French. In 1870, she moved to New Orleans with her husband and had six children before returning, upon his death fourteen years later, to St Louis to take up the serious writing career interrupted by marriage. An early novel, *At Fault*, said to be derivative of Charlotte Brontë's *Jane Eyre*, numerous short stories, and a second novel (destroyed by the author), *Young Doctor Gosse*, preceded the 1899 publication of *The Awakening*. An insanely hostile critical reaction followed, along with her publisher's refusal to publish the third and final collection of short stories. Only sixty years later was her work rescued from oblivion with the 1969 Per Seyersted edition of the *Complete Works*.

Chopin's reading of Spencer, Darwin, Huxley, and other Victorian thinkers led her privately, at least, to renounce much of Catholicism. Her intimate knowledge, as a pianist, of music influenced her style and content, as did her close study of Maupassant and other French realists and naturalists. *The Awakening*, far from being a departure from Chopin's early stories, a little patronisingly described as 'delightful sketches', was the obvious continuation of themes of self-discovery and self-creation that had explicitly shaped her

From *'Modernist' Women Writers and Narrative Art* by Kathleen Wheeler, pp. 51–76. ©1994 by Kathleen Wheeler.

earliest stories and poems, many of which reached national publication in magazines such as *Harper's*, *Vogue*, *Century*, and others. Her handling of controversial themes such as sexual, financial, and emotional independence for women led to considerable critical neglect of her remarkable style, with its Maupassant characteristics of condensation and understatement, economy and clarity, and constant use of irony either as undertone or as explicit narrative stance. Similarly, her ability to capture local intonation and dialect and to portray folk humour gained her recognition as a local colourist but obscured the universality of her literary achievements.

Chopin, herself, awoke to the liberation in style and subject matter that European realism (the 'poison of Europe') offered her as an artist—material too strong, apparently, for her then rather sheltered American audience. Realism initially provided an alternative to the crippling sentimentalism of writers who had idealised marriage, family, and female dependence. Chopin's own style lacks the harsh pessimism and stark bleakness of other local colourists, such as Sarah Orne Jewett, Mary Wilkins Freeman, and McEnery Stewart, enriched as it is with intense and varied symbolism, eroticism, and sensuality (as she explored, for example, the sexual sublimation evident in Catholic rituals). Metaphors of light and warmth, lush visual settings, and colourful surroundings characterise her portrayals of poverty and ordinary life. Even by her most hostile, bullish critics, Chopin was described as 'a writer of great refinement and taste', and Willa Cather called her style 'exquisite and sensitive'.[1]

Chopin's own gradual awakening, however, from the restrictive realist, male techniques (which kept her 'landbound') to the unique and individual style that evolved most fully in *The Awakening*, is dramatised thematically in this last novel as a woman's (female artist's) struggle for her own identity and a self-realisation that undercuts the authority of male (literary and social) conventions.[2] Chopin's ability to create an astounding network of interwoven symbols, images, and metaphors (forming a tight and intricate narrative texture) is surpassed only by her fine use of Sophoclean irony built into the most apparently innocent 'realist' gestures to undercut that very realist authority. As with Jane Austen, the narrative stance is intensely ironic, as is to be expected in a writer seeking to challenge tradition and authority. The simple elegance and severe economy of this novel, where every episode contributes to a final, total effect, are exhilarating as the reader perceives the metaphorical drama of the woman/artist struggling to leave behind imprisoning literary forms, acceptable subject matter, and realist language. Chopin's last, exquisite, and liberating touch in *The Awakening* is her modernist gesture of a refusal of finality at the end of the novel:[3] even into the literal level of the narrative, an uncertainty as to the meaning and value of Edna's action is reinforced by the symbolic and metaphorical implications of her journey as the journey of the soul into the realms of the 'impossible'. Regenerative and 'vital' imagery, along with the indirect appeal to the Aphrodite legend, side by side with indications of fatigue, drowning, death, and hopeless defeat, create an unresolvable ambiguity between victory and defeat. Edna's voyage into the ocean, away from the solid stolidity of the shore, resembles the poet in Shelley's *Adonais*, where 'the spirit's bark is driven / Far from the shore, far from the trembling throng / Whose sails were never to the tempest given; / ... I am borne darkly, fearfully afar ... where the Eternal are'. The drowning and death may be more a symbolical death of the convention-fearing, time-bound ego—the self imprisoned by the morality and convention of its own time and place—to bring about the birth of a self freed from fear and egotism, as in Shelley's poem.[4] Such a theme has applications beyond the liberation of women from male traditions, whether social or literary, to the liberation of the human spirit from the crippling constraints of fear of social condemnation, as well as the recriminations and conflicts within one's own psyche. Other interpretations of the ambiguity of the novel's ending (discussed below) will suggest, however, that any simple account of Edna's death as symbolic of rebirth is misleading and to some extent inconsistent with the details of the text.

The *Awakening* becomes for the alert reader a literary autobiography, and a tragic prognostication of things to come in Chopin's life. For the novel was a literary suicide: Chopin's admirers viciously turned against her 'obscenities'. As a literary autobiography, it portrays Chopin's own awakening from a passive, submissive mother and wife to a woman with autonomy, as she asserted her right to become a fully alive human being (in her case, as an artist). Yet the novel also metaphorically dramatises the related struggle of both the woman artist (and all genuine artists) to break with artistic traditions and conventions in order to create new forms of expression that seem bizarre, offensive, immoral, and ugly to a contemporary audience. For Chopin, every artist is original only to the extent that she can adapt old forms and then create new ones more congruent with the new perceptions and experiences that she needs to express. Chopin showed that to remain within traditional conventions and accepted forms is tantamount to drowning one's individuality, originality, and creativity in a sea of banalities. Indeed, one's identity remains unformed and immature as a result, if not actually non-existent.

To sum, European realism gave Chopin one of the keys to moving out of the sentimentality and crass idealisation of much nineteenth century writing. Yet, after familiarising herself with that form, Chopin found it entirely inadequate to her needs as an artist and as a woman-artist. In her artistic struggle to free herself from these (in part, male) literary constraints, she discovered that she could turn realism against itself, by ironising its own limitations, while using its liberating capacities for her own effects. Chopin's narrative voice has its genius and originality precisely in this fusion of realism and irony, while her style achieved a union of realism and lush, southern symbolism that gives it its unique flavour. By ironising realism, she paradoxically exposed it as itself a decadent and, indeed, nonsensical concept.[5] That is, by her rich symbolism and use of complex imagery and extended metaphors, Chopin undercut realism's most central concept of language as transparent (as directly representative of 'reality'), showing that observation and description are never objective, but always interpretation. Consequently, 'reality' turns out to be plural, always: that is, a reality from a point of view, not the reality from the point of view. *The Awakening* depicts the struggle to establish an individual woman's right to her point of view in both life and art. As such, it explores thematically, at a literal level, the life aspect, while exploring thematically, at a metaphorical level (and through style), the possibility of an art and language more congruent with women's ways of seeing and living than are the styles, forms, and languages established by men. Overt subject matter is, then, a sustained metaphor for Chopin's (and for women-artists') efforts to find languages and forms expressive of their values, beliefs, and experiences. As such, it prophetically reveals the rewards of challenging the male prerogative and the deadly penalties that any woman and any woman artist who dares to do so, will pay.

  The Awakening is a relatively short novel of 140 pages, divided nevertheless into thirty-nine sections of varying lengths.[6] The movement from section to section is often abrupt, with little effort to smooth by transitions the gaps in time, place, and mood from one to another. Indeed, the gaps seem deliberately to be emphasised, giving the reader a sense of profound urgency, as if in the inexorable march toward the conclusion no trifles or literary superfluities can be spared. Yet within the sections themselves, continuity of time and place is almost always strictly and fastidiously maintained. This sectional continuity makes the discontinuity between sections even more noticeable, and more powerfully effective in giving the reader a sense of being propelled toward some dreadful end. Alternation between continuity within sections and discontinuity between often very short sections (less than half a page sometimes) has much the same effect as May Sinclair's use of spacings between paragraphed sections which, in *Mary Olivier*, become shorter and shorter as the book nears its end, seeming thereby to rush headlong toward a powerful finality. In *The Awakening*, however, no speeding up occurs as the novel progresses; rather the speed keeps changing—a slow, emphatic, almost, stately, forward progression within each section, a sudden leap often to the next stage in the new section. This aspect of Chopin's narrative technique creates a potent sense of the subjectivity of time. For while she seems thus to respect the typical realist's objectivity of time within chapters, she rejects realist organisation with her sectionalising of the novel into what are not at all typical length chapters, but short, often choppy sections, mere fragments of narrative in fact (no section is longer than six pages, some are two or less, two are less than a page). Thus, Chopin's narrative 'fragments' are already a step towards modernism, towards liberating herself from the imposition of a false order to human experience characteristic of much realism, as Virginia Woolf was to complain later. The careful, scrupulous even, adherence to 'order' within sections is mocked gently, then, by the fragmentary narrative form that Chopin had selected instead of chapters. However, superimposed on these numerous fragments is a larger whole, structured into three major portions, or, rather, two main portions and a short conclusion. This fragmentation unified by a larger structure is comparable to Jean Rhys' structural technique in *Voyage in the Dark*, not to mention a number of other modernist texts. These various narrative strategies enable Chopin to create a Katherine Mansfield-type dramatic sense, a 'drama' of roughly, three acts, with the same intense emphasis upon inevitability and inexorability that often occurs in dramas, and which helps to make it 'dramatic'. The first act takes place on Grand Isle, during the summer, and consists of sixteen sections, the second, in the city, taking up the next twenty-one pieces, and the third, only one brief fragment of a scene, occurs back at Grand Isle. A further Mansfield-like effect, that familiar Sophoclean irony, reinforces the sense of dread, with its prognostication of things to come and hidden significances studded throughout the novel like carefully placed gems.

Another narrative technique which Chopin employed within her sections, which also acts to reinforce a sense of the rapid acceleration of events, involves a favourite avowed modernist emphasis on understatement, that is, introducing major occurrences, decisions, and discoveries without any build-up or preparation. For example, in fragment twenty-six, Edna suddenly announces to Mlle Reisz, 'Mademoiselle, I am going to move away from my house on Esplanade Street' (p. 134). This is the first the reader has been given any inkling of such a momentous decision. Mlle Reisz is unimpressed, in contrast to the surprise Chopin springs upon her audience. Nor are we prepared for Edna's presence back at Grand Isle, in fragment thirty-nine, with no decision to go narrated, no description of journey, no preparation for Victor, who complains: 'By gimminy! Women have no consideration! She might have sent me word' (p. 174). Expressive also of the reader's response, such self-referral is characteristic of Chopin's ironic style. Equally, the ending of the season at Grand Isle in Part I is dealt with in a boldly perfunctory manner, as is the sudden relocation in

New Orleans, which begins Part II. These artistic gestures of impatience with expected, realist transitions to new scenes and with accepted literary conventions requiring smoother development of plot are reinforced with a rare precision, however, in the thematics of the novel: Edna is hurt and outraged to learn of Robert's sudden decision to, and actual act of, departing. In one short six-page sequence, the reader is equally briskly informed of Robert's decision, presented with his and Edna's painful parting, and, presto! He is gone. Edna, likewise, treats her husband to a parallel briskness: in a letter out of the blue, she informs him of her decision, and, before allowing time for him to answer, she has accomplished her move. This element of surprise, rare in Chopin's novel, is used carefully and only for 'important' events, unlike Jane Bowles, for whom surprise is a major stylistic as well as structural device. Another example of understatement and surprise is Mlle Reisz's sudden revelation to Edna (in fragment twenty-six) that Robert is due back soon. Edna is shocked and desperate to know exactly when he returns, yet, contrastingly and perversely, their reunion is not only delayed until fragment thirty-three, but the meeting is another surprise, an accident. And they meet one another briefly and unexpectedly at Mlle Reisz's while she is out. The 'deferral' of reunion maddeningly continues and suspense mounts until section thirty-six, since until then Robert has refused to declare his love and Edna is in a torture of uncertainty. Curiously contrasting with these *faits accomplis* and arts of surprise and understatement is the preparation, exaggerated importance, and grand build-up given to the 'last supper' in the old house, which, in the event turns out to be a non-event, at least on a surface level. While carrying, no doubt, symbolic significances, the supper party hardly does anything to add to or advance the narrative, or to enhance the dramatic quality. Indeed, this section seems curiously loosely constructed, lacking the economy and pregnancy of meaning of many of the other sections. Much like Mansfield's dinner party in 'Bliss', this 'centrepiece' of the novel falls utterly flat at the level of thematics, so flat that one senses an artistic decision and deliberateness, as if Chopin used its surface meaninglessness to foster a symbolic significance—and that indeed is surely the case, as Sandra Gilbert has convincingly argued (see below, however, for discussion of the limitations of this view).

The dinner party, strategically poised as it is in the narrative between Edna's discovery of Robert's imminent return (xxvi) and her first accidental meeting with him (xxxiii) is in itself of little significance. After a tremendous build-up, Chopin designedly bored her reader with this uneventful evening in order to draw attention to certain qualities in the setting, and especially in Edna, that are maturing into full development:

There was the occasional sound of music, of mandolins, sufficiently removed to be an agreeable accompaniment rather than an interruption to the conversation. Outside the soft, monotonous splash of a fountain could be heard; the sound penetrated into the room with the heavy odor of jessamine that came through the open windows.

The golden shimmer of Edna's satin gown spread in rich folds on either side of her. There was a soft fall of lace encircling her shoulders. It was the color of her skin, without the glow, the myriad living tints that one may sometimes discover in vibrant flesh. There was something in her attitude, in her whole appearance when she leaned her head against the high-backed chair and spread her arms, which suggested that regal woman, the one who rules, who looks on, who stands alone. But as she sat there amid her guests, she felt the old ennui overtaking her; the hopelessness which so often assailed her, which came upon her like an obsession, like something extraneous, independent of volition. It was something which announced itself; a chill breath that seemed to issue from some vast cavern wherein discords wailed. There came over her the acute longing which always summoned into her spiritual vision the presence of the beloved one, overpowering her at once with a sense of the unattainable.

The moments glided on, while a feeling of good fellowship passed around the circle like a mystic cord, holding and binding these people together with jest and laughter. (p. 145)

The last sentence of paragraph two is one example of many occasions when Chopin loaded the narrative with ambiguous, Sophoclean prognostications of both heroic and tragic endings, and a careful look suggests precisely the ambiguity found at the end of the novel. Edna is described as 'the regal woman, the one who rules, who looks on, who stands alone' (a far more apt description of Mlle Reisz, the pianist, in fact), yet, simultaneously, a sense of the unattainable is said to overpower her with hopelessness.

Chopin's abrupt handling of the penultimate dramatic moment— Robert's second desertion of Edna and his brief, pathetic farewell note— combines once again surprise and understatement with a number of ambiguous intimations preceding his largely unexpected flight from Edna, who, during their only love scene, has shocked him with her dismissal of respectability and convention ('I am no longer one of Mr Pontellier's possessions to dispose of or not. I give myself where I choose', p. 167). Sandwiched between their love-making (and that is unconsummated), is the scene in which Edna is called to attend the birth of her friend Adèle Ratignolle's baby, which she had casually promised to do at the beginning of the section in which she and Robert met accidentally at Mlle Reisz's (xxxiii). The tragic consequences of this promise allied with the studied casualness on Kate Chopin's part are exemplary of her dramatic genius, for this casualness is in appalling contrast with the dire results. For in the midst of Edna's and Robert's long-awaited (literally) endlessly deferred union, Edna is forced to leave Robert to attend the birth, in spite of his pleadings that she should remain. Nevertheless, the narrative seems to assure the reader that Lebrun will await Edna, deprived as he is said to be 'of every impulse but the longing to hold her and keep her' (p. 168). Edna's faith in him adds to this unfulfilled expectation, and to the shock of his desertion shortly after. Towards the end of the birth-scene, Chopin introduced hints of possible trouble, as well as loading the narrative with symbolic meanings: the birth of the child is a metaphor for Edna's birth into a new life; the birth is shockingly painful and tortuous, as her own is becoming; insinuations of the meaningless transience of life, of a Nietzschean horror at the wanton profligacy of Nature, and of the futility of bringing children into a world of suffering are implanted in the space of a brief paragraph. Edna is 'seized with a vague dread ... with an "inward agony, with a flaming, outspoken revolt against the ways of Nature", [as] she witnesses the scene of torture' (p. 170). A brief, but symbolically revealing conversation with her friend Doctor Mandelet adds to the forebodings, as Edna remarks 'perhaps it is better to wake up after all—even to suffer, rather than to remain a dupe to illusions all one's life' (p. 171).

Edna's illusions are shown by Kate Chopin to be more complicated, however, than Edna realises consciously; Edna, and the reader, are led for a time to believe the illusions to be marriage, children, and conventional prosperity as sources of fulfilment. Yet Chopin insinuated into the narrative, with admirably subtle artistry, other more fundamental illusions which will confront Edna eventually; namely 'she could picture at that moment no greater bliss on earth than possession of the beloved one' (p. 172); earlier Edna had an acute longing for the presence of the beloved one (see pp. 57–8 above). A leering irony peers out at the reader from the first quotation: '*possession* of the beloved one'? This clearly is the most destructive illusion of all, as Edna herself had known when her husband treated her as one of his possessions, his 'household gods' (p. 99; a play on words for 'goods'). Yet now, apparently, Edna thinks of Robert that way, but fears he is 'unattainable', another ironic word suggestive of the illusion of possession. Thus, Edna's profoundest, most destructive illusion is also revealed in the love scene with Robert, when she cries:

'It was you who awoke me last summer out of a life-long, stupid dream. Oh! you have made me so unhappy with your indifference. Oh! I have suffered, suffered! Now you are here we shall love each other, my Robert. We shall be everything to each other. Nothing else in the world is of any consequence. I must go to my friend; but you will wait for me? No matter how late; you will wait for me, Robert?'

'Don't go; don't go! Oh! Edna, stay with me,' he pleaded. 'Why should you go? Stay with me, stay with me.'

'I shall come back as soon as I can; I shall find you here.' She buried her face in his neck, and said good-by again Her seductive voice, together with his great love for her, had enthralled his senses, had deprived him of every impulse but the longing to hold her and keep her. (p. 168)

For Chopin, Mansfield, Rhys, Richardson, Woolf, and many other women writers, the dream we need to be awakened from is not just that of the (questionable) possibility of complete fulfilment in marriage, child-bearing and mothering alone. Like Rhys, Chopin's novel and stories portray individual, existential self-development as a pre-condition for fulfilment from other spheres. We do not wake from the profoundest dream by embracing 'free love', unconventional relationships, much less promiscuity. We awake only through existential acts creative of individuality. The dream which women must awake from is the myth that fulfilment lies outside themselves, the illusion described in the above three quotations, or as Katherine Mansfield said,

It is the hopelessly insipid doctrine that love is the only thing in the world, taught, hammered into women, from generation to generation, which hampers us so cruelly. We must get rid of that bogey—and then, then comes the opportunity of happiness and freedom. (*Journal*, May 1908)[7]

Throughout the novel, metaphors of sleeping, dreaming, and awakening are used by Chopin to symbolise psychological imprisonment or liberation.[8] Chopin's irony, like that of Jane Austen, however, penetrates more deeply into the text than is at first apparent. Throughout the novel, 'the awakening' is, on the level of surface events and thematics, made out to be, as in 'Bliss', an awakening to sexual love, to passion of the body united with love. (It is never a question of mere lust, as the scenes between Edna and Arobin show.) This surface interpretation of 'awakening' as an opening up to sexual desire

united with love is strengthened in the narrative on numerous occasions, as
for example, when Edna asks Robert, 'Are you asleep' and he answers 'No',
after which they embrace for the first time (p. 166). This contrasts (while
reinforcing the more apparent meaning of awakening) with Edna's sleep in
section thirteen and the narrative comment later that 'Robert ... did not know
she was awake and up' (p. 85). Yet, in spite of this clear thematic interpretation of
'awakening', Chopin used powerfully ironic narrative techniques to construct
the entirely different, indeed to some extent contradictory interpretation of
awakening described in the Mansfield quotation, namely, the shattering of
the illusion that sexual and romantic love can 'be everything', that 'nothing
else in the world is of any consequence' (p. 168).

In order to develop this sub-textual meaning of awakening, Chopin
created a foil for Edna in her characterization of Mlle Reisz, the name playing
on the word 'rights', as is ironically indicated by Chopin in her description
of the pianist: 'she was a disagreeable little woman, no longer young ... self-
assertive and [with] a disposition to trample on the rights of others' (p. 70). The
character of Mlle Reisz has rarely been accorded the attention she deserves.
This neglect of Mlle Reisz's central place in the novel has led to a certain
blindness to the crucial sub-text of *The Awakening*, which transforms the
novel into a more sophisticated literary achievement than is usually realised.
That is, once we 'awake' to Mlle Reisz's dramatic importance, we awake not
only to a consciousness of a double, ironic text–sub-text construction. We
also sophisticate our understanding of the double-awakening in the novel.
The ambiguity of Chopin's ending is also better understood. Let us examine,
then, Chopin's subtle construction of this alternative sub-text with Mlle
Reisz as the central character, a sub-text wherein the meaning of awakening
is different from the sexual liberation of the surface text with Edna as the
protagonist.

Like Edna, whose sanity is seriously questioned by her husband (p. 108)
when she begins to search for a self which is independent of her role as wife
or mother, Mlle Reisz is said by Arobin to be 'partially demented' (p. 138;
Edna finds her 'wonderfully sane' in reply to Arobin). On the other hand,
while Edna overcomes her fear of swimming after hearing Mlle Reisz play
the piano (section ix)—the pianist singling Edna out as the 'only one worth
playing for' (p. 72)—Edna then makes swimming into an obsessional passion,
incurring Mlle Reisz's disapproval. After Robert departs for Mexico (section
xvi, last scene at Grand Isle), Edna is said to spend much time in the water
'since she had finally acquired the art of swimming' (p. 95): 'She felt that she
could not give too much time to a diversion which afforded her the only real
pleasurable moments that she knew' (p. 95). Since Mlle Reisz is the first of
the characters to know Edna's love for Robert (indeed, she also is the only

one to learn of Robert's love for Edna), Edna wants Mlle Reisz to come and swim with her, now that they share this knowledge and Robert is gone. Mlle Reisz rudely rejects the invitation, however, whereupon Edna remembers the pianist's 'aversion for water' and 'avoidance' of the sea (p. 97). Insinuations of danger from the sea were slipped unobtrusively into the text by Chopin, as she had Mlle Reisz watch over Edna's swim; ironically Edna wishes she would not wait, but Mlle does wait throughout the interminable bathe in a dogged, protective way, as if she senses Edna is in some danger from the water. Later, these sinister forebodings are borne out by events, as the water imagery takes on unexpected significance.

Mlle Reisz is also the object of many ambivalences on Edna's part. Edna is drawn to the pianist, yet finds her unbearably disagreeable at times (pp. 98, 114, 133), especially when she seeks to reveal to Edna aspects of Robert's character that are not flattering (pp. 98, 136).[9] Upon closer scrutiny of the structure of Chopin's plot, it becomes evident that she has woven two separate, but artistically complementary stories into her text to correspond precisely to the two contrasting meanings of 'the awakening'. The surface text involves, first, Edna's and Robert's discoveries of their love for each other, then Edna's awakening to sexual and emotional freedom from marriage and from enslavement to husband, children, and conventions, and, finally, Robert's cowardly desertion. The sub-text, which corresponds to the ironic, 'hidden' interpretation of an awakening out of that partial awakening (really another kind of sleep, or, rather, a delightful dream in contrast to the sleep of mediocrity and convention), involves Edna's relationship with the only other major character in the text besides Edna and Robert, namely Mlle Reisz herself. Indeed, the novel in its depth structure, resembles in certain respects, Bowles' *Two Serious Ladies*, with its division into two distinct but not entirely separate plots. Robert and Edna form the main focus of part I (sections i–xvi), while Edna and Mlle Reisz form the main focus of Part II (sections xvii–xxxviii). Part I attends to Edna's awakening from the sleep of repression into sexual fulfilment; part II attends to her failure to 'get rid of that bogey' that 'love is the only thing in the world', to use Mansfield's phrase. It is Mlle Reisz, not Robert, who is presented to Edna as the key to emotional liberation through independence. Part III illustrates the drastic consequences of that failure, but is also a celebration of Edna's success in escaping, at least, the prostitution of mediocrity.

This hidden sub-plot is an ironic commentary on the surface thematics,[10] with Mlle Reisz acting as a detached, critical, authorial observer over the entire sequence of events. Like Lily Briscoe in Woolf's *To the Lighthouse*, Mlle Reisz, an artist of great accomplishment, represents a kind of consciousness which is that other 'awakening'—the genuine independence and autonomy which Miriam Henderson in *Pilgrimage*, or Thea Kronborg in *The Song of the Lark*, or Mary Olivier painstakingly achieve. This autonomy is equated with the status of 'artist' by Kate Chopin, not because only artists can achieve such genuine self-development. For Chopin, the idea of 'artist' applies to the person who has created herself into an original individuality. Genuine autonomy and personal independence is a creative endeavour, and such a person is both a work of art and an artist who achieves that self-creation. By profession one may be a prostitute, as Jean Rhys showed, but self-creation by anyone is the fullest meaning of the word 'artist', and Chopin, like Rhys, thereby fuses art and life in an imaginative stroke. Mlle Reisz is, then, a critical, detached, indeed disturbing and disruptive point of view built into the narrative. It is her point of view which adds the sustained level of powerful dramatic irony to the text, while Kate Chopin wove an intricate pattern of carefully crafted tensions and oppositions throughout the novel with marvellously delicate imagery, to enrich and embellish her multiple, complex design. These oppositions work at the structural level (sub-text versus text, Part II versus Part I), at the thematic level (two types of awakening and the failure to awaken), at the level of character (oppositions between Robert and Edna, Robert and Arobin, Robert and Victor, Arobin and Victor, Edna and Mlle Reisz, Edna and Adèle), and at the stylistic level (realism and the ironisation and transformation of realism into a distinct original style). Oppositions at the detailed level of imagery and tone further enrich the texture of the narrative and lead to sophisticated transvaluations.

More precisely, on Grand Isle (Part I) Edna awakens to her infatuation with Robert, as it is called, and begins a quest for fulfilment of it (p. 94). Chopin's narrative emphasises frequently that Edna's feeling for Robert was a childish infatuation, fast becoming an obsession much like several others Edna had felt as a child and young girl. Yet, the reader, trapped in her own dreams of true love, ignores these danger signals. In Part II, in New Orleans, Edna is, surprisingly, described as having 'started on her quest for the pianist' (p. 109). Throughout Part II, a powerful conflict develops between the two plot levels, with Edna enthralled by her dream of union with Robert as the illusory means of self-fulfilment, at the same time that her deeper self is drawn inexorably on a quest for the, at times, disagreeable and even offensive Mlle Reisz, who can set Edna's spirit free:

> There was nothing which so quieted the turmoil of Edna's senses as a visit to Mademoiselle Reisz. It was then, in the presence of that personality which was offensive to her, that the woman, by her divine art, seemed to reach Edna's spirit and set it free. (p. 133)

Mlle Reisz is ambiguously portrayed by Kate Chopin as a protectress, yet with undertones of a dangerous sorceress. The latter aspect is, ironically, Edna's projection of her own fears of what it would mean to wake up—not only from her conventional sleep as wife and mother, but also from the dream of true love as the source of all meaning in life. This fantasy she clearly shares with Robert; indeed, he is shown to encourage and embellish it. Chopin's text ruthlessly but subtly undermines Edna's dream, and even exposes it on a number of occasions as nothing more than the absurd fantasies of a child, indeed, of two children, Edna and Robert, as in the following two passages:

> When Edna awoke it was with the conviction that she had slept long and soundly ....
>
> 'How many years have I slept?' she inquired. 'The whole island seems changed. A new race of beings must have sprung up, leaving only you and me as past relics. How many ages ago did Madame Antoine and Tonie die? and when did our people from Grand Isle disappear from the earth?'
>
> He familiarly adjusted a ruffle upon her shoulder.
>
> 'You have slept precisely one hundred years. I was left here to guard your slumbers; and for one hundred years I have been out under the shed reading a book. The only evil I couldn't prevent was to keep a broiled fowl from drying up.' (pp. 84–5)

> Yes. On the twenty-eighth of August, at the hour of midnight, and if the moon is shining—the moon must be shining—a spirit that has haunted these shores for ages rises up from the Gulf. With its own penetrating vision the spirit seeks some one mortal worthy to hold him company, worthy to being exalted for a few hours into realms of the semi-celestials. His search has always hitherto been fruitless, and he has sunk back, disheartened, into the sea. But to-night he found Mrs Pontellier. Perhaps he will never wholly release her from the spell. Perhaps she will never again suffer a poor, unworthy earthling to walk in the shadow of her divine presence. (p. 75)

These two episodes could be read as nothing more than the playful banter of two lovers, but they are too carefully constructed as fantasy and fairy-tale not to suspect that Chopin meant them ironically, that is, as parodies of the folly of such a dream of love as Edna and Robert have. Repeatedly throughout the novel, Chopin parodied Edna's love as a pure, childish fantasy, the description of which Edna herself gave most succinctly and most damningly at the first dinner party, for her father: 'She had [a story] of her own to tell, of a woman who paddled away with her lover one night in a pirogue and never came back ...' (p. 123). The narrator ironically comments 'It was pure invention ... perhaps it was a dream she had had' (p. 124). In a further gesture of supreme irony at the expense of the gullible reader, Chopin wrote:

> But every glowing word seemed real to those who listened. They could feel the hot breath of the Southern night; they could hear the long sweep of the pirogue through the glistening moonlit water, the beating of birds' wings, rising startled from among the reeds in the salt-water pools; they could see the faces of the lovers, pale, close together, rapt in oblivious forgetfulness, drifting into the unknown. (p. 124)

Like the listeners to Edna's story, that story of pure invention, a mere dream, Chopin's readers fall under the spell of the story Chopin wrote: 'every glowing word seemed real to those who listened' (p. 124). Only Doctor Mandelet seems to penetrate some distance into the mystery. Indeed, he, like Mlle. Reisz, is another example of a relatively detached point of view—but he never sees Edna as clearly as Mlle Reisz does. For, although he is a type of artist, he is not portrayed as the supremely accomplished artist of life as well as music that the pianist became. Nevertheless, there are repeated suggestions throughout Part II of the novel that Mandelet is a man utterly unlike Robert or Edna's husband; he is a genuine friend, and might have been able to provide Edna with some support; yet somehow she does not let him. Throughout, Chopin relentlessly exposed Edna's dream of true love as a childish fantasy: she had Edna repeat to Adèle Ratignolle her childhood memory (dream/fantasy?) of walking into infinity in a sea of grass (an ominous prognostication of things to come), and admits she was 'a little unthinking child ... following a misleading impulse without question ... I feel this summer as if I were walking through the green meadow again; idly, aimlessly, unthinking and unguided' (p. 61). Chopin, by a stroke of pure irony, has Edna unconsciously expose her own present, adult state as childish folly, albeit of a more deadly kind, and this irony is reinforced over the next few paragraphs as Edna remembers her previous, less dangerous infatuations (p. 62). All these men 'went the way of dreams', as will Robert, in the end, but with far more disastrous results. For her infatuation with Robert, being more emotionally, sexually intense, indeed, being the infatuation of 'true love' (that most dangerous illusion of all), constitutes the most dangerous hindrance to self-development, as the self is submerged in the loved one. Hence Mlle Reisz's hatred of swimming, as a symbol of submergence in emotional dependency.

The sea and the ocean become a metaphoric image of such all-consuming, drowning love, and, as such, they are a source of terrible danger and destruction; hence, Chopin made Mlle Reisz, who is free from such delusions, avoid the water. Over and over again, Chopin portrayed Edna's fantasies of love by means of images of the boundless ocean: 'Edna felt as if she were being borne away from some anchorage which had held her fast, whose chains had been loosening—had snapped the night before when the mystic spirit was abroad, leaving her free to drift whithersoever she chose to set her sails. Robert spoke to her incessantly; he no longer noticed Mariequita' (p. 81 and see p. 73, where Edna is likened to a child who 'grew daring and reckless, overestimating her strength. She wanted to swim far out, where no woman had swum before').

It quickly becomes evident that Chopin used the boundless ocean as an image of liberation only at the surface level of her story.[11] In the sub-text (the text describing the means of liberating oneself from not only the sleep of convention—as Edna does do—but also from the dream of true love as fulfilment—which she fails to do), the sea is, ironically, portrayed not as a state of mind of liberation, but as a state of totally blind, will-less immersion in fantasy, dream, and unreality. The sea is charged with sinister implications in Chopin's ironic, devastating sub-text: it is, indeed, contrasted with art, its opposite. Art is the activity of giving shape and order to oceanic formlessness. Art is a creative process, pre-eminently of the creation (through great labour) of a self which is genuinely original and individual. Art is structured through intelligent work, organised and articulated as a result of powerful imaginative gestures working on initially unformed material. The ocean, on the other hand, represents a kind of primordial unity, a shapelessness, an unarticulated power, unformed force, which, as Willa Cather repeatedly wrote, may well be the source of all art and creativity, but remains beyond the control of the artist's imagination and will, without powerful, imaginative labour and systematic intervention by the human in such an otherwise oceanic, unbounded nature. Ocean and art are images opposed in Chopin's text, though they are not portrayed as contraries which exclude each other. The ocean is the symbol of creative nature in its Nietzchean original oneness and unity, a unity for which there is a powerful longing, and indeed, a death instinct, that desire for reunion into oceanic oneness, the desire to escape from the labour and suffering of individuality and life. Chopin's irony becomes a powerful tool, first, for imaging the sea as a world of partial liberation, then undercutting that image as Chopin deftly, unobtrusively portrayed the sea in her sub-text as the world of death. Twice, out swimming, Edna 'sees' death: 'A quick vision of death smote her soul, and for a second of time appalled and enfeebled her senses. But by an effort she rallied her staggering faculties and managed to regain the land' (p. 74). Frightened, Edna speaks of 'perishing out there', while the narrator describes her swim as 'an encounter with death' (p. 74).[12]

Chopin used the ocean as an image of danger because of its power totally to engulf one, as does love. She also frequently described the sea as seductive; as a force that will lovingly overpower Edna and totally drown her, as does 'love':

> The voice of the sea is seductive; never ceasing, whispering, clamoring, murmuring, inviting the soul to wander for a spell in abysses of solitude; to lose itself in mazes of inward contemplation. The voice of the sea speaks to the soul. The touch of the sea is sensuous, enfolding the body in its soft, close embrace. (p. 57, and see pp. 56, 81).

Not surprisingly, it was Robert who tried to teach Edna to swim, to love the sea, to venture out into such a sea of unbridled, uncontrolled, unbounded love, that 'mystic shimmer' of the Gulf, its waves like sinister white serpents (see also p. 23). On the final page of the novel, Chopin daringly plagiarised herself by describing the ocean in exactly the same sexual, sensuous words as she had used on p. 57, some hundred pages earlier. She also referred to Edna's childish fantasy of the fields like waves rolling into infinity, with 'no beginning and no end'. The deliberate narrative repetitions, which ironise spontaneity, also reinforce the voice of irony and its sub-text, in part by intruding upon the reader a realisation that the lines are not spontaneous outpouring of passion, but a deliberate authorial self-reference. As Edna swims out, on the final page of the novel, the reference to Mlle Reisz is illuminating—for it also is another deliberate narrative repetition of words of warning Mlle Reisz spoke to Edna:

> 'How Mlle Reisz would have laughed, perhaps sneered, if she knew! And you call yourself an artist! What pretensions, Madame! The artist must possess the courageous soul that dares and defies.' (p. 176)

In Edna's quest in the second half of the novel for Mlle Reisz, she is, at the narrative level of conflicting (or completing) sub-text, searching for herself—the 'artist' within herself—in the fullest sense of the word 'artist' as fully developed, original individuality, as a human work of art. Her efforts to sketch and eventually to paint lead her part of the way, to financial independence and setting up her own household. Her lack of further development as a better painter is less a cause than a metaphor, however, for her arrested emotional development as an individual: she wakes from the sleep of conventional notions of fulfilment, but is engulfed in the oceanic dream of love. Yet Mlle Reisz provides her with a model, one which, like herself, others see as mad, as 'imbalanced'. Edna has, both literally and figuratively, lost Mlle's address, lost touch with her, that is, and can only reach her through Mme Lebrun (Robert's and Victor's mother). When she goes to the Lebruns, Victor, Robert's brother, regales her with a story of lust and sexual adventure: Victor is not another Robert, for his role in the novel is primarily at the level of the sub-text. In the surface story, he makes little sense. But in the hidden, ironic sub-plot, where Mlle Reisz is Edna's potential self, Victor is Robert's 'reality'—a light, irresponsible sexual animal, hardly different from Arobin. It is Victor, not Robert, who meets Edna in the final scene, before her swim into oblivion; Victor, not Robert, who comes to her 'Last Supper'; Victor, not Robert, whom she meets on her quest for Mlle Reisz. Victor's presence in the surface plot is, dramatically, almost meaningless; any unrelated person could have served his function. Yet, when the sub-plot is attended to, he becomes a transparent 'figure' for Robert's hidden, actual character, a character only superficially different from Arobin (note the similarity of names: A-robin, not-Robert, yet a variation on a Robert). Victor is exactly like Arobin in his amorous, irresponsible seduction of women, yet he is also Robert's 'brother', indeed, he may be read as Robert's self, in important respects. Robert has achieved a veneer of culture and a veneer of maturity which Mlle Reisz appreciates, since so few achieve even this. Yet Mlle Reisz does not delude herself about his moral being. The novel suggests the possibility that he is a polished, cultivated cad, but nevertheless still a cad, still Victor's spiritual and moral brother. Indeed, his difference from Arobin and Victor may be only a variation on a theme of a fantasy—a false veneer of superficial cultivation passed over as moral development, whereas Victor and Arobin at least have no pretensions. The ambiguity of Robert's character is indissoluble. Nor is it important. Cad or 'sincere lover', the dream of fulfilment through love rather than through self-development is still a delusion. Indeed, Chopin's text suggests that if the love is sincere, it can lead to still more damaging results, especially if the lover lacks courage. Chopin's novel presses, with its ironies, sub-text, and complex imagery, for a disruption of fantasies of romantic love, however morally developed the lover. While it offers Mlle Reisz, however, as an alternative, a more sure basis for life, this does not suggest that Chopin argued for a single, substantial self-identity independent of the world and an entity unto itself. The self is understood as a work of art, as a text, with all the ambiguities, uncertainties, and relativities of interpretation involved in texts.

Hence the impossibility of judging or evaluating Robert becomes a code for
the irreducible 'meaning' of the text.

   Mlle Reisz accuses Edna gently of having pretensions (p. 115), but she
earlier referred to her as 'la belle dame' (sans merci?), suggesting imaginative
possibilities. She, like the marvellous Doctor Mandelet, sees Edna as
awakening so far only from her sleep, but not from her dream. She sees her
as an animal almost (p. 114), while the doctor describes her precisely as a
'beautiful, sleek animal waking up in the sun' (p. 123). Yet Mlle Reisz seems,
while fearing for Edna, also to encourage her out of the dream, since she sees
that Edna has at least awakened from the sleep of repressed sexuality. Already
in section ix, Mlle Reisz had managed with her music to propel Edna out of the
common, mediocre response to art into a realm where she was speechless with
appreciation, while the other listeners mindlessly babbled praise. Later, she
speaks of the need to be able to fly (not to swim!), and prophetically cautions
Edna on birds who seek to 'soar above tradition and prejudice' but, without
strong enough wings, fall exhausted back to earth (p. 138, section xxvii).
The metonymic 'wings' are used as a traditional metaphor for imagination,
rather than the bird itself. Chopin thereby emphasised that strength and
development of one's powers, not just potentiality, are the crucial elements
in becoming an artist. The repetition of the image of broken-winged bird
(p. 175, near the end) is less crass than it seems. Although, it functions only
as a poverty-stricken allegory in the surface plot as an emblem of why Edna
failed, at the level of sub-plot, the image works as a viable convention rather
than a cliché. The failure was one of strength, a failure on Edna's part to
develop her capacities, before launching out into premature 'flights of fancy'
which, if acted upon, lead to death.

   Chopin's text is too rich to do more than mention a few more examples
of her fine intricacy of imagery and narrative complexity, where each episode,
each image is 'worked' for full effect. For example, throughout Part I, a pair of
lovers appear in and out of the narrative; on most occasions they are followed
by 'a lady in black' (pp. 44, 59, 66, 79, 80, where she is 'gaining steadily on
them', pp. 81, 83; and pp. 63, 64, 73, where the lovers are mentioned without
the lady in black, either several children or Robert literally come between
them). This sinister image is an ironic device used by Chopin to image Edna's
oppression, dread, and the 'fatality of love' and is similar to Chopin's repeated
use of the garment as a metaphor for the conventional self. The garment,
faded and unpleasant, Edna casts away to become naked, 'like some new-born
creature' (p. 175). Chopin's sub-text has implied throughout that awakening to
full self-realisation, to the self as an artist–individual, can come only through
breaking the spell of the dream of love and sexual fulfilment as the ultimate
source and ground of fulfilment. For Mlle Reisz, Edna is still submerged in

this powerful fantasy, has not yet worked through it, is not yet strong enough
to escape; yet, the pianist seems to feel that Edna has the chance, unlike
most other people she knows. Hence the careful logic of numerous narrative
details; for example Edna must go via the Lebrun's (via Robert and Victor) to
fulfil her further 'quest' for Mlle Reisz. Chopin missed no chance to imbue
her tapestry with rich emblems, as she sought on behalf of the reader to
reveal the illusion for what it is. She also suggested the means by which one
can 'avoid the terrible, seductive longing' for self-immolation into primeval
nature: one must labour to strengthen the imagination, gradually to articulate
into a work of art the self. Such articulation alone can give the ground and
context for meaning in life. Unarticulated, abyss-like experience condemns
the soul to solitary wanderings, to solipsism, to suicide, and to selfishness (pp.
57, 176). Edna's awakening is only a beginning, then, a beginning which is
essential, absolutely necessary, in fact, to fuller realisation. But in itself it is
quite insufficient as a basis for self-development:

> But the beginning of things, of a world especially, is necessarily
> vague, tangled, chaotic, and exceedingly disturbing. How few of
> us ever emerge from such beginning! How many souls perish in
> its tumult! (p. 57)

Edna's throwing off of clothes, a metaphor for rejecting the conventional
roles of mother and wife which enslave women, is not enough if one goes on
dreaming the child-fantasy of submerging and drowning one's unindividuated
self in an ocean of love (or sex, or anything else). Chopin's complex narratives,
her ironic plottings, and her rich tapestries of imagery urge the reader to
grasp the necessity for articulated, artistic experience, experience that is
shaped and formed, not blindly felt like an animal. Chopin made Edna remark
that expression is what men call unwomanly: 'but I have got in the habit of
expressing myself' (p. 165). Yet, while having 'got in the habit', she had not
yet learned to express herself articulately or artistically. Habit is animal-like;
art requires something more than habit, though it is a start.

Chopin introduced, moreover, a powerful feminist theme which
overshadows the entire novel.[13] It involves the critical, ironical, detached
exposure of the destructiveness of seeing women as oceanic, as primeval
oneness, as beings with those attributes given in the novel to the sea. Women,
according to men (and to too many other women, like Irigaray)[14] are allegedly
endowed with the 'essential feminine'. They are Nature itself in its primeval,
mind-less, unarticulated, procreation-seductive, engulfing, undifferentiated
state. Pre-eminently, women are often viewed as essential Mother Natures,
whose role and essential being is to procreate. That is, they create, but only

in a bodily, sexual, animal way. Women are not supposed to move on from this primordial, animal-like, and primatively powerful stage. They are not to become language users—human beings, that is, much less artists. Many women are attracted to such a Mother-Nature role, partly out of instinct (Freud's combined life-death instinct, Nietzsche's urge for the primordial Dionysiac One), and partly out of a socialised belief that this can lead to fulfilment. It can, but only on an animal level, as Chopin demonstrated in *The Awakening*. To become fulfilled as an individuality (as opposed to a force of nature), as a human being, Chopin, Rhys, Richardson, and many other women writers suggested that women need to articulate experience, use art to become a work of art, not a mere blind product of natural forces. For, miraculous as nature is, as childbirth is, as all life is, art and humanity are something building on that specifically human capacity for self-conscious self-development.

The notion that *The Awakening* represents a celebration of the myth of Aphrodite rising from the waves is suggested by Sandra Gilbert, in her fine introduction to the Penguin edition (1983).[15] Clearly, the argument presented here would suggest, however, that such an interpretation is, in part, at least, an example of falling prey to the illusion or fantasy that the dream seductively offers, whether it be in the form of a dream of all-encompassing love or the analogous dream (fantasy) of returning to Oceanic Oneness. Gilbert's interpretation seems, unintentionally perhaps, to accede to Irigaray's naïve and even destructive celebration of an eternal, essential feminine essence. Aphrodite, Venus, is the Goddess of Love—the Goddess of Oceanic inarticulacy. It was, ironically, Victor, not Chopin, who envisaged and fantasised Edna as Aphrodite, in order to make Mariequita jealous:

> They had been talking for an hour or more. She was never tired of hearing Victor describe the dinner at Mrs. Pontellier's. He exaggerated every detail, making it appear a veritable Lucullean feast. The flowers were in tubs, he said. The champagne was quaffed from huge golden goblets. Venus rising from the foam could have presented no more entrancing a spectacle than Mrs. Pontellier, blazing with beauty and diamonds at the head of the board, while the other women were all of them youthful houris, possessed of incomparable charms. (p. 173)

This, Victor's, view of women, Chopin painted as *the* male fantasy—what men want us to be, what men want us to see ourselves as. While Gilbert astutely realised the ironic undertones of the text which expose Edna's fantasies, her interpretation cuts somewhat short Chopin's critical, ironic exposure of Edna's 'retarded' emotional development. Gilbert is surely warranted in criticising Susanne Wolkenfeld's somewhat over-simplified account of Edna's situation as 'a defeat and a regression, rooted in a self-annihilating instinct, in a romantic incapacity to accommodate ... to the limitation of reality' (p. 31).[16] This, as Gilbert shows, is to miss Chopin's powerful analysis of the processes and stages of self-development. Far from regressing, far from being simply defeated, Edna has taken an enormously courageous step forward, more, as Mlle Reisz argues, than nearly anyone else. She needed to work through that achievement, however, to progress to the next stage, of becoming an individuality, a human work of art. This is the dramatic function of the carefully designed ambiguous ending, an ending which has created much critical controversy. Wolkenfeld's interpretation of Edna's end as essentially regression and defeat is consistent with the text only if one ignores the tremendously rich and subtle artistry of Chopin's complex plottings, ironies, imageries, and characters: all the details of the novel are working in the service of Chopin's analysis of the means and multiple stages toward self-realisation. Rather than simply holding up some distant, undefined ideal of self-knowledge, Chopin charted the way stage by stage, in so far as it can be charted. And of course she realised these stages in her own artistry, the complexity of which has been consistently, indeed systematically overlooked.[17] Readers and critics seem, in the main, unwilling to look at the details of the text—these 'minute particulars' which Blake claimed were all-important. To look at detail requires time and labour, but, as Chopin demonstrated, imaginative labour is precisely what develops one's strength, one's imagination. The neglect of such labour inevitably leads to the reader's becoming a victim of the text's irony. Yet irony and its sister, metaphor are the means by which the artist seeks to fashion her vision, and an awareness of these is crucial to seeing that vision.

Wolkenfeld's evaluation fails, in part, as Gilbert argued, in the face of textual detail, though, admittedly, it does express the spirit of destruction, one element of the text. Hence, it is not by any means entirely at odds with the text. It is, however, an account of one aspect of the text only, though in that capacity it makes a definite contribution. Gilbert's interpretation, though in some ways more subtle than Wolkenfeld's, is nevertheless (and paradoxically) still further at odds with the complexity of the text, for it seems inadvertently to be in the spell of the dream of love, the fantasy of romance and sexual freedom, in spite of perceiving the romantic illusion Edna labours under. That is, Gilbert's interpretation is inconsistent. The ironic sub-text acts contrary to Gilbert's conclusion of the novel as partly, much less pre-eminently, a celebration of Aphrodite, of Love, of Venus. The ambiguity of the ending is devised by Chopin not for this purpose, not to sustain this male fantasy of

Victor's, of seeing Women as goddesses of love and romance. Chopin made her ending impossible to resolve into univocals, either negative or positive, because Edna's situation contains both creative and destructive forces. Edna has made a beginning—a heroic, admirable, rarely achieved beginning, and this partial progress and growth is sustained by the sub-text. The sub-text is, however, a further analysis of this progress as only partial; Edna did not get all the way—she did not succeed in flying, in articulating herself beyond the dream of love, beyond habit, and into the fuller self-development of human artistry: 'How few of us ever emerge from such a beginning! How many souls perish in its tumult!' (p. 57).

Edna, then, is both partially and imperfectly successful, and yet, crucially, she fails; hence the ambiguity of the ending of the book—its triumphant tone and its implication of failure, destruction, and death. Chopin had made indirectly two witty and ironic comments during the course of the novel about endings. Edna tells a story to her children:

> Then she sat and told the children a story. Instead of soothing it excited them, and added to their wakefulness. She left them in heated argument, speculating about the conclusion of the tale which their mother promised to finish the following night. (p. 92)

Much later, Robert, Chopin wrote, tells Edna 'the end, to save her the trouble of *wading* through it, he said' (p. 166). This punning remark is within ten pages of Edna's last swim. Such overt irony is, one could argue, an effort on the author's part to 'awaken' the reader to the persuasiveness of the irony and of the wit of the book, by shocking her out of the fond, sentimental affection for the tale which blunts sensitivity to humour, irony, and to a critical awareness that the novel's analysis goes further than the reader could initially have perceived. Many of the other devices mentioned function with the same dramatic purpose of effecting a more complex, detached level of response in the reader. Such ironic devices often look like crass, rather stilted allegories, such as the broken-winged bird, or the lovers followed by the lady in black, and what can we make of the author's cynical repetition of an apparently spontaneous, 'moving and sensitive' passage on the final page—lifted word for word from page 57! 'The touch of the sea is sensuous, enfolding the body in its soft, close embrace', etc. (p. 176).

Gilbert's fascinating interpretation of *The Awakening*'s ambiguous ending as expressive of the Aphrodite myth of rebirth is, then, based on a failure to perceive Chopin's portrayal of the Edna–Venus relation as ironic. That is, Edna is seen as an embodiment of Aphrodite not by

Chopin, but by the superficial Victor. It is through Victor's eyes that we are presented with this equation; it is Victor's fantasy that Edna is a regal Venus goddess. Chopin explodes this fantasy as one of the most tragically destructive views of women, by narrating it to her readers as Victor's point of view on women.[18] This ironic commentary is a crucial part of Chopin's sub-text, as crucial as Willa Cather's portrayal of Ántonia as Jim Burden's fantasy of the ideal woman, or Virginia Woolf's ambiguous portrayal of Mrs Ramsey as the Woman–Mother. If we fail to see the importance of these authorial ironisings of male points of view, we end up seeing the women as Jim Burden, Victor Lebrun, and Mr Ramsey do, and we imagine that this view is the author's, when it is the view the author is brutally ironising.

In the first paragraph of the novel another of those apparently crass, over-obvious, belaboured images occurs, which bears inspection, placed as it is at the outset of the story:

> A green and yellow parrot, which hung in a cage outside the door, kept repeating over and over:
> 'Allez vous-en! Allez vous-en! Sapristi! That's all right!'. He could speak a little Spanish, and also a language which nobody understood, unless it was the mocking-bird... (p. 43)

The parrot in the cage alone is a lamentable, over-used literary convention—all too worn-out and familiar to be very effective. What a poor, convention-ridden way to start a book that shocked the English-speaking world! Yet, closer scrutiny reveals an increment in complexity, a description of a 'mocking-bird that hung on the other side of the door, whistling his fluting notes out upon the breeze with maddening persistence' (p. 43). A mocking-bird, perhaps an image for the ironist, the two birds being images for the two-sided construction of the plot, for the double voice of Chopin the surface narrator and Chopin the voice behind appearance, ironising and criticising the surface. Such a beginning to a novel alerts the reader to irony, to wit, to double-edged meanings and two-sided texts or multi-layered texts. 'The language nobody understood' is suggestive of the language of Chopin the ironist, sensitive and open to humour even in tragic themes. The phrase also suggests Chopin's understanding of the need to keep an ironic perspective on life and on literature, pre-eminently through such humour as these bird images convey. Chopin did not speak the language of realism, nor that of romantic novels. Or rather, she spoke them both, and something more, an ironic, mocking criticism of both, which 'nobody understood, unless it be the mocking-bird'.[19]

Notes

1. For further biographical material see Emily Toth, *Kate Chopin* (London: 1990) and Per Seyersted, *Kate Chopin: A Critical Biography* (Baton Rouge: 1969). For background, see L. Ziff, *The American 1890s: Life and Times of a Lost Generation* (London: 1967). And see Priscilla Allen, 'Old Critics and New: The Treatment of Chopin's *The Awakening*', in *The Authority of Experience*, ed. A. Diamond and L. R. Edwards (1977) pp. 224–38, for useful critical background. More generally, note Helen Taylor's excellent *Gender, Race, and Region* (London: 1989). And see Anne G. Jones, *Tomorrow is Another Day: The Woman Writer in the South, 1859–1936* (Baton Rouge: 1981). Willa Cather's review of *The Awakening* is reprinted in *The World and the Parish: Willa Cather's Articles and Reviews, 1893–1902*, ed. W. M. Cullin (Lincoln, Nebraska: 1970) vol. II, pp. 693–4.

2. Two decades later, Dorothy Richardson was undergoing a similar dissatisfaction with realism; see Kate Fulbrook, *Free Women* (London: 1990) pp. 114–15 and Elaine Showalter, *A Literature of their Own* (Princeton: 1977) pp. 253–5, on Richardson's repudiation of realism.

3. Chopin anticipated modernist challenges to realist order, with their parodying of structure, specifically by reversals of beginnings and endings or by ironizing definitive conclusions. For such writers as Djuna Barnes, Virginia Woolf, May Sinclair, and others, experiments in structure, unity, and order were designed to reveal the arbitrariness of order and especially of determinate endings, whether in art and fiction or in life. In *Pilgrimage*, Miriam remarks, 'It did not matter. Nothing was at an end. Nothing would ever come to an end again' (vol. III, p. 129); later, she complains of a friend, 'He had never for a moment shared her sense of endlessness' (vol. III, p. 304).

4. Chopin also anticipated modernists' fascination with death portrayed as ambiguous or even as a positive experience. For Djuna Barnes, death is represented as a fortuitous release from a universe of meaninglessness. In Rhys' *Voyage in the Dark*, a comparable ambiguity in Anna's death by abortion is notable (in part due to Rhys' publisher, who apparently protested at the pessimism of a more definitive account).

5. The decadence of realism itself is a theme of some modernist writing as it ironises and undermines the presuppositions and unexamined assumptions of realism. Djuna Barnes' *Nightwood* is as different from Chopin's text as any book could be, yet it shares with it this curious reversal, of seeing realism itself as the decadent ideology, along with many of the assumptions that go unchallenged in it, such as love as possession. Like Chopin's *Awakening*, Barnes' *Nightwood* has as its central theme the futility of possessive love, whether heterosexual or lesbian, while its shadowy character, Robin, eludes any clear gender classifications.

6. The edition used here is Penguin, 1983. See also Per Seyersted's *Complete Works of Kate Chopin*, 2 vols (Baton Rouge: 1969).

7. Katherine Mansfield, *Letters and Journals*, ed. C. K. Stead (Harmondsworth: 1977) pp. 35–6.

8. See Otis B. Wheeler, 'The Five Awakenings of Edna Pontellier', *The Southern Review*, 11 (1975) pp. 118–28, for a discussion of Chopin's recurring metaphors of sleep, dream, and awakening.

9. Unlike Rhys, Richardson, Cather, Wharton, and others, Chopin played down the cruelty of women towards each other.

10. See R. Sullivan and S. Smith, 'Narrative Stance in Kate Chopin's *The Awakening*', *Studies in American Fiction*, 1 (1973) pp. 62–75, for a quite different account.

11. Patricia S. Yaegar, 'A Language Which Nobody Understood: Emancipatory Strategies in *The Awakening*', *The Novel*, 20 (1987), explores Chopin's use of liberation themes.

12. For further discussion of death, see C. G. Wolff, 'Thanatos and Eros: Kate Chopin's *The Awakening*', *American Quarterly*, 25 (1973) pp. 449–72.

13. See Emily Toth, 'Kate Chopin's *The Awakening* as Feminist Criticism', *Louisiana Studies*, 15 (1976) pp. 241–51, and Jane P. Thompkins, '*The Awakening*: An Evaluation', *Feminist Studies*, 3 (1976) pp. 22–9, for analysis of specifically feminist themes of the novel.

14. And Cixous, for that matter, both of whose texts tend to reconstruct a metaphysical account of essential femininity, in spite of declarations to seek to avoid idealist, essentialist definitions.

15. Sandra M. Gilbert, 'The Second Coming of Aphrodite', *Kenyon Review*, 5 (1983) pp. 42–56, also in the Penguin, *The Awakening* (Harmondsworth: 1983), pp. 7–33.

16. Susanne Wolkenfeld, 'Edna's Suicide: The Problem of the One and the Many', in *The Awakening*, ed. M. Culley (New York, 1976) pp. 218–24.

17. But see Wendy Martin's stimulating collection of essays in *New Essays on The Awakening* (1988) and *Louisiana Studies*, xiv: 1 (Spring 1975), 'Special Kate Chopin Issue'.

18. As Showalter argued (*op. cit.*, p. 255) regarding Dorothy Richardson, women must be shown how to stop betraying their own experience, to stop seeing it—and themselves—as men see it.

19. For further secondary literature on Chopin see Gilbert's extremely full bibliography in the Penguin edition of *The Awakening* and see also M. Springer, *Edith Wharton and Kate Chopin: A Reference Guide* (Boston: 1976). Edmund Wilson, in *Patriotic Gore* (London: 1963) was one early 'revivor' of Chopin's fiction.

EMILY TOTH

A Writer, Her Reviewers, and Her Markets

"To be great is to be misunderstood," Ralph Waldo Emerson wrote, in his famous essay on self-reliance.

Kate Chopin, who had learned all about self-reliance from three generations of independent women, was a reader of Emerson, and so is *The Awakening*'s Edna. (Happily alone, Edna "read Emerson until she grew sleepy"—XXIV). And while Chopin might have hesitated to call herself "great" in public, she soon discovered a fact that is a great disappointment to all authors:

Their reviewers do not understand them.

Self-reliant and clever herself, Kate Chopin learned the basics of professional writing on her own initiative. She studied the experts, and she created in her salon a network of friends, supporters, and advisers. But the next career steps were beyond her control. Whatever happened would depend on the reading, writing, and thinking abilities of other people.

Reviewers, she found, were often enthusiastic, but nowhere near so knowledgeable as she expected. Readers were often worse. Chopin had to force herself to be gracious to those who misunderstood or patronized her writing, and when she travelled to her first writers' conference, she wound up as the center of a regional feud.

From *Unveiling Kate Chopin* by Emily Toth, pp. 148–173. © 1999 by Emily Toth.

Chopin sometimes benefited, though, from other people's ignorance. When reviewers of *Bayou Folk* did not recognize the radical things that she was writing about women, they could not stop her from pushing against the boundaries of what was proper for American authors to say in print.

"In looking over more than a hundred press notices of 'Bayou Folk' which have already been sent to me," Chopin wrote in her diary for June 7, 1894, "I am surprised at the very small number which show anything like a worthy critical faculty." In fact, the worthwhile ones "might be counted upon the fingers of one hand. I had no idea the genuine book critic was so rare a bird. And yet I receive congratulations from my publishers upon the character of the press notices."

Bayou Folk was officially published by Houghton, Mifflin on March 24, 1894. It was a simple, beautiful volume bound in dark green and gold, $1.25 a copy, with a respectable first printing of 1,250 copies, and it gained reviews in all the major magazines and newspapers. Most of them described Chopin's twenty-three stories as local color tales from Louisiana—about which the reviewers were very muddled.

The *New York Times*, for instance, gave the book one of its longest notices (five paragraphs), but only two sentences were not weirdly inaccurate pronouncements about Louisiana—such as the claim that the Mississippi River, "like the Nile—lavish and deadly," is the people's "Medusa." Most other reviewers called Chopin's book "quaint" or "charming" or "agreeable" or all three, and praised her use of dialect, and her skill in mingling pathos and romance, humor and nobility of character. Two reviewers recognized Guy de Maupassant as her major influence; two others praised her subtlety and ability to convey a lot with few words.

The powerful *Atlantic* did give well-thought-out praise: "All of the stories are very simple in structure, but the simplicity is that which belongs to clearness of perception, not to meagerness of imagination. Now and then she strikes a passsionate note, and the naturalness and ease with which she does it impress one as characteristic of power awaiting opportunity."

In St. Louis, Chopin got the laudatory reviews she expected, as a local author. But at least one reviewer appeared not to have understood her: the *Post-Dispatch* reporter called "In Sabine"—the story of a battered wife—"full of humor."

Mostly, reviewers seemed to think that Chopin's *Bayou Folk* stories were about colorfully primitive rural Southerners, plus a couple of New Orleanians ("La Belle Zoraïde" and "A Lady of Bayou St. John"). But that was not Chopin's point of view. Like most local color women writers of her day, she was really writing universal stories about women, men, marriage, children, loyalty, and much more. She was saying very frank things about the power of men to limit and punish women. But when she set her stories in a distant, unusual locale, she deflected criticism—which enabled her to sail into print and even be praised by male publishers, editors, and reviewers in the Northeast. They would never have permitted such frank criticisms of patriarchy in their own back yards.

With *Bayou Folk*, Chopin's strategy worked to the extent that her book was published: that was her first goal. How women readers received it we do not know, since most published reviews were anonymous. We also have no diaries or letters from common readers. But virtually all the stories contained some kind of social criticism that was just as applicable to St. Louis—or to Boston—as it was to Louisiana.

Chopin had followed Houghton, Mifflin's request by bringing the "Santien boys" together for the first three stories—but theirs were not the real stories she was telling. In the first, the farmer Placide Santien gives up the young woman he loves ("A No-Account Creole"); in the second, the gambler Hector almost seduces a schoolteacher ("In and Out of Old Natchitoches"). But in the last, Grégoire, nursing a broken heart after his jilting in *At Fault*, actively helps a battered wife to escape ("In Sabine").

The Santien boys are all honorable and attractive, but the women characters are the ones who grow progressively stronger and more individualized. The first story's vulnerable heroine (created in 1888) expects to marry a man she does not love, while the second (February 1893) flirts with a gambler, then returns to a very impulsive man who has a famously bad temper. But the downtrodden heroine of "In Sabine" (November 1893) rides off alone, to a new life. The Kate Chopin of late 1893 was much more independent and self-confident than she had been in 1888—and a contract with a major national publisher had much to do with it.

She arranged the rest of the stories in *Bayou Folk* for variety, and some are quick sketches: children hide and save their new shoes, or an uncooperative servant puts a household through great turmoil ("Boulôt and Boulotte" and "A Turkey Hunt"). But most of the stories that seem lighthearted have a serious edge—which reviewers, charmed by Chopin's style and colorful characters, seemed not to notice.

Many of the stories are about truly terrifying or tragic situations. In two stories, men's violence destroys women's lives; in another, a young girl is almost killed by her father's irresponsibility ("Désirée's Baby," "A Visit to Avoyelles," and "A Rude Awakening"). Former slaves also suffer: one survives only by manipulating her ex-master's family, while another is too frightened to cross the stream separating her from the rest of the world ("Old Aunt Peggy" and "Beyond the Bayou"). The title character in "Ma'ame Pélagie" has lost everything she cares about in the ruin of her home, while the one in "La Belle Zoraïde" loses her child, and then loses her mind. One of the few tender men, a father whose only wish is to spend Christmas with his son, turns out to be terminally senile, and the son is long dead ("The Return of Alcibiade").

The tone in Chopin's stories often seems light, as if—like Guy de Maupassant—she does not care deeply about her story, and refuses to tell readers what to think. Her characters banter or somehow cope or just fall silent, rather than sobbing about injustice. But even romance in *Bayou Folk* is more tense than sunny. Young men confuse falling in love with pity ("Love on the Bon-Dieu," "A Visit to Avoyelles"). Or the young men fall in love impulsively and tempestuously, as in "Désirée's Baby" and "At the 'Cadian Ball." Meanwhile, Chopin's young women characters may cling to men, but her stories show very few marriages, and only one loving husband (Baptiste in "Loka").

Not one reviewer noticed that *Bayou Folk*, as a whole, is an uncompromising critique of marriage. Of the twenty-three stories, seven show fathers without wives; two more have absent husbands who do not appear at all. Three husbands are brutal ("A Visit to Avoyelles," "Désirée's Baby," and "In Sabine"), and the book ends with a young woman who is very happy to be a widow ("A Lady of Bayou St. John").

If Kate Chopin had written such stories and set them among white middle-class people in the Northeast—in a setting that reviewers could not consider florid or strange—she might have gotten damning reviews, as Mary E. Wilkins did for her novel *Pembroke*, about the iron will of a New England patriarch. Chopin considered *Pembroke*

> the most profound, the most powerful piece of fiction of its kind that has ever come from the American press. And I find such papers as the N. Y. Herald—the N. O. Times Democrat devoting half a column to senseless abuse of the disagreeable characters which figure in the book. No feeling for the spirit of the work, the subtle genius which created it.

Chopin's reviewers had the same problem. Not a one recognized, for instance, her unique treatment of domestic violence (then called "wife abuse")—a topic mostly ignored by men, but always written about by women. Among Chopin's contemporaries, Elizabeth Stuart Phelps had managed to publish, in the genteel *Century* magazine, a story about wife abuse in New England ("Jack the Fisherman"), while Alice Dunbar-Nelson wrote about an Italian-American abuser in New Orleans ("Tony's Wife"). But in both stories, the husband wins, and the wife goes off to starve or die. That was true to life, and it was what editors were willing to publish—and it was what Phelps and Dunbar-Nelson had seen in their lives. Both had had troubled and difficult marriages, but Kate Chopin had not. She had also grown up in a household of women where battering did not take place. Unlike Loca Sampite, she had never had to consider it acceptable, or inevitable, for a husband to abuse his wife.

"In Sabine" can be called humorous in that it has a happy ending—but the plot is anything but comical. The isolated wife 'Tite Reine, whose husband Bud regularly beats and chokes her, cannot even write home for help, because she is illiterate. A black woodsman does help 'Tite Reine—another surprising Chopin touch, for few writers in the 1890s dared to portray a black man and a white woman as allies.

Then an unexpected guest, Grégoire, turns up and plies Bud with free whiskey. When the brutal husband wakes up, he learns that his wife has fled on Grégoire's horse, while Grégoire has lit out for Texas on Bud's most prized mustang. The batterer is left fuming, helpless, and horseless.

"In Sabine" is the only published story of its era in which a battered wife escapes. And Kate Chopin had not finished punishing the batterer Bud Aiken. Three years later in "Ti Frère," an unfinished story, Chopin's title character is insulted by Bud and wants to "pound and punch and pummel him" into unconsciousness—and does. Bud loses his horse again.

But with "In Sabine," the battered woman's story with a happy ending, Kate Chopin also came to terms with what Oscar Chopin and Albert Sampite had meant in her life. One of them, in retrospect, was heroic. Oscar, at fourteen, had stood up to his violent, slave-owning father, and helped his mother to escape. Oscar is reflected in Grégoire's soft and generous feelings for women. Meanwhile, Bud Aiken, the wife beater in "In Sabine," not only shares one of Albert Sampite's initials, but also much of his behavior. Like Bud, Albert beat his wife so brutally that she could not work, and drove her out of her home—although Loca, at least, had been able to return to her mother's house. The fictional Bud humiliates his wife by forcing her to mount a horse that will throw her, and by claiming they are not really married—just as the real-life Albert, a great lover of horses, humiliated his wife by taking up with other women, as if his marriage meant nothing to him.

"In Sabine" can be read as a meditation on the men in Kate Chopin's life during her Louisiana years. A decade after she left Cloutierville, no longer blinded by grief nor dazzled by desire, she could see the many virtues of Oscar Chopin. But her story's most tender passage also describes Kate Chopin's own childhood among mother-women, at home and at the Sacred Heart Academy: "Grégoire loved women. He liked their nearness, their atmosphere; the tones of their voices and the things they said; their ways of moving and turning about; the brushing of their garments when they passed him by pleased him."

Bayou Folk not only criticizes men, but praises women, including honorable fiancées, devoted granddaughters, and loving mothers ("A No-Account Creole", "Love on the Bon-Dieu," "Désirée's Baby," "La Belle Zoraïde"). Both slave and free women treat children and old people with loving care ("Beyond the Bayou," "The Return of Alcibiade," "Old Aunt Peggy"). Women are the ones who give charity and second chances ("Loka," "Ma'ame Pélagie").

If the reader pays attention to the roles of women, *Bayou Folk* is not primarily a picture of the odd folkways of Louisiana. Rather, it portrays a world of women who are honorable, generous, kind, and just.

But not one reviewer saw any of that.

"I fear it was the commercial instinct which decided me. I want the book to succeed," Kate Chopin wrote in her diary six weeks after the publication of *Bayou Folk*. Being a successful author required promoting one's book, so Chopin set out gamely to do so. In April she read from her book for the Duodecimo women's club in St. Louis. In May she missed a meeting of her euchre (bridge) club, because "Mrs. Whitmore insisted upon having me go out to her house to meet Mrs. Ames and her daughter Mrs. Turner, who were anxious to know me and hear me read my stories."

Meanwhile, like most published authors, she was set upon by amateurs who thought she somehow knew the secret of publication. She dutifully read a manuscript written by her neighbor, Lizzie Chambers Hull, who "knows she can write as good stories as she reads in the magazines (such belief in her own ability is a bad omen)." The manuscript proved to be very wordy, the first thousand words all about "how a black girl came in possession of her name. It should have been told in five lines." The overall story—about a young woman with mixed blood who loves a white man, gives him up, and dies of tuberculosis—was "commonplace," and the writing had "No freshness, spontaneity or originality of perception. The whole tendency is in the conventional groove."

Those comments are in Chopin's diary, and what she actually told Mrs. Hull was almost certainly more tactful. Mrs. Hull belonged to the Wednesday Club, which by the mid-1890s was the most powerful of St. Louis's women's clubs, and she was also "a delightful little woman." Yet she needed to do what Chopin had done: "study critically some of the best of our short stories. I know of no one better than Miss Jewett to study for technique and nicety of construction. I don't mention Mary E. Wilkins for she is a great genius and genius is not to be studied. We are unfortunately being afflicted with imitations of Miss Wilkins *ad nauseum*."

The New England stories of Sarah Orne Jewett were also considered proper for everyone to read, while the tales of Guy de Maupassant, Chopin's own models, were too racy to be carried in St. Louis's libraries. And so, when she was among the conventional people whose approval she sought, Kate Chopin did not mention Maupassant. She passed as an American, and kept her Frenchness to herself.

But when Chopin did attend a conventional writers' conference, she found it unbearable, and said so—and found herself, for the first time, publicly attacked in print.

It was not supposed to happen that way.

She had gone to the Western Association of Writers convention in Warsaw, Indiana, in late June 1894, with her friend Harriet Adams Sawyer, a St. Louis association vice president and "harmless poet," and Mrs. Sawyer's musically gifted daughter, Bertha, "more rusé than her mother." Chopin was not on the Western Association program, which did include the young poet Paul Laurence Dunbar (almost certainly the only African American there).

Mostly, the four-day conference consisted of amateur poetry readings and papers on such topics as "The Schoolmaster in Literature," "Sanitization, Mentally and Physically," and "The Novel—Its Uses and Abuses." The *Indianapolis Journal* called the convention just an excuse for unpublished poets to "get together and pelt each other with verses."

Kate Chopin was also unimpressed, as she wrote in her diary: "Provincialism in the best sense of the word stamps the character of this association of writers." She called the members amateurs whose writings were "far too sentimental," conventional, and earnest, and out of touch with "human existence in its subtle, complex, true meaning, stripped of the veil with which ethical and conventional standards have draped it." They had, she wrote, "a singular ignorance of, or disregard for, the value of the highest art forms." She sounded very judicious and French in her pronouncements, but her conclusion was a concession to American upbeatness. If, she wrote, the Western Writers' "earnestness of purpose and poetic insights" made them into "students of true life and true art, who knows but they may produce a genius such as America has not yet known."

Until then, Chopin had confined her grumblings about other writers to her diary. She seemed to know that it was wiser not to make public enemies. Yet something chafed. Maybe it was her French background, or her Sacred Heart training, or simply a newcomer's faith—common to novices in any field—that if those already in the field would just learn a few simple things, everything could be improved. (A century later,

Emily Toth in *Ms. Mentor's Impeccable Advice for Women in Academia* gave a name to that belief among people in their first year on a job: "I'm Surrounded By Idiots!")

Somehow Chopin wound up sending her diary entry on "The Western Association of Writers" to *The Critic*, a national journal which had favorably reviewed *Bayou Folk*. She got back an acceptance, a year's subscription to *The Critic*—and a lot of trouble. She had, after all, called the Western Association of Writers "provincial." They knew immediately what she really meant: "bumpkins."

Her piece appeared in *The Critic* on July 7, and it was reprinted in the *Indianapolis Journal* nine days later. It was published on the front page of the Brookville, Indiana *American*—not far from the conference site—and in other newspapers throughout the Midwest. Then the counterattack appeared in the *Minneapolis Journal* on July 21 and was reprinted, verbatim, in the *Cincinnati Commercial Gazette* a week later. But the response may have begun or ended elsewhere—for it seemed the whole Midwest was a-twitter with indignation against Kate Chopin.

The editorialist, unnamed, called her "Kate Chapin" and said she wrote "unkindly and bitterly of the Western Association of Writers, because it is provincial enough to stick to Indiana and meet every year at Spring Fountain Park." With insulting familiarity, the editorialist insisted that "Kate" was wrong: that James Whitcomb Riley, the Hoosier poet, was an Association member who did show great talent and accomplishment. Further, said the editorialist, the Western Association did have members outside Indiana, although "There is much Indiana talent in it, and Indianians are a little clannish; but the association is intended to have a wide, interstate scope, and it will probably have it in time."

The editorialist missed Kate Chopin's main points, and she did not respond. As an author who followed advanced European models, Chopin wanted to reach readers who were sharp and sophisticated appreciators of "the highest art forms." Haggling over the literary honor of Indiana was not what she had in mind.

But three days after the counterattack, while she was staying at The Cedars resort village, Chopin wrote a melancholy meditation: "I am losing my interest in human beings; in the significance of their lives and their actions. Some one has said it is better to study one man than ten books. I want neither books nor men; they make me suffer." But then she shifted to a more sensual mode: "The night came slowly, softly, as I lay out there under the maple tree.... My whole being was abandoned to the soothing and penetrating charm of the night.... The wind rippled the maple leaves like little warm love thrills."

Two days later, she had completely revived her spirits, and wrote a quirky story about a very large young heroine with a "fresh and sensuous beauty" that men find irresistible. She has a baby, and its father—who may or may not be her husband—is a poor, shabby, one-legged man with whom she goes off into the woods, "where they may love each other away from all prying eyes save those of the birds and the squirrels."

"Juanita," the first Chopin story in three years to be set in Missouri, was inspired by the life of a nearby postmaster's daughter. But it also violated at least half a dozen rules for short story writing. The heroine is not conventionally beautiful; the hero is neither handsome nor strong nor rich. There is no real conflict, but there is a distinct hint that the two young parents are unmarried (which would be called "living in sin" in the 1890s). And Chopin's last jaunty lines do nothing at all to make it acceptable: "For my part I never expected Juanita to be more respectable than a squirrel; and I don't see how any one else could have expected it."

Chopin evidently did not expect to publish the story, and it was ten months before she sent "Juanita" and "The Night Came Slowly" to *Moods*, a short-lived artistic magazine published in Philadelphia. Both were accepted immediately and published under the title "A Scrap and a Sketch," but the readership for *Moods* was either very small or very sophisticated. There were evidently no objections to her story of sex outside marriage.

Throughout 1894, Chopin was pushing her own career, trying to fit into some notion of a promotable author—while also, on her own, writing the kinds of stories that would eventually make her impossible to sell to conventional readers.

Three of the most striking were about wives. One is attracted to her husband's best friend; another is wildly happy to hear that her husband is dead; and a third one leaves, after her own death, hints of adultery that drive her living husband to despair ("A Respectable Woman"; "The Story of an Hour"; "Her Letters"). Only the third actually commits adultery—but the first clearly has it in mind.

Chopin had also begun translating some Guy de Maupassant stories, most of them about suicide, disillusionment, solitude, water, night, and illicit love—subjects that later appear in *The Awakening*. She may have chosen translation as a systematic way to study his writing; certainly her translations did not make much money. She was able to publish only three of them, two with Sue V. Moore's *St. Louis Life* ("It?" and "Solitude") and the third ("Suicide") with her old friends, the Knapps, at the *St. Louis Republic*.

Her other Maupassant translations were simply impossible to publish in the United States, where magazines were supposed to preserve the innocence of "the Young Person." Maupassant (who died of syphilis in 1893) had written about parts of the body that did not exist in respectable American fiction, such as thighs and breasts and tongues. And he also imagined scenes where American readers could not go: in his story "Mad?", an insanely jealous man catches the woman he loves in a sexual rendezvous with her horse.

In the spring of 1894, Chopin did finally break into what was, besides the *Century*, the other top magazine of the 1890s. In late 1893, the *Atlantic* had solicited a story from her, but then rejected "At Chênière Caminada," the tale of a humble Grand Isle fisherman who worships a New Orleans belle. ("The motif has been used so much," *Atlantic* editor Horace E. Scudder wrote to Chopin.) He also rejected "In Sabine" and "A Gentleman of Bayou Têche," the story of a travelling artist who wants to draw an Acadian fisherman as an example of "local color."

Finally, just when *Bayou Folk* came out, the *Atlantic* accepted "Tante Cat'rinette," Chopin's tale of a devoted former slave. She received forty dollars, not her highest payment, but an *Atlantic* acceptance was an extraordinary achievement. Her contemporary Agnes Repplier, a Philadelphia writer, used to say that it took fifteen years to make it into the *Atlantic*, which she called "the taste of the brightest corner of the American literary world." Chopin did it in five years.

Still, "Tante Cat'rinette" is a rather conventional story, and right after she got the proofs, Chopin was moved to find something European and racier, according to her diary: "Received Copy of Tante Cat'rinette from Atlantic for correction. Suppose it will appear in September. Read a few delicious comedies of Aristophanes last night."

The next day she translated Maupassant's "Un cas de divorce," about a husband whose "strange sexual perversion" is an erotic obsession with orchids: "their flanks, odorant, and transparent, open for love and more tempting than all women's flesh." She never found a publisher for that.

Kate Chopin's self-promotion in 1894 included one other ritual now common to writers: the interview-profile. In the 1890s, flamboyant authors like Rudyard Kipling and Mark Twain made extended book tours—something that a St. Louis-based mother of six could not manage. But all authors were potential celebrities, and Kate Chopin had been virtually unknown when the famous Houghton, Mifflin brought out her first story collection.

Sue V. Moore was the first to take advantage of readers' curiosity. "Very few authors have made such a success with their first book as has fallen to the share of Mrs. Chopin," Moore wrote in *St. Louis Life* (June 9, 1894). Reviewers had compared Chopin with Mary E. Wilkins, Grace King, and

George W. Cable, but Chopin had particular successes with dialect and descriptions of Louisiana life. She was once "one of the belles of St. Louis," but "has lived much of her life in New Orleans and on her Natchitoches plantation." (Readers in the 1890s liked to think of authors in aristocratic surroundings. To Northerners, "plantation" meant something far wealthier than "farm.")

Moore's profile also placed Kate Chopin into other conventional female categories: unambitious, physically attractive, and motherly. While her favorite authors, Moore wrote, were Guy de Maupassant and Walt Whitman, Chopin was not a driven, ambitious woman. She was "the exact opposite of the typical bluestocking," without "literary affectations," "fads," or "serious purpose in life." In person, Chopin "is a very pretty woman, of medium height, plump, with a mass of beautiful gray hair almost white, regular features, and brown eyes that sparkle with humor. Her five tall sons and pretty young daughter, who have all inherited from some ancestor a height and slenderness that the mother does not possess, make a most attractive family group, the beauty of which is greatly enhanced by the thorough *entente cordiale* that exists among them. They all take the greatest interest in their mother's work."

An autographed sketch of Kate Chopin in a fluffy hat, looking stern, accompanied Sue V. Moore's sketch. When the article was reprinted in *Current Literature* and *Book News*, Chopin was presented as one who conformed to the traditional expectations of women: she was devoted to her family and not serious about her work. Sue V. Moore evidently felt that was the way to "sell" her friend, but she also knew better. Moore knew that Chopin was a dedicated reviser and editor of her own writing, and that she was an eager and serious professional.

During the same time, Chopin's salon visitor William Schuyler wrote a profile for *The Writer*, but his took a different tack—one she preferred, according to her diary: "I don't know who could have done it better; could have better told in so short a space the story of my growth into a writer of stories."

Schuyler, the hawk-nosed, beetle-browed son of an Episcopal minister, was a man of many talents. A novelist and musician who studied the spirituals sung by Southern blacks, he was also one of the first Americans to admire Brahms and Wagner. At Central High School, where Kate Chopin's youngest son Felix ("Phil") was a 140-pound quarterback, Schuyler taught literature and writing, and sometimes on his way home he would stop at Chopin's house for a visit. Later he composed musical settings for three Chopin poems—"In Spring," "You and I," and "The Song Everlasting"— and in 1895 Chopin composed an affectionate Christmas verse to his wife, "To Hidee Schuyler."

Will Schuyler's profile reported that Kate Chopin had been a marvelous story teller as a girl, and "one of the acknowledged belles of St. Louis," and then a wife, mother, and widow, at which point she "developed much ability as a business woman." Schuyler was unusual in stressing Chopin's intelligence and managerial talents rather than her "womanly" attributes. In Louisiana, he wrote, she "not only straightened out her affairs, but put her plantations in a flourishing condition" before returning to St. Louis. She "learned how to economize her time, and all her social and household duties ... were not sufficient to occupy her mind." And so she began to write for publication, studying "to better her style."

Possibly abetted by Chopin herself, Schuyler blithely lied about the hostile reactions she was getting in Louisiana. He wrote, instead, that "The people of Natchitoches always receive her enthusiastically, since they thoroughly endorse her artistic presentation of their locality and its population; for Mrs. Chopin is not, like most prophets, without honor in her own country."

He described Kate Chopin as "a most interesting and attractive woman. She has a charming face, with regular features and very expressive brown eyes, which show to great advantage beneath the beautiful hair, prematurely gray, which she arranges in a very becoming fashion. Her manner is exceedingly quiet, and one realizes only afterward how many good and witty things she has said in the course of the conversation."

Schuyler did touch on some things that made Kate Chopin unconventional—ideas that were no doubt expressed in her salon. Although she preferred French writers, especially Maupassant, she thought that American writers might even surpass the French, "were it not that the limitations imposed upon their art by their environment hamper a full and spontaneous expression." And Chopin herself had been personally hampered: "had Mrs. Chopin's environment been different, her genius might have developed twenty years sooner than it did."

That was evidently on Kate Chopin's own mind in May 1894, when she wrote her only surviving comment on the people she had lost. She did not want to contemplate graves, or those "mounds of earth out at Calvary Cemetery," but she did wonder: what if those closest to her had not died?

> If it were possible for my husband and my mother to come back to earth, I feel that I would unhesitatingly give up every thing that has come into my life since they left it and join my existence again with theirs. To do that, I would have to forget the past ten years of my growth—my real growth. But I would take back a little wisdom with me; it would be the spirit of a perfect acquiescence.

Had her mother lived, Kate Chopin would have been a dutiful daughter, a quiet custodian of her own property. Had her husband lived, Chopin would have remained in Louisiana, and perhaps made peace with her disapproving Cloutierville neighbors—or perhaps not. In either case, she would not have become the center of St. Louis's growing literary colony, admired and pursued and envied.

In the mid-1890s, Chopin remained in the world of women she had known all her life, with lifelong women friends and an intense curiosity about other women—who sometimes, unwittingly and unwillingly, furnished story material. But men, for the first time, were not disappointments, and many were true friends. Some were personal admirers who also provided professional opportunities.

Still, there were things that non-authors would never understand.

Most authors lead rather dull lives, with hours alone at the typewriter or computer, or (as in Kate Chopin's case) with a stub pen, a block of paper, and a bottle of ink bought at the corner grocery store. She did have a favorite spot, she told inquirers: her Morris chair beside the window, where she could see a tree or two and "a patch of sky, more or less blue."

But interviewers, and the curious public, always want to know much more—about where writers get their ideas, and what tricks of the trade they're willing to reveal. Women writers are also usually asked, in some form: How do you combine being a woman and being a writer?—and they are expected to put womanhood first.

Kate Chopin was the subject of many such questions, which she did not always answer patiently. In an 1899 essay, she refused to answer the question, "Do you smoke cigarettes?" and turned aside a query about her children: "A woman's reluctance to speak of her children has not yet been chronicled. I have a good many, but they'd be simply wild if I dragged them into this." Some of her beloved children were away in Louisiana, Kentucky, and Colorado, she conceded, but "I mistrust the form of their displeasure, with poisoned candy going through the mails." And so, "In answering questions in which an editor believes his readers to be interested, the victim cannot take herself too seriously."

Kate Chopin did exactly that. She seriously and deliberately presented herself as a different creature from the dedicated writer she was. When asked about her writing, she was often evasive, and vague if not untruthful. While she did not write directly and exclusively to sell to a predictable market, as Ruth McEnery Stuart did, Chopin did want commercial success. And so she cut her image to suit a certain fashion—and made herself seem more nonchalant and breezy, and far less ambitious, than she actually was.

It began with Sue V. Moore's often-reprinted piece in *St. Louis Life*, with the claim that Chopin "has no 'fads' or 'serious purpose' in life; declares that she has never studied. She takes no notes and has never consciously observed people, places or things with a view to their use as literary material."

Chopin continued promoting that image when she responded to Waitman Barbe, a West Virginia poet who was writing a piece on "representative Southern Writers" in *Southern Magazine*. "I have no fixed literary plans," she wrote Barbe, "except that I shall go on writing stories as they come to me." Her forthcoming story in the *Century* ("Azélie") was "written in a few hours, and will be printed practically without an alteration or correction of the first draught."

Other observers agreed. According to Harrison Clark of the *St. Louis Republic*: "Mrs. Chopin writes fluently, rapidly, and with practically no revision." Similarly, William Schuyler reported that "When the theme of a story occurs to her, she writes it out immediately, often at one sitting, then, after a little, copies it out carefully, seldom making corrections. She never retouches after that." Her son Felix remembered seeing "a short story burst from her: I have seen her go weeks and weeks without an idea, then suddenly grab her pencil and old lapboard (which was her work bench), and in a couple of hours her story was complete and off to the publisher."

Chopin herself said, "I am completely at the mercy of unconscious selection," and that she relied on "the spontaneous expression of impressions gathered goodness knows where." Not that she hadn't tried to be disciplined, she claimed in an essay—but she always failed. "So I shall say I write in the morning, when not too strongly drawn to struggle with the intricacies of a pattern, and in the afternoon, if the temptation to try a new furniture polish on an old table leg is not too powerful to be denied; sometimes at night, though as I grow older I am more and more inclined to believe that night was made for sleep." And so, "I am forced to admit that I have not the writing habit."

That was not, of course, true. By the time Chopin made that ironic claim, in November of 1899, she had published two novels, some seventy short stories, more than a dozen essays, reviews, and poems, and a play. She was undoubtedly St. Louis's finest writer—but she was also, still, caught between the expectations for women and the expectations for professional authors. She knew that a woman who seemed too pushy would have less commercial (and personal) success than one who was charming and self-deprecating. That, after all, was the successful strategy that Ruth McEnery Stuart was pursuing. Although Stuart performed onstage, much as a standup comic does today, she still preserved the façade of a Southern lady.

And so Kate Chopin presented herself as domestic, spontaneous, and casual, drawn to table legs and furniture polish, when in fact her house was organized around her writing life. She had her own writing room, shown in an 1899 drawing in the *Post-Dispatch*, and her wide day bed, specially made by carpenters, was furnished with deep cushions, suitable for napping, meditating, and dreaming. That process of mulling is common to many writers who seem to be spontaneous. For writers who live amid noise and clutter—including the social lives of half a dozen young adults—the creative stillness needed for ideas and words and images is often difficult to find. Writers have to develop strategies to clear the mind, and one of Chopin's was inadvertently revealed in a local newspaper.

"Kate Chopin loved cards, coffee, and a cigarette," everyone knew. Her favorite game was duplicate whist, which she usually played with her sons and their friends, but the *Republic* reported that "it is a sort of standing joke among her intimate friends to say that if they leave Mrs. Chopin alone for five minutes they'll find her with the cards spread out before her, on their return, deep in the fascinations of one of the many combinations of solitaire."

For writers, solitaire is a classic method for clearing the mind of distractions. Without requiring great concentration, solitaire shuts out the world, while its mindlessness and repetition somehow free the mental channels to receive ideas, images, and words. When Kate Chopin turned immediately to solitaire, what she was seeking was solitude—the unique ability true writers have, to be alone in company.

Another way to keep the world away is to claim that one's work is not a struggle—that it is easily tossed off, spontaneously and casually. Most of the surviving manuscripts from Kate Chopin's hand are clear copies, written in ink in finished form, making it appear she made few or no corrections. The stories handwritten in her 1894 diary were published just as she wrote them. Most manuscripts support her claim that she wrote easily and effortlessly—except for the 1900 story "Charlie," the tale of a tomboy transformed. Among the Chopin papers housed in the Missouri Historical Society, that story (which was not published in Chopin's lifetime) exists in at least two different drafts, one called "Jacques."

Still, until 1992 it was easy to believe that Kate Chopin was mostly a natural author, not a hardworking one.

But in 1992, Linda and Robert Marhefka bought an old warehouse in Worcester, Massachusetts, and began clearing out the lockers, some untouched for sixty years. In one they found a cache of fragile newsprint papers and a letter connecting them with Daniel Rankin, Chopin's first biographer. Rankin had evidently borrowed the papers from her descendants and never returned them.

The papers the Marhefkas found include portions and drafts of five known stories ("Alexandre's Wonderful Experience," "Charlie," "The Gentleman from New Orleans," "A Little Country Girl," and "A Vocation and a Voice"), a portion of an essay (now called "Misty," a draft for "In the Confidence of a Story Writer"), and two short story attempts that Chopin abandoned utterly (now called "Doralise" and "Melancholy").

The papers, now called the Rankin-Marhefka Fragments, show that Kate Chopin was far more disciplined and thorough than she claimed. The fragments are scrawled in pencil, with words crossed out and inserted. Her spelling is careless (if not atrocious), and she uses dashes instead of standard punctuation. Some fragments are so written over that they are illegible, and she would have had to copy them over, making revisions, before passing them on to a typist. The fragments show that she was a diligent reviser who thought deeply about minute changes in wording.

The abandoned "Vocation and a Voice" fragment, for instance, shows the protagonist (a nameless boy) trying to get into a monastery with other brothers. That scene is not in the final version, and Chopin may have felt—as some women writers do—that she could not write an all-male scene. Or she may just have lost interest in it. The published version, much faster-paced, cuts abruptly from the boy's leaving his traveling companions to his appearance as the strongest wood chopper in the monastery.

Chopin abandoned at least one other story with a male protagonist: the fragment now called "Melancholy" begins with a lonely man like those in the Guy de Maupassant stories she was translating. She may have felt—with good reason—that it would be a hard story to sell.

More promising was "Doralise," a fragment about a young watercolor artist who tries to sell her paintings on Canal Street in New Orleans. Like Mademoiselle Reisz in *The Awakening*, she wears black lace in her hair. But Chopin abandoned that fragment after a few paragraphs. As she wrote to Waitman Barbe, "It is either very easy for me to write a story, or utterly impossible; that is, the story must 'write itself' without any perceptible effort on my part, or it remains unwritten."

With some stories, though, she did make perceptible efforts, as the drafts show. She vacillated about characters' names, and worked on finding the exact word. At the beginning of "A Little Country Girl," for instance, she debated whether to show the little girl "polishing" or "scouring" her tin milk pail. In the story "Charlie" (also called "Jacques" or "Jack"), she struggled with how to describe the heroine's composing a poem. In the Rankin-Marhefka fragment, "Its composition had cost Jack much laborious breathing, many drops of perspiration that had profusely besprinkled the sheet," but in what is probably the final draft, the text reads, "Its composition had cost Charlie much laborious breathing and some hard wrung drops from her perspiring brow."

The changes are small, but reflect Chopin's efforts to find the exact words and images she wanted for the reader. She was ambitious for financial success, but she also held herself to higher artistic standards than she was willing to admit—at least to her public.

Kate Chopin had had opinions all her life, and once she became a well-known writer, St. Louis periodicals asked her to write essays and reviews. For Sue V. Moore in *St. Louis Life*, Chopin reviewed three books in 1894, and disliked all of them for different reasons.

She thought the edition of the actor Edwin Booth's letters was a violation of his privacy (as someone who had passionate secrets in her past, she may have been especially attuned to that). She thought Émile Zola's *Lourdes* was overdone and full of that creaking, obvious, old-fashioned machinery that she had abandoned as a storyteller. Moreover, Zola's readers were never allowed to forget that "his design is to instruct us," she wrote. When a character appears to be just strolling to the barber shop, "we know better": we know he'll get a lecture about church abuses, or some other set piece that will stop the plot dead in its tracks.

She was a little more positive—or less disappointed—by the third male author she reviewed: Hamlin Garland, for his essay collection called *Crumbling Idols*. She agreed with his appreciation of Impressionism and innovation, but thought him unbecomingly angry for a young man, full of "hammer-strokes" and "clamor and bluster." She also twitted him for one of his pronouncements, that "in real life people do not talk love."

To which Kate Chopin, with all her French sophistication, responded: "How does he know? I feel very sorry for Mr. Garland."

But it was Zola, the French author, who continually irritated her. A few days after writing her review of his *Lourdes*, and after fuming about his overblown novels, Chopin wrote "A Sentimental Soul," with a hero quite a lot like Zola. She also killed him off.

Her character is Lacodie, a locksmith who spouts his radical opinions in Mamzelle Fleurette's shop in the French Quarter. (Mamzelle, another precursor of *The Awakening*'s Mademoiselle Reisz, wears a rusty black lace collar and has hair that is "painfully and suspiciously black.") Mamzelle Fleurette especially admires Lacodie when he gloats about gouging rich capitalists, for "she held a vague understanding that men were wickeder in many ways than women; that ungodliness was constitutional with them, like their sex, and inseparable from it." But Lacodie dies suddenly, of malaria. His widow soon remarries, and the grieving, adoring Mamzelle Fleurette quietly sets up an altar in his memory. She sees herself as his true widow, and is contented.

And so, presumably, was Kate Chopin—having buried Émile Zola, the incarnation of male bluster, in her own carefully contrived grave.

Rather than writing stories about men and men, Kate Chopin after *Bayou Folk* experimented with stories about women and women. She also tried crossing the color line in new ways.

Magazine editors in the 1890s, all of them white, liked stories of unequal relationships between blacks and whites—in which, for instance, the black character sacrifices for his or her "white folks." Chopin had written that kind of story with "For Marse Chouchoute," her first published short story set in Louisiana, in which an earnest young black boy loses his life carrying the mail in place of an irresponsible white boy. She also wrote about former slaves still devoted to their white families in such tales as "The Bênitous' Slave," "Beyond the Bayou," and "Tante Cat'rinette"—but such stories were predictable and unchallenging to write. Even before *Bayou Folk* was published, Chopin had been seeking new challenges. She tried one variation on the black–white devotion theme with "Ozème's Holiday," in which a young white man gives up his vacation to help a starving black woman. But that story still redounds to the credit of the white man, and the *Century* magazine was happy to take it.

Chopin's "Odalie Misses Mass" is a different kind of tale, about a white girl whose friend and "protégée" is a very old and helpless black woman. (Odalie is thirteen, Kate O'Flaherty's age when her great-grandmother died.) In the story, Odalie stops by to show Aunt Pinky her new dress, but finds that Pinky has been left alone. And so Odalie gives up on displaying her finery at church: sitting with her friend is more important. In the warm afternoon, the girl and the old woman sleep—and when Odalie's parents return, they find that Pinky has quietly passed away.

"Odalie Misses Mass," like "In Sabine," was not an easy story to place. Both are quirky stories in which women's needs come first. The *Atlantic*, the *Century*, and *Youth's Companion* all turned down "Odalie Misses Mass," and Chopin finally sent it to the *Shreveport Times*—which published it but paid her nothing.

"Odalie Misses Mass" is also written partly in dialect, which seems cloying or even racist to readers a century later, and they are apt to miss Kate Chopin's radical message. "Odalie Misses Mass" shows that women and girls can be friends across the races: Odalie does consider Pinky her best friend, and Pinky has no doubt about that. The white Odalie sacrifices peer approval—often the most important thing to adolescent girls—to take care of an older black person for whom she has no defined responsibility, except the ties of friendship. "Odalie Misses Mass" describes a warm female friendship that ignores barriers of race and age.

That is still a radical thought.

After *Bayou Folk*, Kate Chopin began seeking new markets for less traditional stories. The genteel tradition, as represented by William Dean Howells, was simply not hospitable to her vision of women. As the powerful editor of the *Atlantic* and then *Harper's*, Howells preferred "the more smiling aspects of life, which are the more American," rather than the tragic or melancholy themes treated by such Europeans as Guy de Maupassant. In particular, Howells insisted that American authors avoid "certain facts of life which are not usually talked of before young people, and especially young ladies." No American, Howells said, would write anything like *Madame Bovary* or *Anna Karenina*, novels about "guilty love" (he would not say adultery). And if an American writer tried to do so, Howells asked, "What editor of what American magazine would print such a story?"

The writers Howells chose to mentor did include one woman: Sarah Orne Jewett, a New Englander who wrote about women's relationships with each other. In those pre-Freudian days, Jewett's writings about women loving women, and her life with her intimate friend Annie Fields, were not at all controversial (the word "lesbian" was not used: Fields and Jewett had a "Boston marriage"). What would distress Howells and the other men of the genteel tradition was the hint, in print, of a sexual relationship between a woman and a man who were not married—or who were married to other people.

Adultery was, of course, the great, enduring theme of European, and especially French, literature. Kate Chopin, from the beginning of her career, had been skirting around the topic of "guilty love." "A Sentimental Soul," with Mamzelle Fleurette's unspoken crush on the married man who visits her shop, was turned down by the *Century*, the *Atlantic*, and *Harper's*, as were many of Chopin's stories after *Bayou Folk*. When she wrote other stories of flirtations and desires outside marriage—among them "The Kiss" and "La Belle Zoraïde"—Chopin did not even offer them to the genteel journals.

Instead, she published them in *Vogue*, which was launched in early 1893 as a New York fashion, society, and fiction magazine. (The same *Vogue* is still being published today, a century later.) In the early 1890s, *Vogue* was almost the only periodical, besides Reedy *Mirror* in St. Louis, to challenge the genteel tradition. "The Anglo-Saxon novelist," *Vogue* editorialized in

November of 1894, "is again imploring the world to free him from the fetters imposed on him by the Young Person.... The pink and white—débutante afternoon tea—atmosphere in which convention says we must present love, means intellectual asphyxiation for us."

No doubt it helped that *Vogue* was a sophisticated women's magazine edited by a woman, Josephine Redding, who was more than a little eccentric. Possibly Chopin met her in her May 1893 trip to New York, for "A Visit to Avoyelles" and "Désirée's Baby" had already appeared in the January issue of *Vogue*, and "Caline" was published in May. Redding, another precursor of the assertive and unusual Mademoiselle Reisz, was known to colleagues as "a violent little woman, square and dark, who, in an era when everyone wore corsets, didn't." She did always wear a hat, however—even at home in bed.

For *Vogue*, Kate Chopin did not have to pretend to be unambitious, or to love housework above all things. In *Vogue*'s collage of "Writers Who Have Worked with Us" in December 1894, Chopin's picture appeared at the pinnacle, in an ethereal, contemplative pose, wearing a small black headdress. *Vogue*'s caption praised both her brains and beauty: "MRS. KATE CHOPIN.—A beautiful woman, whose portrait fails to convey a tithe of the charm of her expressively lovely face, has been an honored contributor to *Vogue* almost from its first number.... Mrs. Chopin is daring in her choice of themes, but exquisitely refined in the treatment of them, and her literary style is a model of terse and finished diction."

In the mid- to late 1890s, *Vogue* was the place where Chopin published her most daring and surprising stories, those most in the French, Guy de Maupassant mold. In early issues, *Vogue* published, among others, "La Belle Zoraïde" and "Dr. Chevalier's Lie," as well as "A Lady of Bayou St. John," "The Kiss," and "The Story of an Hour." In later editions, *Vogue* published Chopin's stories about young women who grow tired and bored with men's excessive devotion ("Two Summers and Two Souls" and "Suzette"). She criticized youthful illusions about beauty ("The Recovery" and "The Unexpected"), and—odd for *Vogue*'s audience—wrote sympathetically about disabled men and poor women ("The Blind Man" and "A Pair of Silk Stockings"). Chopin even wrote about a hallucinogenic cigarette ("The Egyptian Cigarette").

Because she had *Vogue* as a market—and a well-paying one—Kate Chopin wrote the critical, ironic, brilliant stories about women for which she is best known today. Alone among magazines of the 1890s, *Vogue* published fearless and truthful portrayals of women's lives.

Vogue's openness delighted Kate Chopin, but it may also have betrayed her. Because it was eager to publish her raciest stories, *Vogue* may have deluded her into believing that American reviewers—whose failings and shortcomings she knew very well—would somehow be ready for a novel about youthful illusions, excessive devotion, guilty love, and much more.

Vogue, unwittingly, may have deceived her into thinking that *The Awakening* would be welcome.

NOTES

146ff. TKC, chaps. 13, 15–16, 18. The diary quoted in this chapter is the 1894 one, transcribed in KCPP.

146. Local color and universal: The use of local color as a mask for social criticism is discussed in Susan Koppelman's headnote to Mary Austin "Papago Wedding" in *The Other Woman*, 191–192.

147. *Bayou Folk*: The stories in *Bayou Folk* are "A No-Account Creole," "In and Out of Old Natchitoches," "In Sabine," "A Very Fine Fiddle," "Beyond the Bayou," "Old Aunt Peggy," "The Return of Alcibiade," "A Rude Awakening," "The Bênitous' Slave," "Désirée's Baby," "A Turkey Hunt," "Madame Célestin's Divorce," "Love on the Bon-Dieu," "Loka," "Boulôt and Boulotte," "For Marse Chouchoute," "A Visit to Avoyelles," "A Wizard from Gettysburg," "Ma'ame Pélagie," "At the 'Cadian Ball," "La Belle Zoraïde," "A Gentleman of Bayou Têche," and "A Lady of Bayou St. John."

148. *Pembroke*: Chopin's discussion is from June 7 entry, 1894 diary. KCPP.

149. Wife battering stories: Susan Koppelman's studies of U.S. women's battering stories, reported in the introduction to her *Women in the Trees*, are the most complete surveys ever made. Koppelman, who has spent some 25 years reading American women's short stories, has found no other battered wife stories from the 1890s in which a wife escapes. Personal conversation, 1997.

150. "Commercial instinct": *Diary*, May 4 and 12, 1894. KCPP. Western Association of Writers: Chopin's 1894 diary, June 2, June 30, July 5. KCPP.

152. "Idiots": Emily Toth, *Ms. Mentor's Impeccable Advice for Women in Academia* (Philadelphia: University of Pennsylvania Press, 1997), 60.

154. Diary entries: Aristophanes—July 6, 1894; Schuyler—May 28, 1894; Calvary Cemetery—May 22, 1894. KCPP.

154ff. Moore and Schuyler profiles are both reprinted in KCM.

157ff. Writing habits: "On Certain Brisk, Bright Days," CW, 721; TKC, chaps. 13, 16.

159. Rankin-Marhefka Fragments: KCPP.

161. Chopin's reviews are reprinted in CW.

NANCY A. WALKER

'Local Color' Literature and
A Night in Acadie

How immensely uninteresting some "society" people are!

(Kate Chopin, 'Impressions', 1894)

Besides her 1870 honeymoon journal, the only extant diary that Kate Chopin kept was written in 1894 and titled 'Impressions'. Her 4 May notation about the dullness of 'society people' is strikingly similar to her remarks in her commonplace book in the late 1860s about the fatigue and boredom of the debutante season. Then she had been a young woman who resented the time that parties and banal conversation took from her intellectual pursuits; in 1894, she was in a sense reaping the rewards of her intellectual and professional development by being asked to read her stories to people she often did not respect. The paragraph in which this exclamation occurs reveals Chopin reluctantly forgoing her own pleasures in order to promote *Bayou Folk*, which had been published about six weeks earlier:

Have missed the euchre club again because Mrs. Whitmore insisted upon having me go to her house to meet Mrs. Ames and her daughter Mrs. Turner, who were anxious to know me and hear me read my stories. I fear it was the commercial instinct which decided me. I want the book to succeed. But how immensely uninteresting some "society" people are! That class

From *Kate Chopin: A Literary Life* by Nancy A. Walker, pp. 83–110. © 2001 by the Estate of Nancy A. Walker.

which we know as Philistines. Their refined voices, and refined speech which says nothing—or worse, says something which offends me. Why am I so sensitive to manner.

(*KCPP*, 179–80)

As in her commonplace book, Chopin presents herself not as antisocial, but rather as a woman who preferred to choose her own social events—in this case an opportunity to play cards—rather than being compelled to associate with people she considered 'Philistines'. The remark about giving in to her 'commercial instincts' speaks to Chopin as a professional writer, obligated to promote her own work by reading from it to people she presumed were more interested in her celebrity than her artistry.

'Impressions' also offers other evidence of Chopin's status as a professional author with two published books to her credit. She reports on a dinner party with William Schuyler, who had been asked to write a profile of her for *The Writer*, and his wife, and professes to be quite pleased with the account of her life that Schuyler had developed—perhaps because it preserved her feminine gentility and protected her from the epithet 'bluestocking': 'I don't know who could have done it better; could have better told in so short a space the story of my growth into a writer of stories' (*KCPP*, 183). Being a published author also brought with it requests that she critique the work of those who aspired to be writers, and Chopin responded with generosity, while expressing in the privacy of her diary her reservations about their talent. She remarks of a Mrs Sawyer that she is 'a harmless poet', and of a Mrs Blackman that she has 'the artistic temperament—woefully unballanced [sic] I am afraid' (*KCPP*, 185). Chopin devotes the most detailed entry to a neighbor, Mrs Hall, who has asked her to read some stories she has written. While Chopin readily agrees to do so—'I never pick up such a MS but with the hope that I am about to fall upon a hidden talent'—she is critical of both Mrs Hall's naive faith in her own abilities and, ultimately, Mrs Hall's skill as a writer. 'She knows she can write as good stories as she reads in the magazines (such belief in her own ability is a bad omen).' One of Mrs Hall's stories concerns a young mulatto girl who rejects the attentions of a white man who loves her, and finally dies of consumption. Chopin has no objections to the theme, 'which [George Washington] Cable has used effectively', but she finds Mrs. Hall's handling of it conventional: 'no freshness, spontaneity or originality or perception'. The lessons that Chopin had learned about brevity are apparent when she writes that whereas Mrs Hall has taken a thousand words to tell how the girl had gotten her name, 'it should have been told in five lines' (*KCPP*, 180). Most surprising in Chopin's account of Mrs Hall are the remarks about her age, in which the 44-year-old Chopin suggests that it is too late for her neighbor to begin a career as a writer. Having remarked that Mrs Hall is 'nearly fifty', Chopin notes after reading her stories that 'if she were younger I would tell her to study critically some of the best of our short stories' (*KCPP*, 180–1). Coming from a woman who was 39 when she published her first story, such comments seem to suggest either that Chopin was forgetting her own publishing history or, more likely, that she had considered herself a writer serving an apprenticeship long before her work saw print.

A similar sense of self-importance characterizes Chopin's response to attending her first (and only) conference of writers, which she recorded in her diary and which was subsequently published in *The Critic*. The Western Association of Writers met annually in Warsaw, Indiana, and Chopin joined the group in late June of 1894. Besides Chopin, the attending writers whose work was well-known to contemporary readers were the 'Hoosier Poet', James Whitcomb Riley; Mary Hartwell Catherwood, who wrote historical romances set in the midwest; and Lew Wallace, best-known for his 1880 best-seller, *Ben-Hur*. Most of those attending the four-day conference, however, were aspiring poets, whom Chopin found largely untalented and 'provincial': 'Their native streams, trees, bushes and birds, the lovely country life about them, form the chief burden of their often too sentimental songs.' The conference participants seemed to Chopin mired in convention and unwilling to question received wisdom:

> The cry of the dying century has not reached this body of workers, or else it has not been comprehended. There is no doubt in their souls, no unrest; apparently an abiding faith in God as he manifests himself through the sectional church and an over-mastering love of their soil and institutions.... Among these people are to be found an earnestness in the achievement and dissemination of book-learning, a clinging to past and conventional standards, an almost Creolean sensitiveness to criticism and a singular ignorance of, or disregard for, the value of the highest art forms.
>
> (*CW*, 691)

In her critique of these writers' fondness for 'book-learning' and their adherence to conventional forms, Chopin echoes Emerson's call for American writers to break with the past and to value experience over the information to be found in books. Further, by implicitly setting herself apart from these midwestern writers, Chopin claims for herself an originality that they lacked, and despite the popularity of her Louisiana stories, she downplays the significance of region by declaring that the 'big, big world' about which the writer should concern herself was 'human existence in its subtle, complex, true meaning, stripped of the veil with which ethical and conventional standards have draped it' (*CW*, 691).

Chopin also sounds a Transcendentalist note in the 1894 diary when she rhapsodizes about the natural world. Visiting rural Missouri in late May, she reveled in 'the pure sensuous beauty of it, penetrating and moving as love!'. From the porch of a hillside house, she 'could look across the tree tops to neighboring hills where cattle were grazing on the sloping meadows. Through the ravine deep down on the other side in a green basin, a patch of the Meramec [River] glistened and sparkled like silver' (*KCPP*, 184). On 7 June, Chopin noted that 'my love and reverence for pure unadulterated nature is growing daily. Never in my life before has the Country [sic] had such a poignant charm for me' (*KCPP*, 187). And on 2 June she extolled the value of life's simple pleasures: 'There are a few good things in life—not many, but a few. A soft, firm, magnetic sympathetic hand clasp is one. A walk through the quiet streets at midnight is another' (*KCPP*, 186). As rewarding as the intellectual life could be, Chopin expressed distrust for those who sought to live only through books, and preferred Emersonian direct experience. In her 7 June entry, she writes about St Louis *Post-Dispatch* editor Charles Deyo, who had discovered Plato and was living happily in the philosopher's world:

> This is to me a rather curious condition of mind. It betokens a total lack of inward resource, and makes me doubt the value of the purely intellectual outlook. Here is a man who can only be reached through books. Nature does not speak to him, notwithstanding his firm belief that he is in sympathetic touch with the true—the artistic. He reaches his perceptions through others [sic] minds. It is something, of course that the channel which he follows is a lofty one; but the question remains, has such perception the value of spontaneous insight, however circumscribed.
>
> (*KCPP*, 187)

The spontaneity that Chopin favors over the 'channel' of another person's thoughts had its corollary in her preferred method of writing: the rapid capturing of character, scene, and incident as they formed in her imagination.

Other people's books, however, had their uses. Chopin continued to be an avid reader, and the 1894 diary affords insight into her literary preferences in the mid-1890s. Guy de Maupassant continued to be a favorite, and Chopin copied her translations of three of his stories into her diary: 'A Divorce Case', 'Mad?' and 'For Sale'. All three stories deal with obsessive love that leads to madness or bizarre behavior, and none of them was published until they were included in Thomas Bonner, Jr's *Kate Chopin Companion* in 1988. Of Chopin's American contemporaries, those singled out for praise in the diary wrote, as did Chopin, fiction with distinct regional settings. On her excursion to the Meramec River, a 'rough looking fellow bending over a plow' reminds her of 'one of Hamlin Garland's impersonations' (*KCPP*, 184), and the flavor of fresh strawberries somehow makes her think of James Lane Allen's *A Kentucky Cardinal*, which was being serialized in *Harper's* magazine. Calling Allen's an 'exquisite story', she comments on its naturalness: 'What a refreshing idealistic bit it is, coming to us with the budding leaves and the bird-notes that fill the air' (*KCPP*, 181). Chopin reserved some of her highest praise for her female contemporaries. If her neighbor Mrs Hall had been young enough to benefit from a model, Chopin would have recommended that she read the stories of Sarah Orne Jewett, because 'I know of no one better than Miss Jewett to study for technique and nicety of construction' (*KCPP*, 181). But even better than Jewett in Chopin's estimation was Mary E. Wilkins (Mary Wilkins Freeman, following her marriage in 1902). Wilkins cannot serve as a model for the aspiring writer, Chopin believes, 'for she is a great genius and genius is not to be studied' (*KCPP*, 181). If Chopin was disappointed in the quality and depth of the reviews of *Bayou Folk*, she was equally disturbed by reviews of Wilkins' 1894 novel *Pembroke*, which she called 'the most profound, the most powerful piece of fiction of its kind that has ever come from the American press'. And yet, as with her own work, reviewers seemed to miss the point: 'I find such papers as the N. Y. Herald–the N. O. Times Democrat devoting half a column to senseless abuse of the disagreeable characters which figure in the book. No feeling for the spirit of the work, the subtle genius which created it' (*KCPP*, 187).

In addition to her translations of Maupassant's stories, Chopin copied the texts of six of her own stories into the 1894 diary, apparently doing so as soon as she was satisfied that they were finished. All six were published outside of St Louis—two in *Century* and one in *Vogue*—in 1895 and 1896, and three of the stories—'Cavanelle', 'Regret', and 'Ozème's Holiday'— were included in Chopin's 1897 collection *A Night in Acadie*. The first of the stories, 'The Night Came Slowly', seems indistinguishable from one of Chopin's diary entries. Barely a page in length, it is a plotless reverie, with overtones of Maupassant, in which the first-person narrator begins by asserting disillusionment with both books and people—'they make me suffer'—and a preference for nature. Lying under a maple tree at night, the narrator listens to the sound of katydids while 'abandoned to the soothing and penetrating charm of the night'. In the final paragraph, the mood is broken by a man with 'red cheeks and bold eyes and coarse manner and speech' bringing a 'Bible class' and arousing the speaker's anger with his claim to know Christ (*CW*, 366). This brief sketch, together with the next story, 'Juanita', was published in the Philadelphia periodical *Moods*. 'Juanita' begins as though it, too, could be a diary entry, with Chopin recounting an actual encounter with the title character, an overweight, ungainly young woman who, unaccountably, is rumored to have suitors. But the sketch begins to read like an invention as—with interesting foreshadowings of the fiction of Flannery O'Connor—Juanita settles her affections on a one-legged man by whom she becomes pregnant, and the couple is frequently seen heading for the woods, he 'upon a dejected looking pony which she herself was apparently leading by the bridle' (*CW*, 368). The four remaining stories in the diary are more characteristic of Chopin; all except one are clearly set in Louisiana, as opposed to the indeterminate settings of 'The Night Came Slowly' and 'Juanita', and they feature the sympathetic humor with which Chopin often regarded her characters. Not surprisingly, given Chopin's simultaneous work on translations, there are echoes of Maupassant; in 'Cavanelle', the narrator muses about the title character, 'is Cavanelle a fool? is he a lunatic? is he under a hypnotic spell?' (*CW*, 372).

The fact that some of Chopin's stories read initially like diary entries points to a characteristic of her regional stories that differentiates them from the local-color fiction of many of her contemporaries. As Susan V. Donaldson points out in *Competing Voices: the American Novel, 1865–1914*, one of the functions of the regional literature of the late nineteenth century was to reinforce white middle-class values by making people outside the mainstream appear exotic, magnifying the differences between the readers and the characters they read about. Donaldson likens the popularity of local-color fiction to the proliferation of ethnological exhibitions during the same period: 'Like exhibitions of "primitive" and "quaint" peoples, from Bushmen to South Sea Islanders, local-color narratives focused on subjects assumed to be marginal to the norm—New England spinsters and widows, ex-slaves, and newly arrived immigrants.'[1] Both exhibitions of exotic peoples and artifacts and local-color narratives served to define the boundaries of the 'normal' American through the latter's difference from that which was observed or read about. As Donaldson observes:

> What both ethnological collections and local color fiction shared
> was a dynamic demarcating the boundaries between the ordinary
> and the strange, the normative and the eccentric, and, above all,
> spectators and spectacles. These sets of symbiotic relationships
> implicitly situated both the viewer of the ethnological collection
> and the reader of local color fiction as members of the emerging

white urban middle class. By definition the artifacts on display
and the local stories being read represented everything that the
audience was not, whether regional, traditional, quaint, foreign,
or ethnic.

Reviewers of local color fiction reinforce Donaldson's point: by referring
to characters and settings as 'charming', 'quaint', 'exotic', and even 'alien',
reviewers positioned themselves as well as their readers as part of the normative
group. The *New York Times* reviewer of Chopin's *Bayou Folk*, indeed, could
seem to be describing an exhibition of 'Bushmen' or 'South Sea Islanders'
by using the words 'barbarian' and 'primitive' to refer to Chopin's Louisiana
characters.

Yet Chopin herself seldom employed a device used commonly by her
contemporaries to underscore the difference between reader and 'spectacle':
a narrative voice representative of the class and perspective of the reader, who
introduces the 'different' characters and scenes and thus serves as a genteel
barrier between the 'normal' and the 'odd'. Such a device can be traced
back to the tall tales of the antebellum period—arguably the earliest form
of American local-color writing—in which an educated Easterner venturing
to the frontier on horseback or steamboat encounters the backwoodsman
who boasts in dialect about his larger-than-life exploits. Such a narrator is
implicitly somewhat condescending toward the characters who comprise the
tall tale itself, maintaining an identification with the similarly situated reader.
The narrators of late-century local-color stories are more often charmed
by or sympathetic toward the regional characters to whom they introduce
readers, but they are nonetheless outsiders who enter a different culture and
serve as the reader's guide to it. At the beginning of Jewett's *The Country of the
Pointed Firs*, for example, the observer of the Maine coastal town is described
as 'a lover of Dunnet Landing', but she is a summer visitor from the city
who notes the 'quaintness of the village with its elaborate conventionalities;
all that mixture of remoteness and childish certainty of being the center
of civilization of which her affectionate dreams had told'. Mary Wilkins
Freeman's New England stories typically begin with a paragraph or more
establishing the setting from an external perspective. Freeman's 'A Mistaken
Charity' opens with a distant narrative gaze—'There were in a green field
a little, low, weather-stained cottage with a foot-path leading to it from the
highway several rods distant'—and then introduces the characters: 'two old
women—one with a tin pan and old knife searching for dandelion greens
among the short young grass, and the other sitting on the door-step watching
her, or, rather, having the appearance of watching her'. Harriet Beecher
Stowe begins her story 'Uncle Lot' firmly established as the author: 'And so I

am to write a story—but of what, and where?'. Having chosen New England as her setting, Stowe addresses the reader in familiar tones: 'Did you ever see the little village of Newbury, in New England?'.

Kate Chopin's stories, in contrast, are seldom mediated in this way by a perspective external to the setting and characters. When she employs a first-person narrator, as she does in 'Cavanelle', the narrator is neither an authorial voice nor a visitor, but rather a character in the story—in this case, a woman who shops frequently in Cavanelle's drygoods store. Although the narrator finds Cavanelle something of an enigma, their differences are not cultural or geographical, but instead stem simply from the difficulty that one individual has in understanding another's motivations. More commonly, Chopin employs no mediating narrative perspective at all, instead entering directly into the world her characters inhabit and take for granted, and leaving to the reader the task of becoming oriented there. Typical are the opening lines of 'At the 'Cadian Ball': 'Bobinôt, that big, brown, good-natured Bobinôt, had no intention of going to the ball, even though he knew Calixta would be there. For what came of those balls but heartache, and a sickening disinclination for work the whole week through, till Saturday night came again and his tortures began afresh?' (CW, 219). Similarly, the story 'Lilies' begins with action rather than exposition: 'That little vagabond Mamouche amused himself one afternoon by letting down the fence rails that protected Mr. Billy's young crop of cotton and corn' (CW, 194). Occasionally Chopin offers brief explanations for readers unfamiliar with her settings; near the beginning of 'The Return of Alcibiade', for example, she writes, 'Little more than twelve years ago, before the "Texas and Pacific" had joined the cities of New Orleans and Shreveport with its steel bands, it was a common thing to travel through miles of central Louisiana in a buggy' (CW, 249). But French words and Creole syntax pepper Chopin's Louisiana stories without translation, and the names of towns, rivers, and parishes are used as the residents of those places would use them—casually and without geographical coordinates to locate them on a map. Indeed, the story 'A Gentleman of Bayou Têche', which was first published in Bayou Folk, serves as a warning against the external and potentially condescending gaze of the outsider. Mr Sublet is an artist visiting Louisiana looking for 'bits of "local color" along the Têche'. When he sees the Cajun Evariste, he decides to paint this 'picturesque subject' and put the likeness, as Evariste tells his daughter, 'in one fine "Mag'zine"' (CW, 319). But the black servant Aunt Dicey, wise to the ways of exploitation, warns that the caption will read, '"Dis heah is one dem low-down "Cajuns o' Bayou Têche!"' 'I knows dem kine o' folks', Dicey comments (CW, 320), and, consequently, Evariste refuses to have his picture painted. The resolution of the story both establishes Evariste's humanity and allows him to resist being categorized as an exotic specimen; after Evariste saves Mr Sublet's son from drowning, the artist offers to let him choose his own caption for the picture, and Evariste insists on his dignity and individuality: 'Dis is one picture of Mista Evariste Anatole Bonamour, a gent'man of de Bayou Têche' (*CW*, 324).

Chopin thus positions herself as an inhabitant of the culture she depicts in her fiction, not a visitor or observer who wishes to point out the picturesque and exotic features of the region to underscore its difference from the rest of American society. Just as Louisiana is clearly preferable to St Louis in her novel *At Fault*, Chopin's delight in the language, customs, and landscape of the state is palpable in her short fiction. She seems to have been comfortable with the 'regional' label, particularly as her work attracted attention outside Missouri and Louisiana. Certainly, she expressed pleasure in being selected as one of the 'representative Southern Writers' to be featured in *Southern Magazine* in 1894. In early October, Chopin wrote to the author who was writing the sketches for the series, Waitman Barbe, enclosing newspaper articles about her life and work, and answering questions he had posed. In her letter, Chopin reiterates several central themes of the public story she had developed about herself during the previous few years. Describing her writing habits, she once more emphasizes the speed of her composition and effaces her own agency in the process:

> I have no fixed literary plans, except that I shall go on writing stories as they come to me. It is either very easy for me to write a story or utterly impossible; that is, the story must "write itself" without any perceptible effort on my part, or it remains unwritten. There is not a tale in "Bayou Folk", excepting the first ["A No-Account Creole"], which required a longer time than two, or at most three sittings of a few hours each. A story of more than 3000 words ["Azélie"] which will appear in Dec. Century was written in a few hours, and will be printed practically without an alteration or correction of the first draught.
>
> (*KCPP*, 205)

In addition to presenting herself as a writer to whom stories presented themselves whole, Chopin also places herself squarely in the domestic space: 'I work in the family living room often in the midst of much clatter' (*KCPP*, 205).

Even as Chopin continued to present herself to the public as a proper homemaker who dashed off stories at the dining room table, her reputation as a writer of some stature continued to grow, especially following the largely favorable critical reception of *Bayou Folk*. Her St Louis friends were more than once in a position to enhance her national reputation. Not only did *The Writer* call upon St Louis journalist William Schuyler to write a profile of Chopin; in the spring of 1895 her friend and former St Louis resident Rosa Sonneschein touted Chopin as the star author in the first issue of her magazine *The American Jewess*, published in Chicago. Sonneschein, a Hungarian immigrant, had been a leader in St Louis Jewish intellectual circles; following a messy and painful divorce from her rabbi-husband, she moved to Chicago and started *The American Jewess* as a progressive magazine of the arts and culture with a decidedly pro–women's rights stance. In her editorial for the first issue, Rosa Sonneschein extolled both the skill and the celebrity of Chopin, whose story 'Cavanelle' appeared in the issue:

> MRS. KATE CHOPIN whose gifted pen contributes to our initial number a delightful sketch of Creole life, is one of the most interesting and unique writers of the *fin de siècle*. Since the appearance of her book 'Bayou Folk', a collection of most charming tales, Kate Chopin has become an acknowledged literary power.
>
> (Toth, 247)

Although Sonneschein, like other editors and critics of the period, referred to Chopin's work as 'delightful' and 'charming', she nonetheless singled out the darkest and most daring story in *Bayou Folk*, 'Désirée's Baby', for special praise.

By the time Chopin published 'Cavanelle' in *The American Jewess*, her home had become a gathering place for a diverse group of St Louis intellectuals. Although Chopin's first biographer, Daniel Rankin, claimed that during the years between the publication of *Bayou Folk* and *A Night in Acadie* (1897) her life was 'in no way different from what it had been before literary success brought her from local to national prominence', and that she 'refused to be considered a literary person' (Rankin, 141), he was relying on her own public presentation of self. In fact, she was the frequent hostess of the closest thing St Louis had to a literary salon in the 1890s. One of the most notable attributes of the group that met for Sunday suppers and other gatherings at Chopin's unpretentious Morgan Street home was its ethnic diversity. Like many American cities in the late nineteenth century, St Louis had long been divided into separate enclaves based on ethnic and linguistic heritage, with the French and German residents maintaining their distance from one another—a situation exacerbated by the Civil War, when the French supported the Confederacy and those of German heritage were staunch Unionists—and the Irish at the bottom of the socioeconomic heap. Chopin's friend and physician

Frederick Kolbenheyer, who published his liberal political views in German-language newspapers in St Louis, had emigrated from Poland, where he had been a radical antimonarchist. George Johns was a native Missourian and a Princeton graduate, but in the 1890s he was a liberal editorial writer for the St Louis *Post-Dispatch* who was not afraid to take on the powerful conservative elements of the city. William Marion Reedy had grown up in St Louis' Irish ghetto; very much a self-made man, Reedy edited the *St. Louis Mirror*, which, by the time of his death in 1920, had a readership well beyond conservative St Louis. Reedy not only espoused liberal causes, but he also championed writers and challenged tastes: the *Mirror* was one of the first American periodicals to publish James Joyce, Amy Lowell, and Oscar Wilde.

Uniting these people and the others who frequented Chopin's home was an interest in books and ideas. Many in this circle were journalists with strongly held views on political and social issues; all were well-read in both American and European literature, and enjoyed discussing what they read. For some in the group, including Chopin herself, the gatherings represented an opportunity to indulge in behavior as well as ideas that would have been frowned upon by the more conservative elements of St Louis; women as well as men smoked cigarettes, argued, and, by all accounts, flirted. Even as she continued to present herself to the reading public as a mother writing stories in the midst of family chaos, Chopin enjoyed this social and intellectual life that was so different from the etiquette of calling cards and the assigned essays of the Wednesday Club. The views and behavior of some members of Chopin's circle would have been considered extreme by most standards. In the 5 July entry of her 1894 diary, Chopin noted that '[Charles] Deyo talked anarchy to me last night. There is good reason for his wrath against the "plutocrats" the robbers of the public.... He believes in equal opportunity being afforded to all men' (*KCPP*, 188). William Reedy became a figure of public scandal when, in 1893, he married the madam of a St Louis house of prostitution while on a drunken binge. After they were divorced in 1896, he eloped with a respectable young woman after the Catholic church refused to annul his earlier marriage, and he was excommunicated. Chopin, never a reformer or even a particularly political person, did not often share her friends' most radical views; in the diary entry about Charles Deyo, she expresses her view that his anarchic rhetoric seems based more in personal ambition than in concern for the public welfare, and wonders why he has not tried harder to effect change in his role as a journalist: 'He has had a pen in his hand for the past five years or more—what has he done with it?' (*KCPP*, 188). But Chopin was loyal to her friends, and Reedy, in particular, was a favorite, not least, perhaps, because he consistently championed women writers. When, toward the end of the decade, the New York periodical *Town Topics* put together a

list of writers who should be selected for an American Academy of Letters if
one were to be created, Reedy noted in the *Mirror* the complete omission of
women, and asserted that 'we can turn over the best work that comes to mind
and note that a great deal of it has been achieved by women'. Reedy's list of
female nominees included, in addition to Kate Chopin, Mary E. Wilkins,
Margaret Deland, Agnes Repplier, Gertrude Atherton, and Elizabeth Stuart
Phelps (Toth, 267).

While her journalist friends made known their political views, Kate
Chopin confined her public pronouncements primarily to matters of art
and literature. Two review articles that she published in the fall of 1894
in her friend Sue V. Moore's *St. Louis Life* reveal a good deal about her
taste and sensibility. An avid theater-goer, Chopin particularly admired
the artistry of Edwin Booth, who was famous for his Shakespearian roles,
and who may well have served as the model for the 'great tragedian'
with whom the young Edna Pontellier is infatuated in *The Awakening*.
Chopin's reaction to the announced posthumous publication of some of
Booth's letters, however, is quite negative; not only does she feel that such
publication is an invasion of Booth's privacy, she also believes that the 'real
Edwin Booth'—so proposed the title of the *Century* article announcing
the publication—was to be found in his theatrical interpretations, not in
his correspondence. 'No,' she writes, 'it is not here that we are to look for
the real Edwin Booth, in a puerile collection of letters, expressions wrung
from him by the conventional demands of his daily life.' Chopin defends
the right of the artist to choose his own mode of public presentation: 'The
real Edwin Booth gave himself to the public through his art. Those of us
who most felt its magnetic power are the ones who knew him best, and as
he would have wished to be known' (Rankin, 144). Her review of Émile
Zola's novel *Lourdes* in the 17 November *St. Louis Life* bears directly on
her own fiction-writing practices. She rejects as boring and overly didactic
Zola's journalistic realism, making clear her preference for a compelling
narrative over documentary detail:

> [T]he story is the merest thread of a story running loosely
> through the 400 pages, and more than two-thirds of the time
> swamped beneath a mass of prosaic data, offensive and nauseous
> description and rampant sentimentality. In no former work has
> Mons. Zola so glaringly revealed his constructive methods. Not
> for an instant, from first to last, do we lose sight of the author
> and his note-book and of the disagreeable fact that his design is
> to instruct us.
>
> (Rankin, 145)

Chopin's dislike of Zola's methods also found Its way into her fiction. In her story 'Lilacs', also written in 1894, the French actress Adrienne Farival, annoyed by her servant, Sophie, threatens to throw a book at her: 'What is this? Mons. Zola! Now I warn you, Sophie, the weightiness, the heaviness of Mons. Zola are such that they cannot fail to prostrate you; thankful you may be if they leave you with energy to retain your feet' (*VV*, 140).

Chopin's resistance to both sentimentality and didacticism are demonstrated clearly in her story 'Azélie', which was published the following month in *Century*. Although on a fundamental level the story deals with social-class disparities in the post–Civil War south, Chopin frames the narrative as a gentle love story, allowing social issues to emerge subtly rather than using Zola's documentary detail. The title character, the daughter of an impoverished and lazy Cajun sharecropper, is first observed by the owner of the plantation, Mr Mathurin, 'from his elevation upon the upper gallery' (*CW*, 289), as she approaches the plantation store to secure, on credit, provisions for her family. The perspective then moves to that of 'Polyte, who, as the proprietor of the small store, occupies a social level between those of Mr Mathurin and Azélie, and who has the authority to determine what supplies Azélie may charge to her family's account, allowing her salt meat, coffee, and sugar, but denying her requests for tobacco, whiskey, and lard. But even as he thus exercises power over her family's desires and comfort, 'Polyte is falling in love with Azélie, and this feeling only increases when she breaks into the store one night to get what he had denied her: 'the very action which should have revolted him had seemed, on the contrary, to inflame him with love' (*CW*, 294–5). 'Polyte neither informs his employer about Azélie's burglary nor analyzes his own feelings, but he begins to charge her purchases to his own account and finally declares his feelings to her, hoping she will marry him. But Azélie resists him, neither offended by nor responsive to his kisses, and with the same passivity she accepts her family's move to Little River, an admission of their failure as sharecroppers. Rather than dwelling on the family's poverty, Chopin instead focuses the conclusion of the story on 'Polyte's decision to quit his job and follow Azélie to Little River. By giving the human love story primacy, Chopin manages to depict the complexities of the southern class structure without delivering a moralistic message. The issue of race, in fact, enters the story just once, in a casual although revealing way. When 'Polyte discovers Azélie in the store at night, she defends herself by claiming that her father is being discriminated against in favor of blacks: 'you all treat my popa like he was a dog. It's on'y las' week Mr. Mathurin sen' 'way to the city to fetch a fine buckboa'd fo' Son Ambroise, an' he's on'y a nigga, après tout' (*CW*, 294). Neither 'Polyte nor Chopin comments on Azélie's assumption of white superiority; it was merely a fact of southern life.

The matter-of-fact realism of Chopin's stories of Creole and Acadian life—often, as in 'Azélie', touched with whimsy and wit—is quite different from the thorough reportage of Zola or the intense psychological drama of Maupassant's stories, but she continued to be drawn to the work of the latter author. Between 1894 and 1898, she translated eight of Maupassant's stories, and at one point she approached Houghton Mifflin, which had published *Bayou Folk*, about bringing out a collection of them, but the idea met with no enthusiasm. Chopin's career as a translator was thus limited to the publication of four stories, all in St. Louis periodicals: Adrien Vely's 'Monsieur Pierre' in the *Post-Dispatch* in 1892, and Maupassant's 'Solitude' and 'It?' in *St. Louis Life* (1895) and 'Suicide' in the *St. Louis Republic* (1898). Unlike those in Chopin's coterie, most American readers would have found Maupassant's fiction decadent or worse, and it was very likely Chopin's stature as a writer in St Louis that allowed publication of even these few stories. All three of the published Maupassant translations deal with extremes of human isolation. While the main speaker in 'Solitude' simply attempts to convince his companion of the essential unknowability of one human being by another, 'It?' and 'Suicide' depict characters driven to desperate action by their loneliness. The speaker in 'It?' explains that he is getting married, even though he considers 'legal mating a folly', in order 'to feel that [his] home is inhabited' so that he can avoid the hallucinations that beset his isolation (*KCC*, 189); 'Suicide' consists mainly of a suicide note in which a man explains the bleakness of his life, no 'great catastrophes', but instead 'the slow succession of life's little miseries' (*KCC*, 203). Bleak as these stories are, they were less controversial than those in which Maupassant presents traditional social institutions, such as marriage, in a perverse light. In 'A Divorce Case', a man becomes obsessed with the purity of flowers to the point that his wife's body disgusts him, and in 'Mad?' a woman transfers her affections from her husband to her horse, provoking the man to shoot both of them. The language as well as the themes of these stories would have made then unacceptable to many 1890s readers. Even *Vogue*, which published some of Chopin's more daring stories, would have hesitated at the following passage from 'Mad?': 'When she walked across my room, the sound of her every footfall awakened a turmoil in my whole being: and when she began to remove her garments, letting them fall about her to the floor, and emerging infamous and radiant, I felt in every member a fainting ignoble but infinitely delicious' (*KCC*, 186).

If Maupassant inspired Chopin to be more daring in her subject matter than were many of her contemporaries, the resulting fiction deals more with challenges to social convention than with states of obsession and despair. Some of these stories—including 'Désirée's Baby' and 'The Story of an Hour'—are among the best-known of Chopin's fictional works; the former deals with a young woman doomed by the suspicion that she is part Negro, and the latter presents a woman's relief at being widowed. These two stories, and more than a dozen others that Chopin published between 1893 and 1900, appeared in *Vogue*, a magazine more open than most to the experimental and unorthodox. Unlike *The Atlantic* and *Century*, the young *Vogue*, which began publication in December of 1892, did not attempt to reach a large segment of the American reading public, but rather was consciously intended for an economically and to some extent intellectually elite class. Founded as a weekly magazine of 'fashion, society, and "the ceremonial side of life",' and initially aimed at New Yorkers, *Vogue* had among its original backers Cornelius Vanderbilt, Mrs Stuyvesant Fish, and Mrs William D. Sloan.[2] In addition to forecasting trends in fashion, *Vogue* established a reputation for seeking out what was new in the arts, including literature. Chopin published six stories in *Vogue* during the magazine's first year: 'Désirée's Baby', 'A Visit to Avoyelles', 'Caline', 'Ripe Figs', 'A Lady of Bayou St. John', and 'Dr. Chevalier's Lie'. Two of these stories—'A Visit to Avoyelles' and 'A Lady of Bayou St. John'—deal with unrequited love, in both cases the love of a man for a married woman, although in both stories proper decorum is ultimately maintained. The short sketch 'Dr. Chevalier's Lie' depicts a physician who hides the truth about a young prostitute, whose death by gunshot he attends, from her rural family, who a year earlier had been 'proud as archangels of their handsome girl, who was too clever to stay in an Arkansas cabin, and who was going away to seek her fortune in the big city'. Gossip ensues when Dr Chevalier arranges for the girl's funeral, but the matter is quickly forgotten: 'Society thought of cutting him. Society did not, for some reason or other, so the affair blew over' (*CW*, 147–8). Such stories went beyond the 'charming' and 'picturesque' to reveal extremes of human degradation and kindness.

Even as she paid homage to Maupassant in her translations and in some elements of her own fiction, Chopin also deepened her associations with the other regional writers with whom she was inevitably classified. One of these was Ruth McEnery Stuart, whom she met in St Louis in February of 1897. Stuart, a native of New Orleans, had moved to Arkansas upon her marriage, and returned to New Orleans to support herself by writing following her husband's death in 1893. There are striking parallels between the lives of Chopin and Stuart. Both had immigrant Irish fathers and mothers from distinguished southern families. Almost exact contemporaries (Ruth McEnery was born in 1849), both women became widows in the early 1880s and returned to their native cities to become writers; Stuart's first story was published in 1888. There are, however, significant differences. While Kate Chopin had several sources of income following Oscar's death, Stuart was dependent upon her writing to support herself and her son, a fact which may have a bearing on the themes and form of her work, which is more conventional and sentimental than is Chopin's. As Edwin Lewis Stevens wrote in the *Library of Southern Literature* in 1909: 'The anti-Christmas, anti-holiday, unchristianlike or unhappy side of life finds small expression from Mrs. Stuart's pen, for she is everywhere cheerful, looking on the bright side, and turning the flow of her drama away from tragedy and toward wholesome living, lightened by the play of comedy.' By the time she met Chopin, Stuart was living in New York and traveling around the country reading from her very popular stories set in Louisiana and Arkansas. Despite their differences, Chopin professed admiration for both Stuart and her work. After meeting her, Chopin wrote an admiring note to Stuart, crediting her with dispelling the chill of a snowy February day: 'the snow lay everywhere; but its silence and its chill no longer touched me. For the voice of the woman lingered in my ears like a melting song, and her presence, like the warm red glow of the sun still infolded [sic] me' (*KCPP*, 215–16). Later in the month, Chopin praised Stuart's fiction in the *Criterion*, noting first the 'fidelity' of her portrayal of the inhabitants of New Orleans and then sounding the same note that Stevens would by singling out the 'wholesome, human note sounding through and through' her stories (Rankin, 155–6).

But the *Criterion* article also reveals that Chopin was somewhat overwhelmed by her meeting with Stuart, and some of her comments about Stuart's fictional practice seem inexplicable unless seen in the context of a sense of personal awe. Chopin acknowledges that Stuart is a 'celebrity', one 'recognized throughout the length and breadth of these United States'. It is this very celebrity that initially made Chopin reluctant to meet Stuart: 'I had met a few celebrities, and they had never failed to depress me.' Stuart's sense of humor quickly dispelled Chopin's reservations: 'I might have known that a woman possessing so great an abundance of saving grace—which is humor—was not going to take herself seriously, or to imagine for a moment that I intended to take her seriously.' Given this personal 'saving grace', it is not surprising that Chopin praises Stuart for the 'rich and plentiful' humor in her fiction. More difficult to reconcile with a general avoidance of racial stereotypes in Chopin's own work is her endorsement of Stuart's portrayal of 'that child-like exuberance which is so pronounced a feature of negro character, and which has furnished so much that is deliciously humorous and pathetic to our recent literature'. Although there is little reason to doubt the sincerity of Chopin's admiration of Ruth McEnery Stuart and her talent as a writer, the *Criterion* article seems to be her attempt to present Stuart to the reading public as she presented herself to that public; toward the end of the article, Chopin insists on Stuart's femininity, calling her 'a delightful womanly woman', and she remarks that despite her intentions, when she met

Stuart she 'did not speak of her stories', thus maintaining the social rather than the professional nature of their conversation (Rankin, 156–7).

Chopin's effusive remarks about Stuart are certainly not echoed in her *Criterion* articles about the work of two of her male contemporaries in March of 1897. Her commentary on Thomas Hardy's *Jude the Obscure* (1895) is framed as a larger discussion of book-banning, which Chopin, like the visitors to her salon, deplored. Hardy's novel has, she asserts, 'for some inscrutable reason ... been withdrawn ... from circulation at our libraries', and a visitor is shocked to see a copy of it in her home, 'with so many young people about'. But it is not for any offensive material that she criticizes Hardy's book, but rather for its dullness. 'The art is so poor that scenes intended to be impressive are at best but grotesque. The whole exposition is colorless. The hero arouses so little sympathy that at the close one does not care whether he lives or dies.' The novel *is*, Chopin concedes, 'immoral', but only because 'it is not true'. The sense of humor so important to Ruth McEnery Stuart's fiction is missing in Hardy's: 'From beginning to end there is not a gleam of humor in the book' (Rankin, 51–3). Chopin was far closer in spirit to Joel Chandler Harris, who had begun publishing his 'Uncle Remus' stories in 1879. Reviewing Harris' 1896 novel *Sister Jane: Her Friends and Acquaintances*, Chopin had the greatest praise for his creation of southern characters, 'every one of [whom] is a masterpiece of his creative genius'. Not surprisingly, Chopin admired most those traits of Harris' writing that were most similar to her own; individual chapters of *Sister Jane*, which read like local-color sketches, 'stand out like flaming torches'. But Chopin did not believe that Harris had the 'constructive faculty' to write a novel, and she found the plot of *Sister Jane* 'weak, unjointed [and] melodramatic'. She concludes her review by asking Harris to write more stories about 'those old-time people in their quiet, sleepy corner of Middle Georgia' (Rankin, 154–5).

As early as the fall of 1894, Chopin had envisioned a second collection of short stories. In her letter to Waitman Barbe in October, she noted, 'I have ready another collection of Creole tales which I hope to have published in book form after they have made their slow way through the magazines' (*KCPP*, 205). Her success to this point in her career had been with the short-story form, and she saw no reason to depart from it. When, however, she approached Houghton Mifflin, the publisher of *Bayou Folk*, about bringing out a second volume of her stories, the editors were not enthusiastic. When the firm's H. E. Scudder finally responded to her early in 1897, he complained that some of her stories seemed to have little plot. Further, he had made 'inquiries' about the success of *Bayou Folk*, and 'the result was not encouraging', despite the fact that the initial printing had sold out and 500 additional copies had been printed in 1895. Houghton Mifflin did wish to remain loyal to its published authors, Scudder told Chopin—'[we are] always loth to seem inhospitable to one whom [we] have once included in the lists'— but he suggested that a novel would be more successful than a collection of stories: 'You have now and then sent me a story long enough to run through two or three numbers in [*The Atlantic*]. Have you never felt moved to write a downright novel?' (Toth, 296). Scudder was apparently unaware of Chopin's novel *At Fault*, which she had privately printed in St Louis, and he shared the common perception that both fiction writers and their readers preferred novels to shorter forms.

However Chopin may have responded to Scudder, she pressed ahead to find a publisher for her collection of stories. Despite her criticism of Hamlin Garland for predicting that cities such as Chicago would soon rival Boston and New York as centers of publishing, she next tried the Chicago publishing company Stone & Kimball, which published the avant-garde *Chap-Book*, a *fin-de-siècle* periodical that prided itself on the modernity of its authors, including Aubrey Beardsley, George Bernard Shaw, and Stéphané Mallarmé. Chopin's collection of 'Creole tales' may have seemed entirely too tame to Stone & Kimball, which had also rejected *Young Dr. Gosse and Théo*. Chopin had been for some time eager to publish with Stone & Kimball, especially in the *Chap-Book*, perhaps because such publication would give her the stamp of the 'modern' author—which some of her work surely deserved—as opposed to the more staid category of 'local-color' writer. In January of 1896, after she had sent Stone & Kimball her short-story manuscript, she wrote to suggest that two of the stories, 'Lilacs' and 'Three [Two] Portraits', might be appropriate for the *Chap-Book*, and closed her letter with an almost abject plea: 'I would greatly like to see one of them—some of them—something— anything over my name in the Chap-Book' (*KCPP*, 209). The two stories that Chopin identified as appropriate for the *Chap-Book* are definitely not local-color stories; both deal with the attractions of convent life in unconventional ways, and neither appeared in *A Night in Acadie*, but were deferred to the ill-fated *A Vocation and a Voice*. 'Lilacs' is the story of an actress for whom the convent-school of her youth is an annual refuge until, because of either the extravagant gifts she brings or the homoerotic relationship with a nun at which the story hints, she is forbidden to return. The 'Two Portraits' are of 'The Wanton' and 'The Nun', which together serve as a cautionary tale about the effects of the childhood environment on the development of a woman's self-esteem. The 'wanton' is raised with beatings and sexual promiscuity, and becomes a prostitute, and the 'nun', early taught the need to submit to God, has rejected the flesh in favor of the spirit, and is said to have visions. In presenting such extremes, Chopin implicitly argues for a middle ground, in which girls are taught to respect themselves without being abject. The

Chap-Book accepted neither story, and Stone & Kimball rejected the story collection, which Chopin eventually placed with their Chicago competitor Way & Williams, which published *A Night in Acadie* in 1897.

A Night in Acadie differs in several respects from *Bayou Folk*. Only four of the 21 stories—'Polydore', 'A Matter of Prejudice', 'Mamouche', and 'The Lilies'—were initially published in a periodical for children, the first three in *Youth's Companion* and the last in *Wide Awake*. And although 'Mamouche' and 'Polydore' depict orphaned children who repent of behaving badly and are consequently rewarded with the love of wealthy benefactors, the stories are more complex than were Chopin's earlier brief cautionary tales, and much of the focus is on the stories' adult characters. In 'A Matter of Prejudice', an elderly Creole woman who, like Oscar Chopin's father, believes that 'anything not French had ... little right to existence' (*CW*, 282), has broken off relations with her only son for marrying an 'American' girl and living outside the French Quarter of New Orleans. When a little girl becomes ill at her grandson's birthday party, however, her maternal instincts are awakened and she goes to see her son, whereupon she discovers that the little girl is her own grandchild. 'Mamouche' is a sequel to 'The Lilies'. In 'The Lilies', the 'little vagabond Mamouche' appears only at the beginning of the story to perform the prank of letting down fence rails to allow the Widow Angle's calf to eat Mr Billy's cotton crop. When Mamouche reappears in the story that bears his name, he becomes the agent by which the reclusive Doctor John-Luis decides that he needs human companionship. Although the story involves the rehabilitation of the 'little vagabond,' Chopin is at least as interested in John-Luis, who had known Mamouche's grandfather and, it is suggested, was in love with his grandmother. Three of the stories in *A Night in Acadie* had appeared in *Vogue*, and three each in *Atlantic* and *Century*; none of the stories had been published in St. Louis periodicals, although three had appeared in the New Orleans *Times Democrat*.

The titles of the two collections suggest differences as well, 'bayou folk' conveying a sense of the picturesque and different, and 'night in Acadie' promising more sophisticated pleasures. Chopin biographer Emily Toth suggests that the name 'Acadie' was selected as a deliberate echo of the title of James Lane Allen's *Summer in Arcady*, a novel first serialized under the title *Butterflies* in *Cosmopolitan* between December 1895 and March 1896 and published in somewhat revised form by Macmillan in 1896. Allen's novel pushed at the limits of propriety, describing the sexual attraction of a young man and woman during a hot summer in Kentucky. Although the consummation of their relationship does not take place until after they are married, in one scene the act is averted only by the intrusion of an angry bull. In language as well as in plot, Allen's novel was daring for its time, with such descriptions as 'laughing round-breasted girls', and the natural world is presented as conspiring with human desires: 'lashing everything—grass, fruit, insects, cattle, human creatures—more fiercely onward to the fulfillment of her ends'. Critical reaction to *Summer in Arcady* was predictable. *The Sewanee Review* wanted a story of a 'purer love' than that which Allen had presented, and even the more liberal *Vogue* called the book 'unclean'. Yet Allen remained a popular novelist, better able, as a man, to weather such criticism, and Chopin and her publisher may have wished to take advantage of that popularity (Toth, 297–8).

The title story of Chopin's second collection—the only story not previously published—is not nearly as daring as Allen's *Summer in Arcady*. A mere plot summary, in fact, reveals elements of melodrama. Twenty-eight-year-old Telèsphore, with time on his hands and seeking a respite from trying to decide which of the neighboring young women to marry, takes the train from his plantation near Natchitoches to Marksville, a small town in central Louisiana. On the train he meets Zaida, who invites him to go to a dance that night. When, shortly after midnight, Zaida abruptly leaves the dance, Telèsphore discovers why she is dressed in white: she intends to meet her fiancé at the home of a justice of the peace and marry him over her family's objections. When the fiancé arrives drunk, Zaida's illusions about him are shattered, the two men fight, and the victorious Telèsphore drives Zaida away in her buggy, so infatuated that 'for the first time in his life, [he] did not care what time it was' (*CW*, 499). But despite the melodramatic elements of the chance meeting, the lovers' planned tryst, and the gallant Telèsphore besting the scoundrel, Chopin resists the closure of the melodramatic plot: the story ends with the couple riding slowly through the woods, making no plans for the future. One of Chopin's main concerns in 'A Night in Acadie' is depicting the rebelliousness of her two central characters. Zaida's is the more conventional rebellion, declaring her parents 'perfec' mules' (*CW*, 494) for believing the rumors that her fiancé drinks, and prepared to marry him against their will. Telèsphore's rebellion is less orthodox, and verges on the comic. Named for an uncle to whom his family has been fond of comparing him, Telèsphore has determined to be his own person: 'His whole conduct of life had been planned on lines in direct contradistinction to those of his uncle Telèsphore', and the result has made him a successful young man. Because his uncle was illiterate, Telèsphore has learned to read and write; his uncle preferred hunting and fishing to work, and so young Telèsphore devotes himself to farming. 'In short, Telèsphore, by advisedly shaping his course in direct opposition to that of his uncle, managed to lead a rather orderly, industrious, and respectable existence' (*CW*, 485).

Many of the stories in *A Night in Acadie* deal with personal transformations, some of them as self-willed as that of Télèsphore, but most occurring because of external agency. The title characters in 'Polydore' and 'Mamouche', both young boys, learn to give up bad behavior, and the reclusive Mr Billy, in 'Lilies', gains a sense of the value of human contact after Marie Louise impulsively brings him an armful of lilies to make up for her calf's destruction of his cotton crop. While such stories, like the title story, have a touch of whimsy, Chopin seems to devote the most love and sympathy to her female characters who undergo transformative experiences, such as Madame Carambeau's decision to become reunited with her son in 'A Matter of Prejudice'. Two very different stories depict the complexities of the marital relationship and explore women's emotions regarding it; for different reasons, these stories were potentially the most controversial ones in the collection. The title character in 'Athénaïse', which had been published in the *Atlantic* in August and September of 1896, married for only a short time to the much older successful planter Cazeau, leaves him to return to her parents' house, not because of any mistreatment or discord—indeed, Cazeau loves her tenderly—but because she finds marriage itself oppressive: 'I can't stan' to live with a man; to have him always there; his coats an' pantaloons hanging in my room; his ugly bare feet—washing them in my tub, befo' my very eyes, ugh!' (*CW*, 431). When her parents cannot convince Athénaïse to return to her husband, her brother spirits her away to a boarding house in New Orleans, where she vaguely plans to become self-supporting, and where she is befriended by a journalist, Gouvernail, who becomes infatuated with her. Athénaïse pays scant attention to Gouvernail or to much of anything else until she discovers that she is pregnant, whereupon she returns happily to Cazeau, and 'her lips for the first time respond to the passion of his own' (*CW*, 454). Gouvernail reappears in 'A Respectable Woman', which had appeared in *Vogue* in February of 1894, as a houseguest of Mrs Baroda and her husband. Imagining that her husband's friend will be 'tall, slim, cynical; with eyeglasses, and his hands in his pockets' (*CW*, 333), Mrs Baroda is prepared to dislike him, but as they talk one evening, she is drawn to him quite sensually:

> She wanted to reach out her hand in the darkness and touch him with the sensitive tips of her fingers upon the face or the lips. She wanted to draw close to him and whisper against his cheek—she did not care what—as she might have done if she had not been a respectable woman.
>
> (*CW*, 335)

Instead of giving in to her passionate impulse, Mrs Baroda goes to visit her aunt for the duration of Gouvernail's visit, but some months later she suggests to her husband that he come to visit again; the story concludes with her suggestive remark, 'This time I shall be very nice to him' (CW, 336).

In 'Athénaïse', Chopin makes a brief, ironic comment on regional literature and its readers. When Gouvernail is looking through his books for something that Athénaïse would enjoy reading, he suspects correctly that she has no 'literary tastes', and rejects philosophy, poetry, and novels before deciding to loan her a magazine. She later reports that 'it had entertained her passably', although 'a New England story had puzzled her ... and a Creole tale had offended her' (CW, 446). Chopin does not specify what 'puzzles' and 'offends' Athénaïse, but she seems to suggest that portrayals of life in distant regions might indeed present 'alien' people and customs, while depictions of ways of life with which a reader was familiar—as Creole culture would have been to Athénaïse—could offend through inaccuracy or condescension. After nearly ten years of writing and of testing the literary marketplace, Chopin had arrived at a balance between the 'picturesque' elements that editors demanded of regional writers, and ways of presenting the themes of human desire and self-fulfillment that interested her. While a few of the stories in A Night in Acadie are dependent upon the specific settings of central and southern Louisiana, most, without the place names and speech patterns, could take place anywhere. The very brief story 'Ripe Figs' is one of the former; Maman-Nainaine times family visits according to seasonal signals such as the ripening of the figs and the blooming of chrysanthemums. The story 'Regret', in contrast, could easily be transplanted to New England. The self-sufficient Aurélie had 'promptly declined' the proposal of marriage she received at the age of 20, and 'at the age of fifty she had not yet lived to regret it' (CW, 375). But when a neighbor must leave on a family emergency and asks Aurélie to care for her four small children, they quickly become an important part of her life, and after the children's mother comes to collect them, 'she cried like a man, with sobs that seemed to tear her very soul' (CW, 378).

As had been the case with Bayou Folk, however, reviewers of A Night in Acadie tended to evaluate Chopin's stories on the basis of their regional qualities rather than their thematic messages. The reviewer for the St Louis Post-Dispatch stressed Chopin's knowledge of 'the black race', 'the pure Congo African', and singled out for praise the story 'Tante Cat'rinette', which deals with a black woman's gratitude toward the white owner who had freed her (Toth, 303). Alexander DeMenil, reviewing the book in The Hyperion, which he had founded in 1894, was even more élitist, speaking of all of Chopin's Louisiana characters when he praised Chopin's depiction of 'a race and a life which are as innocent of the refinements and knowledge of higher civilization as it is possible for an exclusive, strongly opinionated, and self-isolated people clinging to the forms and traditions of a past civilization ... to be' (Toth, 305). The reviewer for the *Nation* pegged Chopin firmly as a regional writer, writing that 'her stories are to the bayous of Louisiana what Mary Wilkins's are to New England, ... in seizing the heart of her people and showing the traits that come from their surroundings' (Toth, 299). Chopin was also compared—favorably—to Joel Chandler Harris and George Washington Harris. In short, with the publication of her second volume of short stories, Chopin was critically ensconced as a major regional writer, a position which had both positive and negative effects on her career and her subsequent literary reputation.

While the reviews of *A Night in Acadie* were largely favorable, there were quibbles. The reviewer for *The Critic* noted that 'Athénaïse' was 'marred by one or two slight and unnecessary coarsenesses'. While this reviewer was not specific about what elements of the story were 'coarse', there are some obvious candidates for such an accusation: Gouvernail's undisguised attraction to the married Athénaïse, the clear references to her pregnancy (although the word is never used), and the passion of the embrace that closes the story. The St. Louis *Republic* wanted some of Chopin's stories to have more conclusive endings. The ending of the title story would have been more 'satisfactory' if the justice of the peace had arrived to join Telèsphore and Zaïda in marriage (Toth, 301)—the melodramatic 'marriage plot' ending that Chopin deliberately resists in the story. The reviewer for the St Louis *Globe-Democrat*, like others, concentrated primarily on Chopin's black characters and children, paying scant attention to the adult dramas in the stories. One of the risks of writing fiction that was immediately categorized in a sub-genre such as local color, as Chopin knew well by this point, was that reviewers brought to it a set of expectations against which to measure the work; as Chopin increasingly worked against the conventions of the genre, her friend Bill Reedy was one of the few who understood, as he wrote in the *Mirror*, that Chopin was dealing with 'human nature that is old as mankind and as puzzling and new to-day as when the first murderous instinct awoke to life in the heart of Cain or the first grand passion of love entered Eden' (Toth, 301).

By the time the reviews of *A Night in Acadie* appeared, Chopin had begun to work on *The Awakening*, and was thinking about a publisher for her third collection of stories, to be titled *A Vocation and a Voice*. Although she continued to wish for greater national visibility—she may briefly have considered a reading tour such as the one that had brought Ruth McEnery Stuart to St Louis—there was comfort in being a local literary celebrity. Almost all of the St Louis reviews of her second collection of stories, whatever their evaluation of the work, drew proud attention to the fact that Chopin was a resident of the city. Her satiric sketches of parts of St Louis society in *At Fault* and her attack on hypocritical do-gooders in 'Miss McEnders' had angered some, and others had been at least slightly offended by what they perceived as 'coarseness' or 'indelicacy' in some of her stories, but no one could deny that Chopin was a widely known and respected writer. When, in mid-February of 1898, Chopin was invited to read two of the stories in *A Night in Acadie* to the St Louis Chart Club, the tribute to her by the club's president, reported in the *Post-Dispatch*, evidenced great pride at the same time that it offered a narrowly circumscribed view of her contribution to American literature:

> We are proud of the fact that a sister St. Louisan has made such valuable contributions to literature. The portrayal of characters, habits and manner in the Gulf States, with their phrases of French and Spanish creole, negro and Indian, is a marked feature of nineteenth century literature. Writers on these subjects have drawn on a deep mine of poetry and romance, and will give the next generation correct ideas of an institution and regime that has passed away. In the front ranks of the dialect writers stands Mrs. Kate Chopin.
>
> (Toth, 308)

In the view of the Chart Club president, Chopin's role as a writer was to chronicle a nearly bygone era, preserving its folkways for future generations; categorized as a 'dialect writer', her art is confined to the mimetic. But if such assessments continued to overlook the adult passions and the thematic emphasis on self-fulfillment in Chopin's fiction, she had already, by February of 1898, finished the manuscript of the novel that would challenge any reductive critique of her work.

NOTES

1. Susan V. Donaldson, *Competing Voices: The American Novel, 1865–1914.* New York: Twayne, 1998. Subsequent references will be page numbers in the text.
2. Theodore Peterson, *Magazines in the Twentieth Century.* Urbana: University of Illinois Press, 1964, p. 64.

MAUREEN ANDERSON

Unraveling the Southern Pastoral Tradition: A New Look at Kate Chopin's At Fault

Nine years before Kate Chopin unveiled *The Awakening* (1899), she self-published her first novel, *At Fault*. The novel, considered by critics as a worthy piece of fiction, established Chopin as a new and talented writer. The story of a widow running a plantation in the Natchitoches Parish of Louisiana, *At Fault* reflects Chopin's own life. After two years of widowhood and successfully running her husband's business, Chopin left the Natchitoches Parish for St. Louis in mid-1884, partly because of her involvement with Albert Sampite, a married man.[1] After a year in St. Louis and shortly after her mother's death, Chopin began writing for publication.[2] Like Thérèse in *At Fault*, Chopin faced a decision between love and traditional ethics in her relationship with Sampite. Because Sampite was a southern Catholic, he could not divorce. In Louisiana when a couple did divorce, civil law prohibited either partner from marrying a lover. Consequently, Chopin had reason to question what she called an old southern "code of righteousness" that prevented her as well as her female protagonist in *At Fault* from happiness.

At Fault (1890) exhibits the same genius and skill characteristic of all Kate Chopin's writing. Yet, despite the revitalization of interest in Chopin's works during the twentieth century, Chopin's first novel has been, for the most part, forgotten in academic study. Still, *At Fault* is no exception to Chopin's authorial skill through which she elegantly addresses society's flaws. Since

From *Southern Literary Journal* Vol. 34, No. 1 (2001), pp. 1–13. © 2001 by the University of North Carolina Press.

the plot of *At Fault* appears on the surface to be contrived or stereotypical, some scholars have dismissed the novel as a weak attempt by Chopin to gain recognition as a new writer. What is not immediately apparent in *At Fault* is Chopin's careful manipulation of nineteenth-century southern pastoral conventions in the novel to address flaws in southern society.

Southern pastoral, a genre addressing southern political issues, was popular during Reconstruction. Educated and well read, Chopin would have been familiar with the southern pastoral literary conventions of her time. Sidney Lanier, Thomas Nelson Page, and Joel Chandler Harris had all published southern pastoral fiction by the time Chopin completed *At Fault*. And like writers before her, Chopin provides enough information in *At Fault* for her reader to determine that the novel is southern pastoral. Like a traditional southern pastoral, *At Fault* opens with the rural and secluded setting of Place du Bois that contrasts to an urban world encroaching from the outside. Even in the opening chapters when Thérèse first assumes her husband's role, change is implied at Place du Bois. For instance, a new railroad "squats" at the edge of the plantation (5). Moreover, the southern pastoral setting is altered throughout the novel until the setting is no longer traditionally pastoral.

Like the setting, characters in *At Fault* are also shaped in a pastoral mold. Yet the pastoral gender roles in *At Fault*, such as the pastoral love interest of the master of the plantation, invert when the female protagonist assumes the traditionally male pastoral role. Jane Hotchkiss, in her "Confusing the Issue: Who's 'At Fault'," suggests the possibility of gender reversal in *At Fault* by applying Carol Gilligan's study of gender-based ethics to Chopin's characters. According to Hotchkiss, the male ethical character follows what Chopin described as a "code of righteousness" of what is right and wrong to "deal out judgements," while the female ethical character observes the individual circumstances of each moral dilemma before making a conscientious decision (34). Hotchkiss asserts that Thérèse embodies a male ethical character while Hosmer personifies a female ethical character (34). What Hotchkiss does not consider is how her assertions are related to Chopin's use of pastoral conventions. While Chopin associates male ethics with an old pastoral ideal, she relates female ethics to a contemporary or urban ideal in *At Fault*. By inverting the pastoral gender roles, Chopin emphasizes how old pastoral roles cannot function in a changing South.

The changes that occur within the novel are most evident in the character of Thérèse, as the master of the plantation. In the first sentence of *At Fault*, Thérèse assumes Jérôme Lafirme's role of the patriarch: "When Jérôme Lafirme died, his neighbors awaited the results of his sudden taking off with indolent watchfulness. It was a matter of unusual interest to them that a plantation of four thousand acres had been left unincumbered to the disposal of a handsome, inconsolable, childless Creole widow of thirty" (3). The *"bêtise"* her neighbors expect never occurs. Instead, the widow "successfully follows the methods of her departed husband" (3). Yet as soon as Thérèse successfully transforms from the feminine role to the masculine role, other pastoral conventions at Place du Bois reflect that inversion. Influences from outside of Place du Bois perpetuate change in the setting and its characters after Thérèse assumes her husband's position. Both the railroad and the timber industry enter Place Du Bois after Thérèse becomes master. While the typical southern pastoral asserts that changes to a traditional way of life are both negative and undesirable, in *At Fault*, changes are progressive and beneficial. *At Fault* is the story of what happens to the old southern pastoral when the traditional setting changes, when pastoral character roles are reversed, and when the old southern pastoral model is unraveled. Unlike traditional pastoral that is reflective of an old culture, *At Fault* is about change. *At Fault* deconstructs the conventional southern pastoral, revealing a progressive South of industry and social equality.

The society depicted in southern pastoral is an archetype with which Chopin declaims the archaisms of an Old South. The pastoral landscape in *At Fault* is fertile, pure, and removed from urban society, portraying a free and unhurried lifestyle that contrasts to the outside urban society that is confined, structured, and fast-paced. Lucinda MacKethan states in *The Dream of Arcady* that southern pastoral writers idealized and preserved in literature class distinctions, contempt for material values, freedom of a slow and leisurely rural environment, and an austere code of honor of an Old South (37). However, by preserving an Old South in literature, writers also preserved the inequalities, particularly strict racial and gender roles, represented in an idealized Old South. Chopin may use southern pastoral conventions, but she is not interested in preserving or in justifying the pre–Civil War ideal. *At Fault* is set during Reconstruction, not in an ideal past. And although Place du Bois is rural and removed from urban society, Chopin's pastoral landscape benefits from urban encroachments. By placing *At Fault* during Reconstruction, Chopin does not directly address or justify race issues. Rather, the slave-like characters in *At Fault* are retired plantation workers, representative of an outdated way of life.

The novel begins by establishing Place du Bois as a pastoral setting that seems safely removed from the outside world:

The short length of this Louisiana plantation stretched along Cane River, meeting the water when that stream was at its highest, with a thick growth of cotton-wood trees; save where a

narrow convenient opening had been cut into their midst, and
where further down the pine hills started in abrupt prominence
from the water and the dead level of the land on either side of
them. (4)

Place du Bois, a rural setting that appears naturally and safely secluded from
the outside world, is separated from the outside world by deep forest and a
river that is often too rough to cross (4). In traditional pastoral, the gentleness
of springtime emphasizes the easy and ideal life of a golden age. By scanning
the setting, Chopin establishes the pastoral springtime atmosphere of Place
du Bois: "The negro quarters were scattered at wide intervals over the land,
breaking with picturesque irregularity into systematic division of field to
field; and in the early springtime gleaming in their new coat of whitewash
against the tender green of the cotton and corn" (5). The fertileness of Place
du Bois, "rich in its exhaustless powers of reproduction," reflects a golden
age of easy life with its abundant yields of vegetation and "bursting cotton"
(5, 52). Within the setting, nature provides for its inhabitants. For example,
Hosmer stops to let his horse drink "at the side of the hill where the sparkling
spring water came trickling from the moist rocks, and emptied into the long
out-scooped trunk of a cypress, that served as a trough" (31). The leisurely
lifestyle of the pastoral's inhabitants in a traditional pastoral is also reflected
upon in *At Fault*. Thérèse observes that "beneath the spreading shade of an
umbrella-China tree, lay burly Hector, but half awake" while "Betsy, a piece
of youthful ebony in blue cottonade was crossing leisurely on her way to the
poultry yard" (6). Casual and dreamy, the landscape of Place du Bois appears
to be the ideal pastoral landscape.

Shortly after establishing that Place du Bois is a pastoral setting, Chopin
details the changes to the plantation since the death of Jérôme Lafirme. As
Thérèse leisurely surveys her land, her eye scans to the far edge of her land
where "squatted a brown and ugly intruder within her fair domain," a new
railroad (6). As a symbol of movement and progress, the railroad at this
point in the novel is an "ugly intruder" to the tranquil setting. By describing
the railroad as "ugly" and the pastoral setting as "fair," Chopin implies the
traditional rural-beautiful/urban-ugly contrast (6). Changes after Lafirme's
death are of "questionable benefit" and part of what drives "Thérèse to seek
another domicile," abandoning her former homestead for a more secluded
location. At the end of the first chapter, Chopin foreshadows future changes
to the pastoral setting when Thérèse enters the woods and "bades a tearful
farewell to the silence" (8). The setting evolves even though Place du Bois is
at first established as a traditional plantation.

As the novel continues, outside influences continue to affect the traditional pastoral setting. The two distinct barriers, the forest and the river, keep Place du Bois safe from the outside world. Yet as the novel progresses, these barriers erode. The first chapter concludes when an outsider introduces the timber industry to Place du Bois. Thérèse knows that Hosmer is "no Southerner" when he offers her the "privilege of cutting timber from her land for a given number of years" (8). According to Karen Cole, even though southern literature seized an idealized version of a pre–Civil War plantation, "the rawer landscape of the Great Pine Woods" stretching from the Mississippi region into Texas was "not particularly well suited for agriculture" (65). Cole continues, adding that "northern interests in timber bolstered a depressed, postwar southern economy" and that the pre–Civil War plantation was an oasis carved out of the woods by the hardship and toil of slavery (66, 67). Slave labor constructed the plantations of the Old South, separating the land from the outside world by woods. Whereas slaves construct boundaries in typical southern pastoral, in *At Fault* workers at the timber industry erode the pine boundaries.

The pines and other species of trees at Place du Bois are significant as representations of old and new ways of life. For instance, Hosmer and Thérèse embrace beneath a live oak tree. As a literary symbol, the oak is associated with strength and longevity. The oak cannot flourish within the confines of the dark pine forest because it needs open, well-lit spaces. In *At Fault*, these spaces exist only on the plantation. Because the oak tree grows specifically at the plantation, not in the pine forest, the oak is also associated with family and home. By diminishing the pine barrier, the timber industry enables the outside to influence the traditional homestead. Plantation outsiders who accompany the new timber industry influence Thérèse and other inhabitants at the plantation. As a result, inhabitants at the plantation can no longer maintain their former way of life by secluding themselves from an outside world. When an oak appears at the novel's conclusion, it signifies that a new homestead has been established.

In contrast to the oak, the "great rose tree" beside the cabin of Thérèse's old nurse, Marie-Louise, symbolizes the old Catholic ways of the plantation and blooms because "of a blessing from Père Antoine," the parish priest (70). According to Cole, because Marie Louise is Thérèse's old nurse and Marie Louise's cabin is surrounded by Catholic symbolism, the cabin is a refuge for old world attributes and is set deep in the pine woods: "Marie Louise represents both the refinements and responsibilities of the old order. She offers good coffee, eau sedative, and the link to Catholicism that reminds Thérèse of why she had meddled in David Hosmer's marriage" (70). Marie

Louise's cabin with its blooming rose tree, a symbol of an old world, is surrounded and protected by the pines.

Representative of an old way of life, the pine woods of Place du Bois harbor many old southern symbols. Ole MacFarlane's grave is nestled in the pine woods, and according to Grégoire, Thérèse's nephew, "folks 'round yere says he walks about o' nights; can't res' in his grave fur the niggas he's killed" (19). Plantation inhabitants also "say he's the person that Mrs. Wa'at's her name wrote about in *Uncle Tom's Cabin*" (19). The past literally haunts the present at Place du Bois. However, when Melicent, Hosmer's sister, is introduced to the legend of ole MacFarlane, her reason shatters the old superstition and the legend dies. Melicent informs Grégoire upon visiting the grave that she does not believe in ghosts or hell. Melicent reflects the reason of an outside world, which contrasts to the superstition of the old plantation. Outside influences exorcise Place du Bois of its old world ghosts.

A river also borders Place Du Bois. As a symbol of movement and change at Place du Bois, the river continually erodes its banks. The river is a consistent "worry to Thérèse, for when the water [is] high and rapid, the banks cave constantly, carrying away great sections from the land" (109). Place du Bois' own natural border hastens progress as it erodes parts of the plantation. Marie Louise's cabin, while nestled in the pine woods, sits perilously close to the river's banks even though her cabin has been moved previously "away back in Dumont's field" (113). When Thérèse suggests that the cabin be moved again, Marie Louise insists that she "will move no more; she's too old" (113). Chopin foreshadows the cabin's destruction when Marie Louise calls on the god from her old Catholic religion of the plantation to protect her, replying that "if the good God does not want to take care of me, then it's time for me to go" (113). Marie Louise explains to Thérèse that she must be safe because Père Antoine, the local priest, has blessed her cabin: "I called him in, and he blessed the whole house inside and out, with holy water—notice how the roses have bloomed since then—and he gave me medals of the holy Virgin to hang about" (113). As important representations of an Old South, Marie Louise and her cabin are fated victims to the ongoing transformation of the plantation. Chopin provides the character of Marie Louise with little depth beyond the stereotypical mammy character so that when the old nurse is washed into the river, the reader feels little sympathy for the character. Instead, because of the Catholic symbolism that surrounds the cabin and Marie Louise, when the cabin washes into the river, the sacrament of baptism is implied. Baptism, the Christian sacrament of cleansing and rebirth, washes away the influences of a past world when the river overwhelms Marie Louise's cabin. The river, as a symbol of motion and change, cleanses Place du Bois of its Old South symbols.

Without its natural barriers, additional change influences Place Du Bois. By the novel's conclusion, Place du Bois is no longer a traditional southern pastoral setting. As though it had undergone a hard winter, the plantation emerges at the height of spring: "the air was filled with the spring and all its promises" (201). Influences from the outside have turned Hosmer's timber industry into a thriving business. Financiers to Hosmer's business freely enter Place du Bois and examine the pine woods. Hosmer explains, "they didn't leave a stick of timber unscrutinized"; moreover, as the financiers look at Place du Bois, they are "like ferrets into every cranny" as though the men examine every recess of the plantation to discover any remaining old world symbolism still hidden in the pine woods (209). Consequently, Place du Bois is no longer the traditional pastoral setting, free from industry and outside influence.

Characters at Place Du Bois are also influenced by change. Thérèse's character, as Place du Bois' pastoral master, best emphasizes those transitions. Introduced as the "Mistress of Place du Bois," Thérèse is portrayed as an ideal, albeit feminine, pastoral model of a master. As a pastoral master of the plantation, Thérèse is also a stronghold against outside forces at Place du Bois. Like the traditional pastoral shepherd who protects his sheep, in the southern pastoral, the master protects his plantation. The first chapter of the novel relates how Thérèse fulfills the pastoral role when Hiram informs her that "things is a goin' wrong" (4). After receiving the knowledge of things "goin' wrong," Thérèse is roused and moved to action, completely fulfilling her husband's duties: "The wrong doing presented as a tangible abuse and defiance of authority, served to move her to action" (4).

Thérèse's awakening to her role as master is where the novel begins. As the master of the plantation, Thérèse "bristles with objections" to future change and "in building, she avoids the temptations offered by modern architectural innovations" (5). Thérèse also fears "a visionary troop of evils coming in the wake of the railroad, which, in her eyes no conceivable benefits could mitigate" (5). Furthermore, Thérèse "dreads an endless procession of intruders forcing themselves upon her privacy" (5). At the opening of *At Fault*, Thérèse is as secluded from the outside world as Place du Bois is.

Thérèse is no longer secluded when Hosmer and other outsiders arrive at Place du Bois. Each visitor brings to Place du Bois a different ethical code from the outside world that is different from the traditional moral code that Thérèse ascribes to. According to Hotchkiss, Melicent brings to Place du Bois "moral precepts" that are "mere platitudes" (37). Melicent "delivers the time worn aphorisms with the air and tone of a pretty sage, giving utterance to an inspired truth" (55). Fanny, on the other hand, brings with her a lack of conscience, exhibited by her alcoholism. After Fanny steals a flask of whiskey

from Morico, Morico blames his son Joçint. Instead of confessing, Fanny
turns away asking Grégoire, "Is it just this same old thing year in and year out,
Grégoire? Don't any one ever get up a dance, or a card party or anything?"
(120). Fanny's lack of morals is contrary to a sunken and stereotypical deserted
wife. Instead, when Hosmer returns to St. Louis for his wife, he finds that she
has coped rather well after the divorce. Hosmer discovers the home he had
formerly shared with his ex-wife "much changed" with new rugs, wallpaper,
and wall hangings (60). However, alcoholism and lack of conscience in
Fanny's character evoke little sympathy from Chopin's readers, making Fanny
a shallow character and easily expendable at the novel's conclusion. Ethical
decisions outside of Place du Bois are not hampered by outdated rules from
a lost past, so the solution to Hosmer's ethical dilemma seems simple. Mrs.
Dawson, from outside of Place du Bois, states the obviousness of Hosmer's
situation: "I thought he had more sense than to tie himself to that little gump
again, after he'd had the luck to get rid of her" (81). By the end of the novel,
Thérèse is no longer as secluded as she once was; Thérèse has traveled to
Paris, rides a train, and wears stylish Parisian clothing.

In addition to protecting Place du Bois from change as the novel
opens, Thérèse, as a male ethical character, protects the old southern "code
of righteousness" (119). Thérèse "was little given to the consideration of
abstract ideas" (40). When an early reviewer of *At Fault* claimed Fanny,
Hosmer's wife, was the character who was "at fault," Chopin replied to the
criticism in the 18 December 1890 issue of the *Natchitoches Enterprise*, in an
effort to clear the reader's misconception. According to Chopin, Thérèse was
to blame because of her old world ethics:

> Thérèse Lafirme, the heroine of the book is the one who was
> at fault—remotely, and immediately. Remotely—in her blind
> acceptance of an undistinguishing, therefore unintelligent code
> of righteousness by which to deal out judgements. Immediately—
> in this, that unknowing the individual needs of this man or this
> woman, she should yet constitute herself not only as mentor, but
> an instrument in reuniting them. (qtd in Toth 194)

Thérèse's masculine and old southern ethics shape her character into an
ideal plantation master of the traditional southern pastoral and emphasize
the control she has over, and the responsibility she takes for, those at her
plantation. According to the love-blinded Hosmer, "Thérèse was love's
prophet" while Melicent declares that "she's positively a queen" (Chopin 61,
34). After Fanny has a difficult time riding Torpedo, a slow and stubborn
horse, Thérèse says, "I can't forgive myself for such a blunder" (122). Thérèse

also advises Grégoire, "I hope that your heart is not too deep in this folly," when she discovers his hopeless obsession with Melicent (100). Morico, the elderly father of Joçint and a retired plantation worker, is given special care by Thérèse when she supplies him with chickens and eggs. Yet the most explicit display of Thérèse's control in *At Fault* is when she insists that Hosmer is a coward for divorcing his wife and should repair the relationship immediately: "'You left her then as practically without moral support as you have certainly done now, in deserting her. It was the act of a coward.' Thérèse spoke these last words with intensity" (47). Hosmer asks her what he should do, and Thérèse replies, "I would have you do what is right" (48). Apparently, what is "right" for Hosmer according to Thérèse's old code of ethics is to "face the consequences of his own actions" by repairing relations with his ex-wife, regardless of the outcome (47).

Like the traditional object of the pastoral master's love, in his relationship to Thérèse, Hosmer is submissive: Thérèse moves him "to a blind submission" (48). Transformation and self-denial is also a large part of Hosmer and Thérèse's relationship. Harold Toliver explains in his *Pastoral Forms and Attitudes* that what is expected of the pastoral lover/shepherd character "is a purification of his love through self-denial, and thus his transformation from one level of love to another" (21). The pastoral romance as described by Toliver is similar to what passes between Thérèse and Hosmer. After Chopin establishes Thérèse's male characterization, it is also evident that, like the tortured love that is never acted upon in the traditional pastoral, Thérèse also suffers from love that is never acted upon. Old world ethics and Thérèse's position as a pastoral master prevent her from pursuing a relationship with the divorced David Hosmer. When Thérèse thinks of Hosmer's divorce "with the prejudices of her Catholic education coloring her sentiment, she instinctively [shrinks] when the theme confront[s] her as one having even a remote reference to her own clean existence" (40). Thérèse's character also resembles Toliver's definition of a pastoral lover after Thérèse transforms because of her self-denial. When Thérèse denies herself a relationship with Hosmer, she is forced to see the consequences of her involvement as a pastoral master in Hosmer's affairs. Thérèse arrives at Hosmer's house to see Fanny drunk and incoherent: "Thérèse was so shocked that for awhile she could say nothing" (151). Thérèse is forced to ask herself "with a shudder 'was I right—was I right?'" (158). She also questions her own actions: "When left alone, Thérèse at once relapses into the gloomy train of reflections that has occupied her since the day she had seen with her bodily eyes something of that wretched life that she had brought upon the man she loved" (158). Thérèse changes because she sees the error of her ways; furthermore, as a pastoral lover, Thérèse transforms from one level of love to another.

Like Thérèse, Hosmer also undergoes change. However, unlike Thérèse's transformation, Hosmer's change is both sudden and dramatic. When Fanny is swept into the river with Marie Louise and the cabin, Hosmer dives into the water to save his wife. For the first time in the novel and without Thérèse's advice, Hosmer actively tries to help his wife. When she discovers that Hosmer is divorced, Thérèse claims that Hosmer was "deserting" Fanny by divorcing her. And before Hosmer reunites with Fanny, he tells Thérèse, "What ever I do, must be because you want it" (48). When Hosmer reunites with Fanny, he tells Thérèse, "I didn't do it because I thought it was right, but because you thought it was right" (123). When Hosmer attempts to rescue his wife, it is the first time in the novel that he tries to do what is "right" for Fanny. By following for the first time what he thinks is "right," Hosmer is no longer completely submissive to Thérèse. Chopin implies that Hosmer has been changed by the experience when Thérèse, finding him on the train a year later is "aware of some change in him which she had not the opportunity to define; but this firmness and fullness of the hand was part of it" (205). Thérèse "looks up into his face then, to find the same change there, together with a new content" (205).

As *At Fault* concludes, Chopin surrounds her characters with implications of change. The novel both begins and ends during spring. However, there is also the gap of exactly a year between when Thérèse and Hosmer first meet in the first chapter and the following chapter, as well as between Fanny's death and Hosmer and Thérèse's reunion. Four springs occur over the course of the novel: when the novel opens, when Hosmer and Thérèse realize their feelings, when Fanny's dies, and finally when Hosmer and Thérèse reunite. Most of the story takes place during the second year in which Chopin details the passing of seasons and the relationships among Hosmer, Thérèse, and Fanny. During this time, the parlor within the house signifies the season change: "this was a room kept for most part closed during the summer days" (41). When Thérèse secludes herself within the parlor, the reader knows that it is summer. However, when the parlor has a fire blazing, the open room and the fire imply that it is winter.

At the conclusion of the novel, Place du Bois is experiencing springtime: "the air was filled with the spring and all its promises" (201). After establishing a gap of time and the springtime atmosphere, Chopin reunites Thérèse and Hosmer on the train. The train, a symbol of industry, movement, and progression, is no longer an "ugly intruder," but a vehicle in which Thérèse and Hosmer are reunited (5). The novel concludes as the moon climbs "over the top of that live-oak" beside the house (212). The moon, used in many of Chopin's works as a feminine symbol, such as in *The Awakening*, is significant as the last image of Place du Bois in the novel. Used in *The Awakening* as a symbol of Edna's self-discovery, the climbing moon in *At Fault* suggests Thérèse's achievement in transforming from the pastoral master role into a partner and wife. The fact that the moon climbs over a "live-oak," a symbol of home in *At Fault*, indicates an accomplishment at the plantation itself. The oak promises a future to a new Place du Bois. The plantation successfully transforms from an old pastoral homestead into a contemporary setting. Consequently, the symbols at the conclusion of *At Fault* imply a positive change for the characters at Place du Bois.

With the marriage of Thérèse and Hosmer at the conclusion of *At Fault*, Chopin reinforces and promises a future for the South in the novel. Whereas Chopin utilizes the pastoral convention of marriage, their marriage ensures the demise of an old way of life. In *At Fault*, the marriage promises a future for a new way of life, not for a traditional pastoral lifestyle. The springtime atmosphere combined with Hosmer and Thérèse's parenting-like role to Melicent at the conclusion of the novel implies the possibility of children in their future. By the novel's end, Place du Bois is no longer the pastoral setting it was, for the plantation and its inhabitants are no longer secluded from the outside world.

Melicent's letter emphasizes that communication is open to the outside world from Place du Bois. However, perhaps more important than the letter's arrival, is the letter's content. As the last outside influence to Place du Bois that is mentioned in the novel, the letter details Melicent's future travel and study with her new friend Mrs. Griesmann: "We're going to take that magnificent trip through the West—Yosemite and so forth. It appears the flora of California is especially interesting" (210). Melicent's letter promises future communication and information about places much farther away than the borders of Place du Bois. Because the letter mentions the flora of other regions, the letter also implies the existence of beauty and gardens outside of the traditional pastoral plantation. The letter also emphasizes that Thérèse's resistance to the outside has changed into curiosity. Melicent's letter details information about people in St. Louis. Although Hosmer assures Thérèse that it is "a piece of scandal concerning people you don't know; that wouldn't interest you," Thérèse insists, "but it would interest me" (211). Thérèse has changed from the woman who "bristled with objections" with the appearance of a stranger to someone curious about strangers far removed from Place du Bois. Thérèse has also become adventurous outside of Place du Bois: Thérèse "had sailed from New Orleans for Paris, whither she had passed six months" (203).

Finally, when Hosmer and Thérèse do marry, neither Hosmer nor Thérèse assume the role of a pastoral master of the plantation. Instead, Hosmer and Thérèse create a compromise as to what their roles will be. Unlike traditional pastoral, neither Hosmer nor Thérèse will assume responsibility of the entire plantation as the plantation master. Hosmer asserts that he will not rob Thérèse of her occupation and will "put no bungling hand into" her concerns (209). Instead, the commerce at Place du Bois is separated into two halves. The timber industry run by Hosmer and the traditional cotton industry run by Thérèse coexist side by side at Place du Bois, as do Hosmer and Thérèse's responsibilities. The marriage of Hosmer and Thérèse does not ensure or reinforce a future to the traditional pastoral. Instead, their marriage guarantees the demise of an old order and the future of a new one.

At Fault is perhaps more personal to Chopin's experience than all her later works. Like Thérèse, Chopin underwent the "indolent watchfulness" of her neighbors after assuming her husband's responsibilities (3). Chopin became involved in a relationship that was doomed because of old ethics and rules, as did Thérèse. Unfortunately, Chopin was unable to reach the happy conclusion that Thérèse does in At Fault. Toth asserts that "if Kate Chopin had wanted to marry Albert Sampite, she could never do so, not so long as Loca Sampite was still alive" (174). Yet by writing At Fault, Chopin challenges the old "code of righteousness" that prohibited her from happiness. Chopin exposes the old ideals and morals as obsolete in a new South by manipulating the conventions of southern pastoral. The strict gender roles and the golden age islands carved into the pine landscapes of an Old South are exposed in At Fault as archaic ideals of a dysfunctional age. In At Fault, Chopin successfully deconstructs the pastoral conventions that represent an ideal Old South. In her subsequent works, such as The Awakening (1899) and Bayou Folk (1894), Chopin abandons literary stereotypes and her characters directly and consciously rebel against their roles in society. However, At Fault remains significant as an early novel by Chopin that addresses society's flaws. Chopin was unable to reach the happy ending that Thérèse does in the novel. But by writing At Fault, Chopin was able to accomplish what she was unable to do in real life: expose the ideals of an Old South as outmoded and detrimental in a new South.

NOTES

1. Emily Toth explains that Chopin's involvement with Sampite and her mother's worsening illness were deciding factors in her returning to her mother in St. Louis (172).

2. After her mother's death, and at the suggestion of family friend and obstetrician Dr. Fredrick Kolbenheyer, Chopin began channeling her grief by writing for publication. Chopin had considerable success with her early short stories from the time she wrote her first story for publication in 1888 to when she began At Fault on 5 July 1890 (Toth 178–179).

Works Cited

Chopin, Kate. *At Fault*. Cambridge: Green Street, 1986.

Cole, Karen. "A Message from the Pine Woods of Central Louisiana: The Garden In Northup, Chopin, and Dormon." *Louisiana Literature* 14.1 (Spring 1997): 64–74.

Hotchkiss, Jane. "Confusing the Issue: Who's 'At Fault'?" *Louisiana Literature* 11.1 (Spring 1994): 31–43.

MacKethan, Lucinda Hardwick. *The Dream of Arcady*. Baton Rouge: Louisiana State UP, 1980.

Toliver, Harold. *Pastoral Forms and Attitudes*. Los Angeles: U of California P, 1971.

Toth, Emily. *Kate Chopin: A Life of the Author of "The Awakening."* New York: William Morrow, 1990.

Chronology

1850	Katherine O'Flaherty (Kate Chopin) is born in St. Louis, Missouri on July 12.
1855	Kate Chopin's father, Thomas O'Flaherty, dies in a railroad accident.
1863	Chopin's great-grandmother and teacher, Victoire Verdon Charleville, dies; half-brother, George, a Confederate soldier, dies; banishment of good friend Kitty Garesche and family.
1868	Chopin graduates from the St. Louise Academy of the Sacred Heart.
1870	Chopin marries Oscar Chopin in St. Louis; they honeymoon in Europe, return in the fall, and relocate to New Orleans.
1871	Chopin's first son, Jean, is born on May 22 in New Orleans.
1873	Chopin's second son, Oscar Jr., is born in St. Louis; Chopin's brother dies.
1874	Chopin's third son, George, is born in St. Louis.
1876	Chopin's fourth son, Frederick, is born in St. Louis.
1878	Chopin's fifth son, Felix, is born in New Orleans.
1879	Chopin's only daughter, Lelia, is born in New Orleans. Husband Oscar's business collapses and the family relocates to Cloutierville, Louisianna.

1882	Husband Oscar dies in December; romantic relationship with Albert Sampite begins.
1884	Chopin moves back to her family in St. Louis.
1885	Chopin's mother dies.
1889	On October 27, Chopin's first published story, "A Point at Issue" is printed in the *St. Louis Post-Dispatch*.
1890	In September, Chopin publishes at her own expense her first novel, *At Fault*. She also writes her second novel, "Young Dr. Gosse," which she later destroys after multiple rejections. In March, *Bayou Folk*, her first volume of short stories is published.
1897	Her second volume of short stories, *A Night in Acadie*, is published.
1898	In July, she writes, "The Storm."
1899	In April, Chopin publishes *The Awakening*. Critics call both Chopin and her work immoral. As a result, Chopin stops writing and publishing.
1904	In August, Chopin dies of a cerebral haemorrhage after spending the day at the World's Fair.

Contributors

HAROLD BLOOM is Sterling Professor of the Humanities at Yale University. He is the author of 30 books, including *Shelley's Mythmaking*; *The Visionary Company*; *Blake's Apocalypse*; *Yeats*; *A Map of Misreading*; *Kabbalah and Criticism*; *Agon: Toward a Theory of Revisionism*; *The American Religion*; *The Western Canon*; and *Omens of Millennium: The Gnosis of Angels, Dreams, and Resurrection*. *The Anxiety of Influence* sets forth Professor Bloom's provocative theory of the literary relationships between the great writers and their predecessors. His most recent books include *Shakespeare: The Invention of the Human*, a 1998 National Book Award finalist; *How to Read and Why*; *Genius: A Mosaic of One Hundred Exemplary Creative Minds*; *Hamlet: Poem Unlimited*; *Where Shall Wisdom Be Found?*; and *Jesus and Yahweh: The Names Divine*. In 1999, Professor Bloom received the prestigious American Academy of Arts and Letters Gold Medal for Criticism. He has also received the International Prize of Catalonia, the Alfonso Reyes Prize of Mexico, and the Hans Christian Andersen Bicentennial Prize of Denmark.

ELAINE SHOWALTER is the Avalon Foundation Professor of the Humanities and Professor of English at Princeton University. Her books include *The Female Malady: Women, Madness, and English Culture, 1830–1980*, and *Sexual Anarchy: Gender at Culture at the Fin de Siecle*.

MARY E. PAPKE is Professor of English and Associate Dean of Graduate Studies at the University of Tennessee. She is the author of *Verging on the Abyss: The Social Fiction of Kate Chopin and Edith Wharton*; *Susan Glaspell: A*

Research and Production Sourcebook; and *Twisted from the Ordinary: Essays on American Literary Naturalism*.

ELLEN PEEL is Professor of Comparative and World Literature and English at San Francisco State University. She is the author of *Politics, Persuasion, and Pragmatism: A Rhetoric of Feminist Utopian Fiction* and a number of articles.

BERT BENDER is Professor Emeritus of American Literature at Arizona State University. He authored three books: *Sea-Brothers: The Tradition of American Sea Fiction from Moby-Dick to the Present*; *The Descent of Love: Darwin and the Theory of Sexual Selection in American Fiction, 1871–1926*; and *Evolution and "the Sex Problem": American Narratives during the Eclipse of Darwinism*.

MARTHA FODASKI BLACK was a Professor of English in the special baccalaureate degree honors for adults and in the master's degree programs at Brooklyn College, CUNY. She authored *Shaw and Joyce: The Last Word in Stolentelling* as well as a number of scholarly articles.

KATHLEEN WHEELER is the author of *'Modernist' Women Writers and Narrative Art*; *Sources, Processes and Methods in Coleridge's Biographia Literaria*; and *Romanticism, Pragmatism, and Deconstructionism*. She is a Fellow of Darwin College and University Lecturer at the University of Cambridge.

EMILY TOTH is a Professor of English at Louisiana State University. Her books include *Unveiling Kate Chopin*; *Kate Chopin's Private Papers*; *Ms. Mentor's Impeccable Advice for Women in Academia*; *A Vocation and a Voice: Stories by Kate Chopin*; and *Kate Chopin: A Life of the Author of "The Awakening."*

NANCY A. WALKER was a professor of English and the first director of Women's Studies at Vanderbilt University. Her many books include *Shaping Our Mothers World: American Women's Magazines* and *Kate Chopin: A Literary Life*.

MAUREEN ANDERSON is completing her Ph.D. in Comparative Literature at Illinois State University in Normal, Illinois. Recent publications include a number of entries (Edgar Allan Poe, Mercy Otis Warren, Edith Wharton, et al.) in *The Greenwood Encyclopedia of American Poets and Poetry* and "The White Reception of Jazz in America" in *African American Review* (vol. 38, no.1).

Bibliography

Anderson, Maureen. "Unraveling the Southern Pastoral Tradition: A New Look at Kate Chopin's *At Fault*." *The Southern Literary Journal* 34:1 (Fall 2001), pp. 1–13.

Bartley, William. "Imagining the Future in the Awakening." *College English*, Vol. 62, No. 6. (Jul., 2000), pp. 719–746.

Beer, Janet. *Kate Chopin, Edith Wharton and Charlotte Perkins Gilman: Studies in Short Fiction*. Basingstoke: Palgrave Macmillan, 2005.

———. *Kate Chopin's* The Awakening*: A Sourcebook*. New York: Routledge, 2004.

Bender, Bert. "The Teeth of Desire: *The Awakening* and *The Descent of Man*." *American Literature*, Vol. 63, No. 3. (Sept., 1991), pp. 459–473.

Benfey, Christopher. *Degas in New Orleans: Encounters in the Creole world of Kate Chopin and George Washington Cable*. New York: Knopf, 1997.

Birnbaum, Michele A. ""Alien Hands": Kate Chopin and the Colonization of Race." *American Literature*, Vol. 66, No. 2. (Jun., 1994), pp. 301–323.

Boren, Lynda S. and Sara deSaussure Davis, ed. *Kate Chopin Reconsidered: Beyond the Bayou*. Baton Rouge: Louisiana State University Press, 1992.

Bradley, Patricia L. "The Birth of Tragedy and *The Awakening*: Influences and Intertextualities." *The Southern Literary Journal*, 37:2 (Spring 2005), pp. 40–61.

Corse, Sarah M. and Saundra Davis Westervelt. "Gender and Literary Valorization: 'The Awakening' of a Canonical Novel." *Sociological Perspectives*, Vol. 45, No. 2. (Summer, 2002), pp. 139–161.

DeKoven, Marianne. "Gendered Doubleness and the "Origins" of Modernist Form." *Tulsa Studies in Women's Literature*, Vol. 8, No. 1, Toward a Gendered Modernity. (Spring, 1989), pp. 19–42.

Dyer, Joyce. "Reading *The Awakening* with Toni Morrisson." *The Southern Literary Journal*, 35:1 (Fall 2002), pp. 138–154.

———. The Awakening: *A Novel of Beginnings*. New York: Twayne Publishers, 1993.

Elz, Elizabeth. "*The Awakening* and A Lost Lady: Flying with Broken Wings and Raked Feathers." *The Southern Literary Journal*, 35:2 (Spring 2003), pp. 13–27.

Emmitt, Helen V. ""Drowned in a Willing Sea": Freedom and Drowning in Eliot, Chopin, and Drabble." *Tulsa Studies in Women's Literature*, Vol. 12, No. 2. (Autumn, 1993), pp. 315–332.

Evans, Robert C. *Kate Chopin's Short Fiction: A Critical Companion*. Connecticut: Locust Hill Press, 2001.

Gebhard, Caroline. "The Spinster in the House of American Criticism." *Tulsa Studies in Women's Literature*, Vol. 10, No. 1, Redefining Marginality. (Spring, 1991), pp. 79-91.

Grey, Jennifer B. "The Escape of the "Sea": Ideology and *The Awakening*." *The Southern Literary Journal*, 37:1 (Fall 2004), pp. 53–73.

Higonnet, Margaret. "Suicide: Representations of the Feminine in the Nineteenth Century." *Poetics Today*, Vol. 6, No. 1/2, The Female Body in Western Culture: Semiotic Perspectives. (1985), pp. 103–118.

Hoder-Salmon, Marilyn. *Kate Chopin's* The Awakening: *Screenplay as Interpretation*. Gainesville: University Press of Florida, 1992.

Jones, Anne Goodwyn. *Tomorrow Is Another Day: The Woman Writer in the South, 1859–1936*. Baton Rouge: Louisiana State University Press, 1981.

Kearns, Katherine. "The Nullification of Edna Pontellier." *American Literature*, Vol. 63, No. 1. Mar., 1991), pp. 62–88.

Koloski, Bernard, ed. *Approaches to Teaching Chopin's* The Awakening. New York: The Modern Language Association of America, 1988.

LeBlanc, Elizabeth. "The Metaphorical Lesbian: Edna Pontellier in The Awakening." *Tulsa Studies in Women's Literature*, Vol. 15, No. 2. (Autumn, 1996), pp. 289–307.

Maguire, Roberta S. "Kate Chopin and Anna Julia Cooper: Critiquing Kentucky and the South. *The Southern Literary Journal*, 35:1 (Fall 2002), pp. 123–137.

Martin, Wendy, ed. *New Essays on* The Awakening. Cambridge: Cambridge University Press, 1988.

McHaney, Pearl Amelia. "Women's Voices, Black and White." *The Southern Literary Journal*, 33:1 (Fall 2000): pp. 158–164.

Muirhead, Marion. "Articulation and Artistry: A Conversational Analysis of *The Awakening*." *The Southern Literary Journal*, 33:1 (Fall 2000), pp. 42–54.

Papke, Mary E. *Verging on the Abyss: The Social Fiction of Kate Chopin and Edith Wharton*. New York: Greenwood Press, 1990.

Parvulescu, Anca. "To Die Laughing and to Laugh at Dying: Revisiting *The Awakening*." *New Literary History* 36.3 (2005): 477–495, 498.

Peel, Ellen. "Semiotic Subversion in 'Désirée's Baby'." *American Literature*, Vol. 62, No. 2. (Jun., 1990), pp. 223–237.

Ringe, Donald A. "Romantic Imagery in Kate Chopin's *The Awakening*." *American Literature*, Vol. 43, No. 4. (Jan., 1972), pp. 580–588.

Schweitzer, Ivy. "Maternal Discourse and the Romance of Self-Possession in Kate Chopin's *The Awakening*." *Boundary 2*, Vol. 17, No. 1, *New Americanists: Revisionist Interventions into the Canon*. (Spring, 1990), pp. 158–186.

Seyersted, Per. *Kate Chopin: A Critical Biography*. Baton Rouge: Louisiana State University Press, 1969.

Shaker, Bonnie James. *Coloring Locals: Racial Formation in Kate Chopin's Youth's Companion Stories*. Iowa City, University of Iowa Press, 2003.

Skaggs, Peggy. *Kate Chopin*. Boston: Twayne Publishers, 1985.

Showalter, Elaine. "*The Awakening*: Tradition and the American Female Talent." *Sister's Choice: Tradition and Change in American Women's Writing*. Oxford: Clarendon Press, 1991.

Taylor, Helen. *Gender, race, and region in the writings of Grace King, Ruth McEnery Stuart, and Kate Chopin*. Baton Rouge: Louisiana State University Press, 1989.

Thornton, Lawrence. "The Awakening: A Political Romance." *American Literature*, Vol. 52, No. 1. (Mar., 1980), pp. 50–66.

Toth, Emily. "Kate Chopin on Divine Love and Suicide: Two Rediscovered Articles." *American Literature*, Vol. 63, No. 1. (Mar., 1991), pp. 115–121.

————. *Kate Chopin*. New York: William Morrow and Company, Inc., 1990.

————. *Unveiling Kate Chopin*. Jackson: University Press of Mississippi, 1999.

Walker, Nancy A. *Kate Chopin: A Literary Life*. New York: Palgrave, 2001.

Wheeler, Kathleen. "Kate Chopin: Ironist of Realism." *"Modernist" Women Writers and Narrative Art*. New York: New York University Press, 1994.

Yaeger, Patricia S. ""A Language Which Nobody Understood": Emancipatory Strategies in 'The Awakening'." *NOVEL: A Forum on Fiction*, Vol. 20, No. 3, Twentieth Anniversary Issue: III. (Spring, 1987), pp. 197–219.

Acknowledgments

"Tradition and the Female Talent: *The Awakening* as a Solitary Book" by Elaine Showalter. From *New Essays on* The Awakening, Wendy Martin, ed., pp. 33–57. © 1988 by Cambridge University Press. Reprinted with the permission of Cambridge University Press.

"Kate Chopin's Social Fiction" by Mary E. Papke. From *Verging on the Abyss: The Social Fiction of Kate Chopin and Edith Wharton*, pp. 31–88. Copyright © 1990 by Mary E. Papke. Reproduced with permission of Greenwood Publishing Group, Inc., Westport, CT.

Ellen Peel "Semiotic Subversion in 'Désirée's Baby'" in *American Literature* Vol. 62, No. 2 (June, 1990), pp. 223–237. Copyright © 1990 Duke University Press. All rights reserved. Used by permission of the publisher.

Bert Bender "The Teeth of Desire: *The Awakening* and *The Descent of Man*" in *American Literature* Vol. 63, No. 3 (Sept., 1991), pp. 459–473. Copyright © 1991 Duke University Press. All rights reserved. Used by permission of the publisher.

"The Quintessence of Chopinism" by Marth Fodaski Black. Reprinted by permission of Louisiana State University Press from *Kate Chopin Reconsidered: Beyond the Bayou*, Lynda S. Boren and Sara deSaussure Davis, ed., pp. 95–113. © 1992 by Louisiana State University Press.

"Kate Chopin: Ironist of Realism" by Kathleen Wheeler. From *'Modernist' Women Writers and Narrative Art* by Kathleen Wheeler, pp. 51–76. ©1994 by Kathleen Wheeler. Reprinted by permission.

"A Writer, Her Reviewers, and Her Markets" by Emily Toth. From *Unveiling Kate Chopin* by Emily Toth, pp. 148–173. © 1999 by Emily Toth. Reprinted by permission.

"'Local Color' Literature and *A Nigth in Acadie*" by Nancy A. Walker. From *Kate Chopin: A Literary Life* by Nancy A. Walker, pp. 83–110. © 2001 by the Estate of Nancy A. Walker. Reprinted by permission.

"Unraveling the Southern Pastoral Tradition: A New Look at Kate Chopin's *At Fault*" by Maureen Anderson. From *Southern Literary Journal* Vol. 34, No. 1 (2001), pp. 1–13. © 2001 by the University of North Carolina Press. Reprinted by permission.

Every effort has been made to contact the owners of copyrighted material and secure copyright permission. Articles appearing in this volume generally appear much as they did in their original publication with few or no editorial changes. Those interested in locating the original source will find bibliographic information in the bibliography and acknowledgments sections of this volume.

Index

Characters in literary works are indexed by first name (if any), followed by the name of the work in parentheses

Adèle Ratignolle (*The Awakening*), 22, 97, 130
  beauty, 62–63, 107–109, 115
  childbirth, 4–5, 21, 72, 93, 126
  faultless Madonna, 16–20, 33, 60–61, 67–68, 107–111, 115–116, 132
Adonais (Shelley), 121
"After the Winter" (short story)
  alienation in, 45
  Michel in, 45
Alcée Arobin (*The Awakening*)
  rake, 18, 22, 135
  seduction of Edna, 15, 20, 69–70, 97–99, 110–111, 114, 116, 127–128, 130
Alcott, Louisa May
  Diana and Persis, 12
  Moods, 19
"Alexandre's Wonderful Experience" (short story), 160
Alienation and solitude themes, 44
  in "After the Winter," 45
  in *The Awakening*, 21, 29–30, 53, 58, 63, 68, 71, 73, 96, 111
  in "Beyond the Bayou," 45

  in "Emancipation: A Life Fable," 29–30
  in "The Story of an Hour," 51–53
Allen, Grant
  The Woman Who Did, 13
Allen, James Lane
  A Kentucky Cardinal, 171
  Summer in Arcady, 185–186
American
  female literary tradition, 8–16, 18–19, 21–24, 27–30, 32, 36, 38, 45, 80–82, 89–93, 103–104, 108, 110–111, 114, 120, 127, 138, 141, 146–147, 150–151, 153–155, 157–159, 163–164, 168–169, 171, 177, 181, 190
  Nineteenth-century females, 10–14, 19, 22, 27, 82, 95, 103–106, 121, 172–173, 176, 192
  sentimentalists, 10–11, 13, 19, 36–37, 121
  South, 27–28, 32, 37–38, 43, 45, 47–48, 105, 179, 191–203
  transcendentalism, 2, 8, 110, 170
Anderson, Maureen, 208
  on Chopin and the Southern pastoral tradition, 191–203

Anna Karenina (Tolstoy), 163
Anthony, Susan B., 11
Aristophanes, 14, 154
Arner, Robert D.
    on "Désirée's Baby," 80
"Art for Truth's Sake" (Phelps), 11
"At the 'Cadian Ball" (short story),
    148, 174
"At Chênière Caminada" (short
    story), 154
At Fault, 1, 184
    controversial context in, 36–37,
        40–41, 191
    criticism, 37, 43–44, 192, 198
    David Hosmer in, 36–43, 192–
        202
    divorce in, 37, 89, 198–199, 201
    Fanny Hosmer in, 36, 38–42, 90,
        198–200
    flaws of Southern society in,
        191–202
    gender roles in, 192, 199, 202
    Grégoire Santien in, 36–38,
        42–34, 147, 198–199
    Homeyer in, 40–41, 43
    industrial capitalism, 37–38, 40,
        43
    Jérôme Lafirme in, 192, 194
    McFarlane in, 38
    Melicent Hosmer in, 36–38, 43,
        198–199, 201
    narrative, 15, 41
    problematic love in, 36, 39–40,
        56
    publication, 91, 119, 191
    racism in, 47
    religion in, 41
    setting of, 175, 190, 192–194
    sexual selection in, 89–91
    symbolism in, 195, 200–201
    Thérèse Lafirme in, 36–43, 48,
        50, 89–90, 191–202

"Athénaïse" (short story)
    Athénaïse Miché in, 54, 187–188
    Cazeau in, 187
    Gouvernail in, 187–188
    motherhood in, 54–55
Atherton, Gertrude, 178
Austen, Jane, 120, 127
Awakening, The, 75, 191
    alienation in, 21, 29–30, 53, 58,
        63, 68, 71, 73, 96, 111
    banning of, 8
    considerations of the literary
        market in, 145–163
    criticism, 1, 8, 12–13, 15, 23–24,
        119–121, 137, 139, 145, 165
    Darwin's influence on, 89–101
    feminist criticism of, 1–26, 74,
        93–94, 103–105, 114, 124,
        138–140, 200
    gender roles in, 103–105, 110–
        111
    Grand Isle in, 7, 16, 18, 20–21,
        60, 66–68, 73, 93, 104, 108–
        109, 111–112, 114, 123, 128,
        130
    irony, 117, 120, 122–123, 126–
        131, 133–134, 136–141
    motifs and images in, 15–16,
        18–19, 44, 56–57, 73, 122, 126,
        130, 133–137, 139, 202
    narrative of, 1–6, 15–16, 18, 117,
        120, 122–126, 128, 130, 132,
        134, 136–137, 141
    publication, 119
    satire of, 15
    Schopenhauer's influence on,
        5–6
    sexual awakening in, 1–5, 7, 15–
        19, 22, 24, 31, 34, 57, 65, 70,
        103, 110, 113, 115, 119–123,
        127–130, 136–137, 201
    sexual selection in, 90–100

structure, 18–19, 72, 122–123, 129–130
uncompromising realism in, 103–118
Whitman's influence on, 1–6, 89–101
writing of, 51, 56, 91, 189
"Azélie" (short story), 175
    amoral, 51–52
    Azélie in, 51–52, 179–180
    Mr. Mathurin in, 179
    narrative, 179
    'Polyte in, 51–52, 179

Barbe, Waitman, 160, 175, 183
Bashkirtseff, Marie, 114
Battleground for self theme, 44
Bayou Folk, 1
    critique of marriage, 146–148
    praise of women in, 150, 202
    publication, 146–147, 150, 154, 162–163, 167, 174, 176, 180, 183
    reviews of, 146–148, 150, 152, 171, 173, 175, 183, 188
    romance in, 148
    stories in, 146–150, 174–176, 185
Beardsley, Aubrey, 184
Beauvoir, Simone de
    The Second Sex, 115
"Belle Dame Sans Merci, La" (Keats), 115
"Belle Zoraïde, La" (short story), 146, 164
    desire versus duty theme in, 50, 163
    motherhood in, 148, 150
Bender, Bert, 208
    on Whitman's and Darwin's influence on *The Awakening*, 89–101

Ben-Hur (Wallace), 169
"Bênitous Slave, The" (short story), 162
"Beyond the Bayou" (short story)
    alienation in, 45
    female roles in, 150
    La Folle in, 45
    suffering slaves in, 147, 162
Black, Martha Fodaski, 208
    on the uncompromising realism in *The Awakening*, 103–118
Blake, William, 139
"Blind, The" (short story), 164
Bloom, Harold, 207
    introduction, 1–6
    on the less feminist narrative of *The Awakening*, 1–6, 94
Bonner, Thomas Jr.,
    Kate Chopin Companion, 171
Booth, Edwin, 161, 178
Boren, Lynda, 115
"Boulôt and Boulotte" (short story), 147
    Boulotte in, 44
Bowles, Jane
    Two Serious Ladies, 129
Brontë, Charlotte
    Jane Eyre, 119

Cable, George Washington, 14, 154, 168
"Caline" (short story), 164, 181
Cather, Willa, 24, 133, 141
    on Chopin, 120
    The Song of the Lark, 130
Catherwood, Mary Hartwell, 169
"Cavanelle" (short story), 171–172
    narrative, 174, 176
"Charlie" (short story), 159–160
Chopin, Felix (son), 119, 155, 158
Chopin, Frederick (son), 119
Chopin, George (son), 119

Chopin, Jean (son), 119
Chopin, Kate
  birth, 119
  childhood, 18, 149
  death, 119
  diary, 150–152, 154, 167, 169–
    171
  education, 13, 119, 151
  marriage, 119
Chopin, Lelia (daughter), 119
Chopin, Oscar (husband), 149, 185
  death, 13, 107, 119, 156–157, 181
Chopin, Oscar, Jr. (son), 119
Civil War
  fiction, 10–12, 23, 27, 47, 176,
    179, 193, 195
Clark, Harrison, 158
Cole, Karen, 195
Competing Voices: the American Novel
  (Donaldson), 172–173
Complete Works of Kate Chopin, The,
  1, 119
Colonel (*The Awakening*), 97, 111
Conrad, Joseph, 79
Cott, Nancy F., 10
Country of the Pointed Firs, The
  (Jewett), 12, 173
Craik, Dinah Mulock
  The Woman's Kingdom, 13, 15
Crumbling Idols (Garland), 161
  Ida Wilbur in, 105

D'Arcy, Ella, 13
Darwin, Charles
  Descent of Man and Selection in
    Relation to Sex, 89–94, 96–98
  The Expression of Emotions, 95
  influence on Chopin, 12, 14,
    89–101, 119
  On the Origin of Species, 94
  skepticism, 12
Deland, Margaret, 178

DeMenil, Alexander, 188
Descent of Man and Selection in
  Relation to Sex (Darwin)
  sexual selection in, 89–94, 96–98
"Désirée's Baby"(short story), 164,
  176
  Armand Aubigny in, 45–47, 49,
    76–85
  baby, 76–81, 83–85
  La Blanche in, 77–79, 81, 85
  class issues in, 75, 80–82, 85–86
  Désirée Aubigny in, 45–47, 62,
    75–86
  destructive will to power in,
    45–48
  female roles in, 150
  men's violence in, 147–148, 180
  namelessness in, 77–79
  poetic justice of, 78–79
  publication, 75
  racism in, 46–47, 49, 75–86, 181
  sexism in, 75–76, 80–86
  slavery and woman's response to
    in, 28
  tragic mulatto in, 80–81
  Valmondés in, 45–47, 50–51,
    76–77, 85
Diana (Warner), 19
Diana and Persis (Alcott), 12
"Divorce Case, A" (Maupassant)
  influence on Chopin, 92, 154,
    170, 180
Doll's House, A (Ibsen), 105
Donaldson, Susan V.
  Competing Voices: the American
    Novel, 172–173
"Doralise" (short story), 160
Dowling, Linda, 13
"Dr. Chevalier's Lie" (short story),
  164, 181
Dream of Arcady, The (MacKethan),
  193

Dreiser, Theodore
Sister Carrie, 23
Dunbar-Nelson, Alice
"Tony's Wife," 148–149

Edna Pontellier (*The Awakening*), 178
appetite, 15
beauty, 17, 19, 22, 125, 138–139, 141
birthday party, 22, 99, 124–125
childhood, 62, 132–133, 139
conflicts between love and work, 12, 16, 131
consciousness, 15, 21, 58, 63, 66, 69
death, 3–6, 22–23, 58, 73, 85, 93, 95, 106, 109, 113–114, 121, 133–136, 140
freedom from social obligations, 8–9, 19, 59, 61–62, 65, 93, 109–111, 113, 115, 123, 129–131
infatuation with Robert, 2, 4–5, 16, 18–21, 59–61, 63–66, 68–72, 93–96, 98–99, 104, 108, 112–116, 124–134, 136–137, 140
marriage, 15–16, 19–22, 58, 62, 64, 68, 104, 110–111, 113, 124, 126, 129, 133
passion of, 1–6, 15–20, 23, 34, 56, 97, 106, 113, 116, 128, 132–133, 136–137
self-gratification, 2–4, 7–9, 17–18, 22, 53, 60–61, 64–73, 91–98, 105, 109–113, 121, 125–129, 201
terror of solitude, 21, 29
Egerton, George, 13
"Egyptian Cigarette, An" (short story), 51

dream in, 57–58
Elfenbein, Anna Shannon, 47, 63
Eliot, George
Middlemarch, 104
"Emancipation: A Life Fable" (short story)
alienation and solitude in, 29–30, 52
awakening in, 30–32, 107
moral of, 30–31
wish-fulfillment, 30
Emerson, Ralph Waldo
influence on Chopin, 3, 94, 110, 112, 145, 169
law of Compensation, 4, 6
on self-reliance, 145
"Euphrasie." *See* "No-Account Creole, A"
European realism
and Chopin, 120–123, 177
Evans, Augusta
St. Elmo, 15
Expression of Emotions, The (Darwin), 95

Farival, Adrienne, 179
Flaubert, Gustave, 2
influence on Chopin, 14
Madame Bovary, 106, 163
"For Marse Chouchoute" (short story), 162
Fox-Genovese, Elizabeth
on Chopin and the woman question, 103, 106
Franklin, Rosemary F.
on *The Awakening*, 70, 72
Freeman, Mary Wilkins, 14, 120
"A Mistaken Charity," 173
"A New England Nun," 23
Pembroke, 148, 171
work of, 150–151, 154, 171, 178, 189

Friedan, Betty, 107
Fuller, Margaret, 110

Garesche, Kitty, 13, 24
Garland, Hamlin, 171, 184
    Crumbling Idols, 105, 161
"Gentleman of Bayou Têche, A"
    (short story), 154
    Aunt Dicey in, 174
    Evariste in, 174–175
    Mr. Sublet in, 174–175
"Gentleman from New Orleans,
    The" (short story), 160
Gilbert, Sandra M.
    feminist review of *The
        Awakening*, 3, 14, 16, 22, 124,
        138–140
Gilligans, Carol
    on *At Fault*, 192
Glasglow, Ellen, 23
Grand, Sarah, 13
    The Heavenly Twins, 15

Hardy, Thomas, 15
    Jude the Obscure, 183
Harris, Joel Chandler, 189
    *Sister Jane: Her Friends and
        Acquaintance*, 183
    Uncle Remus stories, 183
Heavenly Twins, The (Grand), 15
Hedda Gabler (Ibsen), 105
"Her Letters" (short story)
    adultery in, 153
    female passion in, 56
Hotchkiss, Jane
    on *At Fault*, 192
House of Mirth, The (Wharton),
    16
Howells, William Dean, 163
Hull, Lizzie Chambers, 150
Huxley, Aldous
    influence on Chopin, 14, 119

Ibsen, Henrik
    A Doll's House, 105
    on the feminist heroine, 103–
        111, 117
    Hedda Gabler, 105
    influence on Chopin, 14
"In and Out of Old Natchitoches"
    (short story)
    Hector Santien in, 147
"In Sabine" (short story), 154, 162
    battered wife story, 146–149
    Bud Aiken in, 149
    Grégoire Santien in, 147,
        149–150
    heroine escape in, 147, 149
    Tite Reine in, 149
"In Spring" (poem), 155
"It" (Maupassant), 92, 153, 180

"Jack the Fisherman" (Phelps)
    wife abuse in, 148–149
James, Henry, 16
Jane Eyre (Brontë, C.), 119
Jewett, Sarah Orne, 11, 14, 120
    The Country of the Pointed Firs,
        12, 173
    New England stories of, 150–
        151, 163
Johns, George, 177
Joyce, James, 177
"Juanita" (short story), 172
    sex outside marriage, 153
Jude the Obscure (Hardy), 183

Kate Chopin (Skaggs), 47, 54
Kate Chopin Companion (Bonner),
    171
"Kate Chopin and the Fiction of
    Limits" (Wolff)
    change in Chopin's fiction, 29
Keats, John
    "La Belle Dame Sans Merci," 115

Kentucky Cardinal, A (Allen), 171
King, Grace, 14, 154
Kipling, Rudyard, 154
"Kiss, The" (short story), 164
  guilty love in, 163
Kolbenheyer, Frederick, 177

Ladenson, Joyce Ruddel
  on *At Fault*, 37
"Lady of Bayou St. John, A" (short story), 146, 164, 181
  happy widow in, 148
Lattin, Patricia Hopkins, 55
Leary, Lewis, 38, 106
  on Whitman's influence on *The Awakening*, 4
Leaves of Grass (Whitman)
  offense of, 2
Lebrun, Madame (*The Awakening*), 68
  living through offspring, 109, 135
  pension, 16
  sewing machine, 21
Lee, Brian
  on *The Awakening*, 67
Leónce Pontellier (*The Awakening*)
  assumptions about women, 112, 117
  club life, 20, 22, 59
  freedom, 104, 108, 110–111, 132
  obsessions, 16, 58, 60–61, 64, 67–72, 96, 99, 124–125
"Lilacs" (short story), 184
  desire versus duty theme in, 50
"Lilies" (short story), 187
"Little Country Girl, A" (short story), 160
"Loka" (short story)
  Baptiste in, 148
  female roles in, 150

Lourdes (Zola)
  Chopin's review of, 161, 178–180
"Love on the Bon-Dieu" (short story)
  female roles in, 150
  love and pity in, 148
Lowell, Amy, 177

"Ma'ame Pélagie" (short story)
  destructive will-to-power, 45, 47–48
  female roles in, 150
  living in the past, 48–50
  Pauline Valmêt in, 47–51
  Pélagie Valmêt in, 47–50, 147–148
  La Petite in, 48–50
  racism in, 49–50
  the South in, 47–48
MacKethan, Lucinda
  The Dream of Arcady, 193
"Mad?" (Maupassant), 154, 170
Madame Bovary (Flaubert), 163
  obscenity in, 106
"Maid of Saint Phillippe, The" (short-story)
  Marianne in, 44–45
  survival in, 45
"Mamouche" (short story), 185, 187
Mansfield, Katherine
  modernism, 123–124, 127–129
Marhefka, Linda, 159–160
Marhefka, Robert, 159–160
Marlarmé, Stéphané, 184
Marx, Karl, 37
Mary Olivier (Sinclair), 122, 130
"Matter of Prejudice, A" (short story), 185, 187
Maupassant, Guy de
  Chopin's translations of, 153, 160, 171, 180

death, 154
"A Divorce Case," 92, 154, 170,
    180
influence on Chopin, 9, 14, 56,
    82, 119–120, 146, 148, 151,
    155–156, 163–164, 170–172,
    180–181
"It," 92, 153
"Mad?," 154, 170, 180
"Solitude," 7, 93, 153, 180
"Suicide," 153, 180
"Melancholy" (short story), 160
Melville, Herman, 22
Middlemarch (Eliot), 104
Miller, Nancy K.
    on women's writing, 18
"Miss McEnders" (short story),
    190
    blind social consciousness in, 50
    moral guardianship theme in, 50
"Mistaken Charity, A" (Freeman),
    173
"Misty" (short story), 160
Moods (Alcott), 19
Moore, Susan V., 153, 161, 178
    profile of Chopin, 154–155, 158

"New England Nun, A" (Freeman),
    23
Nietzsche, Friedrich
    on woman, 104, 126, 133, 138
"Night Came Slowly, The" (short
    story), 171
    sex outside marriage, 153
    setting of, 172
Night in Acadie, A, 1
    reviews of, 188–189
    publication, 171, 176, 185
    stories in, 171, 184–188, 190
"Night in Acadie, A" (short story)
    Telèsphore in, 186–187, 189
    Zaida in, 186, 189

"No-Account Creole, A" (short
    story), 175
    Euphrasie in, 31–33
    female roles in, 150
    Placide Santien in, 31–32, 36,
        147
    Wallace Offdean in, 31–32
    woman reaching self-
        consciousness in, 31–33, 147
Nostalgia and progress myths
    in Chopin's short stories, 27

O'Connor, Flannery, 172
"Odalie Misses Mass" (short story)
    female friendship in, 162–163
O'Flaherty, Katherine. *See* Chopin,
    Kate
O'Flaherty, Thomas (father), 105,
    119
Ohmann, Richard, 105
"Old Aunt Peggy" (short story)
    female roles in, 150
    suffering slaves in, 147
On the Origin of Species (Darwin),
    94
"Out of the Cradle Endlessly
    Rocking" (Whitman), 95
"Ozème's Holiday" (short story),
    162, 171

"Pair of Silk Stockings, A" (short
    story), 164
    dark side of motherhood in,
        55–56
    Mrs. Sommers in, 55–56
Papke, Mary E., 207–208
    on Chopin's shorter fictions,
        27–74
Parr, Susan Resneck
    on *The Awakening*, 71
Pastoral Forms and Attitudes
    (Toliver), 199

Pater, Walter, 3
Pearl of Orr's Island (Stowe), 11
Peel, Ellen, 208
   on Chopin's shorter fictions,
     75–87
Pembroke (Freeman), 148
   reviews of, 171
Perfect Wagnerite, The (Shaw),
   115
Phelps, Elizabeth Stuart, 178
   "Art for Truth's Sake," 11
   "Jack the Fisherman," 148–149
   The Story of Avis, 12
Pilgrimage (Richardson)
   Miriam Henderson in, 130
"Point at Issue, A" (story)
   Charles Faraday in, 34–36
   Eleanor Gail in, 34–36
   woman divided in, 31, 34–36, 43
"Polydore" (short story), 185, 187
Porcerh, Frances
   on Edna's desire for self in *The
     Awakening*, 2–3

Quintessence of Ibsenism, The (Shaw)
   "The Womanly Woman" in,
     103–115, 117

Rankin, Daniel, 14, 159–160, 176
"Recovery, The" (short story), 164
Redding, Josephine, 164
Reedy, William Marion, 177–178
"Regret" (short story), 171, 188
   motherhood in, 54
Reisz, Mademoiselle (*The
   Awakening*), 160–161
   art of, 17–19, 63, 68, 70, 94–95,
     115, 125, 128, 137
   independence and individuality
     of, 9, 18–19, 22, 34, 71, 98,
     113–116, 123–126, 128, 130–
     136, 139

obsession with Edna, 17, 19, 66,
   68–69, 115, 129, 134, 136–137
Repplier, Agnes, 154, 178
"Respectable Woman, A" (short story)
   Mrs. Baroda in, 91–92, 187–188
   Gouvernail in, 187–189
   sexual selection in, 91, 153
"Return of Alcibiade, The" (short
   story), 174
   female roles in, 150
   senile father in, 148
Rhys, Jean, 127, 130, 138
   Voyage in the Dark, 123
Richardson, Dorothy, 127, 138
   Pilgrimage, 130
Riley, James Whitcomb, 152, 169
"Ripe Figs" (short story), 181, 188
Robert Lebrun (*The Awakening*)
   desertion, 124–125, 129
   Edna's infatuation with, 2,
     4–5, 16, 18–21, 59–61, 63–66,
     68–72, 93–96, 98–99, 104, 108,
     112–116, 124–137, 140
Roller, Judi
   on *The Awakening*, 74
Rossetti, Dante Gabriel, 3
"Rude Awakening, A" (short story)
   Lolotte Bordon in, 44–45
   men's violence in, 147
Ryan, Mary
   on the women's culture, 10–11

Sampite, Albert, 149, 191, 202
Sand, George, 115
Sanity of Art, The (Shaw), 113
Sawyer, Harriet Adams, 151
Schopenhauer, Arthur
   influence on Chopin, 5–6
Schreiner, Olive, 13
Schuyler, William
   profile of Chopin, 155–156, 158,
     168, 176

Scott, Anne Firor
  on the Southern woman, 28
Scudder, H.E., 183–184
Second Sex, The (Beauvoir), 115
Sedgwick, Catherine, 10
"Sentimental Soul, A" (short story)
  guilty love in, 163
  Lacodie in, 161–162
  Mamzelle Fleurette in, 161–163
Seyersted, Per
  on Chopin, 23, 104, 115, 119
"Shameful Affair, A" (short story)
  heroine in, 105
Shaw, George Bernard
  The Perfect Wagnerite, 115
  The Quintessence of Ibsenism,
    103–115, 117
  The Sanity of Art, 113
Shelley, Percy Bysshe
  Adonais, 121
Showalter, Elaine, 207
  on the feminism in *The
    Awakening*, 7–26
Sinclair, Mary
  Mary Olivier, 122, 130
Sister Carrie (Dreiser), 23
*Sister Jane: Her Friends and
  Acquaintance* (Harris), 183
Skaggs, Peggy, 108
  Kate Chopin, 47, 54
Slavery issues
  in "La Belle Zoraïde," 28
  in "Désirée's Baby," 28
"Sleepers, The" (Whitman)
  sensuous atmosphere of, 3
Smith-Rosenberg, Carroll, 9
Social stratification themes
  in *At Fault*, 37, 43, 47
  in Chopin's short stories, 27–29,
    45, 47
"Solitude" (Maupassant), 93, 153, 180
  melancholy wisdom in, 7

"Song of Everlasting, The" (poem),
  155
Song of the Lark, The (Cather)
  Thea Kronborg in, 130
Song of Myself (Whitman)
  self of, 2, 93–94
Sonneschein, Rosa, 176
Southworth, E.D.E.N., 9
Spenser, Edmund
  influence on Chopin, 14, 119
Stanton, Elizabeth Cady, 13
  on womanliness, 103, 110–112
St. Elmo (Evans), 15
Stevens, Edwin Lewis, 182
Stevens, Wallace, 6
"Storm, The" (short story), 51
  expressive freedom in, 24
Story of Avis, The (Phelps), 12
"Story of an Hour, The" (short
  story), 164
  awakening in, 53, 55, 92
  Bently Mallard in, 52, 54, 56, 92
  Louise Mallard in, 52–56, 68,
    92, 153, 180–181
  self-alienation in, 51–53
Stowe, Harriet Beecher, 9, 13
  Pearl of Orr's Island, 11
  "Uncle Lot," 173–174
  Uncle Tom's Cabin, 28
  on the woman question, 10
Stuart, Ruth McEnery
  writings of, 120, 157–158, 181–
    183, 189
"Suicide" (Maupassant), 153, 180
Summer in Arcady (Allen, J.),
  185–186
"Suzette" (short story), 164
Swinburne, Algernon, 3
  influence on Chopin, 14

"Tante Cat'rinette" (short story), 188
  devoted slave in, 154, 162

"Ti Frère" (short story)
Bud Aiken in, 149
"To The Friend of My Youth"
(poem)
emotional bonds between
women in, 24
Toth, Emily, 208
on Chopin, 103, 105, 185
considerations of the literary
market in The Awakening,
145–165
on "Désirée's Baby," 76
"To Hidee Schuyler" (poem), 155
To the Lighthouse (Woolf), 22
Lily Briscoe in, 129
Toliver, Harold
Pastoral Forms and Attitudes,
199
Tolstoy, Leo
Anna Karenina, 163
"Tony's Wife" (Dunbar-Nelson)
wife abuse in, 148–149
"Turkey Hunt, A" (short story),
147
Twain, Mark, 154
Two Serious Ladies (Bowles), 129
"Two Summers and Two Souls"
(short story), 164

"Uncle Lot" (Stowe), 173–174
Uncle Tom's Cabin (Stowe), 28
Simon Legree in, 38
"Unexpected, The" (short story),
164

"Very Fine Fiddle, A" (short story)
Fifine in, 44
Victor Lebrun (The Awakening), 94
view of women, 123, 130, 134,
138–139, 141
"Visit to Avoyelles, A" (short story),
164, 181

love and pity in, 148
men's violence in, 147–148
Vocation and a Voice, A
stories in, 189
"Vocation and a Voice, A" (short
story), 160, 184–185
Voyage in the Dark (Rhys), 123

Walker, Nancy A., 208
on Chopin's irony in her short
stories, 105, 167–190
Wallace, Lew
Ben-Hur, 169
Warner, Susan, 9, 13
Diana, 19
Warnken, William P.
on Chopin, 105–106
Wharton, Edith
The House of Mirth, 16
womanhood themes, 27–28
Wheeler, Kathleen, 208
on Chopin's irony, 119–143
"When Lilacs Last in the Dooryard
Bloom'd" (Whitman)
hermit's song of death in, 3, 6, 95
Whitman, Walt
death, 2–3
erotic perspective of, 1–3, 94
influence on Chopin, 1–6, 14,
89–101, 155
Leaves of Grass, 2
"Out of the Cradle Endlessly
Rocking," 95
"The Sleepers," 3
Song of Myself, 2, 93–94
"When Lilacs Last in the
Dooryard Bloom'd," 3, 6, 95
Wilde, Oscar, 3, 177
Williamson, Joel
on "Désirée's Baby," 78
Williams, Raymond
on The Awakening, 73

Wilson, Edmund, 106
"Wiser Than a God" (short story),
   51
   art over love in, 33
   George Brainard in, 33, 33–34
   Max Kuntzler in, 33–34
   Paula Von Stoltz in, 18, 31,
      33–34, 52, 63
Wolff, Cynthia Griffin
   on "Désirée's Baby," 82
Wolkenfeld, Susanne, 139
Wollstonecraft, Mary
   on woman, 104
Woman's Kingdom, The (Craik), 13
Woman Who Did, The (Allen), 13, 15

Woodhull, Victoria, 110
Woolf, Virginia, 123, 127, 141
   To the Lighthouse, 22, 129

Yeazell, Ruth Bernard
   on Darwin, 91–92
"You and I" (poem), 155
Young Dr. Grosse and Théo
   rejection, 44, 119, 184

Ziff, Larzer, 111
Zlotnick, Joan
   on Chopin, 105
Zola, Émile, 15, 105, 162
   Lourdes, 161, 178–180